True Stories of the Foreign Legion

TRUE STORIES
OF THE
FOREIGN LEGION

ROBIN HUNTER

Virgin

First published in Great Britain in 1997 by
Virgin Books
an imprint of Virgin Publishing Ltd
332 Ladbroke Grove
London W10 5AH

A catalogue record for this book is available from the
British Library.

ISBN 0 7535 0130 9

Typeset by TW Typesetting, Plymouth, Devon

Printed and bound by
Mackays of Chatham PLC, Lordswood, Chatham, Kent

CONTENTS

A PERSONAL INTRODUCTION TO THE FRENCH FOREIGN LEGION, 1955–97

If I pause before writing this line, and probe my right jaw with my tongue, I am instantly reminded of my first contact with the French Foreign Legion. It was the late summer of 1955 and I was in the Algerian port of Arzew, a young Royal Marine commando, as tough as a buttered bun and suffering from violent toothache.

I had been suffering from toothache for about a week, since before the advance party of my unit had arrived in this grubby little garrison town, and such was the present level of pain that, clearly, something had to be done. The question was what, for our own medics were still at sea. I therefore begged leave from my troop sergeant-major, who had been keeping me going with whisky, and set out to find a dentist somewhere in the town.

Arzew in 1955 was not the most salubrious of towns. It might be best imagined as the French colonial version of Aldershot, a place teeming at the time with sullen *matelots*, even more sullen French fusiliers-marines, some husky colonial paratroopers and, most of all, a large number of foreign legionnaires, recently released from prison camps in Vietnam and all in a very bad mood. The town consisted of a harbour full of warships, various barracks for the soldiery, a large collection of bars and brothels and a great quantity of whores. Signs of civilisation, like dentists, were rather harder to come by.

The search for relief eventually took me to a decommissioned French warship, the cruiser *Duquesne*, which was rusting away by the harbour wall, and serving as a storeship, a prison for the rougher elements of the soldiery, washrooms for my commando detachment – and a medical centre. The person in charge of the latter facility was a hard-looking bloke who wore a grubby apron and the *képi blanc* of the Légion Etrangère. I explained my problem. He ushered me into a chair and ordered me to open my mouth.

'This is the one, right?' he asked, prodding my jaw with his finger. Terrible pain!

It is not easy to talk with a fist in your mouth but I nodded assent. He then produced a pair of metal forceps and rapped them smartly against my tooth . . . agony!

'That will have to come out,' he said. He was now kneeling on my chest and, before I could say 'anaesthetics', he had inserted the forceps, seized hold of the offending tooth and ripped it from my mouth, taking with it a large piece of jawbone. Forty years later that gap in my jaw is still a fair size; at the time the pain was indescribable.

I do not recall much of the next few minutes but before five of them had passed I was back on the *quai* with a handful of aspirin and a mouthful of blood, wondering what had hit me. When our own MO arrived, a couple of days later, he peered into my mouth, saw what had been done, whistled softly, offered me some brandy and said, 'Just thank your lucky stars you joined the Royal Marines and not the Foreign Legion. What a butcher!'

In spite of that inauspicious start, the doc was wrong. I was very happy in the Corps but I soon acquired a great respect for the Foreign Legion, partly because they ran rings round us in the subsequent exercises, the reason for my commando unit being in Algeria in the first place, but mostly because they seemed to run their affairs on sensible, soldierly lines. It was noticeable, for example, that when we visited the Legion headquarters at Sidi Bel Abbès, square pegs were firmly in square holes. Those who could cook, cooked, and Legion food was excellent, as were the facilities at Sidi Bel Abbès – swimming pools, bars, barracks, all of them designed and built by legionnaires, all in excellent condition; such things matter to commando soldiers and we noticed them.

The legionnaires were also tough; those at Arzew in 1955 had to be tough or they would have been dead, killed in the fighting at Dien Bien Phu a year before, or dead of ill-treatment and neglect in Vietminh prison camps during the captivity that followed. We heard the tale of one Legion sergeant-major, wounded in the fighting at Dien Bien Phu, who had cut off his own gangrenous arm with a jack knife and gone back to the battle. This tale turned out to be true, and when I realised that I knew why only wimps needed Novocaine.

Now the Legion were back in their Algerian home, where yet another war was brewing nicely in 1955, but they still marched and fought and sang – the Legion seemed to do a lot of singing and (here was a new one to me) they *never* complained. Their officers were competent and their NCOs were first-class, the soldiers were excellent, everyone knew their business and they just got on with it. It was very apparent, even to my young eyes, that this was a regiment with a difference, and a formidable fighting force.

Nor was I the only one to feel this. We were all impressed with the Legion, and the fighting men of my stern corps were not easily impressed. We may have been a little disappointed to discover that the legionnaires did not actually wear those rather fetching little caps with a hankie at the back to keep the sun off their necks, the kind we had seen in the movies, but we were wise enough not to comment. What these legionnaires did wear were numerous medals, about which they would say no more than '*Indochine*' or '*Extrême Orient*' when we asked where they got them. They were hard, hospitable, silent men, from half a hundred countries, and though they made us welcome there was no fuss about it. They were soldiers, and so were we, but they were legionnaires, *c'est tout*.

So we exercised against them in the *bled*, and landed to attack them from the sea, and eventually we even got to the point where we were holding our own in these trial affairs. We went to Sidi Bel Abbès and saw the Voie Sacrée and the wooden hand of Captain Danjou and heard the story of Camerone. We even spent Camerone Day with the Legion, sharing in the celebrations, with it, if not of it, and we sent our brigade band and a fighting troop from 45 Commando to march through Oran on the Fête Nationale. There we got gloriously lost in the back streets of the city and marched past the saluting base no less than four times, the last time coming from the wrong direction, which caused something of a stir in military circles but delighted the crowd.

Then we embarked onto our grey ships and sailed back to Malta and the Legion went off into the *bled* and another bitter war. Having been with the advance party, I was also with the rear party, so I stayed on for a few extra days and was in the port when the Legion marched out. Having nothing else to do for once, I went up to see them go. They could probably have left in trucks but they elected to march, long files of heavily armed troops, every one a professional fighting man. They looked superb.

Since that long-ago time I have taken an interest in the Legion and its doings. When I worked in Mexico I hired a car in Veracruz to visit the site of Camerone, where a Legion company fought the definitive Legion battle and endowed the Legion with its most enduring souvenir. I have seen them leaping into the sea from aircraft circling off Corsica, and scaling the walls of the fortress in Collouire. I have visited their barracks and the museum at Aubagne and watched them march down the Champs-Elysées behind their pioneers on the Quatorze Juillet, moving with that slow and stately Legion stride. Most magnificent they looked, but no sight since 1955 has erased the memory of those splendid infantry soldiers, the cutting edge of the Légion Etrangère, marching from their barracks to a new, hard war.

This is the story of one of the world's finest and most unusual military formations and, if you like soldiers and brave tales, I commend their story to you.

1

THE OLD LEGION, 1831–37

'What difference does it make if a hundred thousand rifles fire in Africa? Europe does not hear them'

Louis-Philippe, King of France, 1831

The Foreign Legion exists today to fight France's more unpopular wars and maintain French influence in insalubrious places, but that is not why the Legion was created, 160 years ago. The idea behind the Royal Ordinance, issued by King Louis-Philippe, authorising the formation of 'a legion, composed of foreigners, to be called the Foreign Legion', issued on 9 March 1831, was to rid France of the large number of foreign nationals who had arrived in France as Europe gradually fell into chaos after the conclusion of the Napoleonic Wars.

On that chilly day at the end of winter, no one could have foreseen that this new formation would go on to make a name for itself, a name that would become a byword among the armies of the world and among professional soldiers for over 150 years, a unit noted for its military prowess, harsh training and relentless discipline far beyond the boundaries of metropolitan France. France had plenty of fine regiments in the early decades of the nineteenth century, and memories of the late emperor's Imperial Guard, which had carried the Napoleonic eagles from the sierras of Spain to the freezing wastes of Russia, were still vivid in France, where there were plenty of 'old moustaches' still alive to tell the old tales, even in these less stirring days. This new formation was to eclipse these veterans but that hardly seemed likely at the first Legion parade.

This new legion was organised as a normal French Army infantry battalion, with eight companies, each of 112 men, with men of the same nationality mustered into the same company – a practice that was later abandoned. The men were also dressed in standard French Army uniforms – red trousers, blue tunics, a black shako and a grey overcoat. The glamorous *képi* with the flap to cover the neck did not make its appearance for several decades, being introduced in 1859, and the white *kèpi* and neck flap emerged only around 1900. In 1831 their new clothes did not immediately make the Legion a smart regiment, and those who saw it form were far from impressed. One observer commented that these first legionnaires resembled 'a mob, of every age from 16 to 60, clad in the oldest rags the depots could find'.

On the other hand, many of these men were old and experienced soldiers, hard-bitten veterans who had served in a variety of armies, men who had joined this new legion to return to the only life and trade they knew. The officers – all of them French – had seen service in the Napoleonic armies, and certainly in the early months Frenchmen were allowed to join as rankers, though the ones who did so usually pretended to be Swiss or Belgians. Many of the first Legion volunteers came from the disbanded Hohenlohe Regiment, a unit created in September 1815, three months after Waterloo, to accommodate all those foreign soldiers who had served in the armies of the recently deposed Napoleon. These men introduced the Legion's famous, impressive and majestically slow parade marching pace of 88 paces to the minute, a pace that had formerly been used by the Hohenlohe and one that has been retained to this day by the Legion.

Even after Waterloo and the reverses and losses of the Napoleonic Wars, France had still not given up on the idea of military glory. The only problem was where to find it. Continental Europe had had more than enough of French ambition since 1779, and starting a new war in Europe would be inadvisable. The excuse for further military adventures came in North Africa in the spring of 1830 when the Bey of Algiers, Hussein, was alleged to have struck the French consul with his fly whisk. That might seem a puny excuse for starting a war but there was a slightly more substantial reason, the allegation that the bey had not yet paid some local merchants who had been supplying wheat to France. These merchants needed a debt collector and Charles X, *faut de mieux*, took on the task and despatched a small army to the coast of North Africa.

A force of some 35,000 men landed on the North African coast near Algiers in June 1830. This force was commanded by General M. le Comte de Bourmont, who had the curious distinction in France – especially for a general officer – of being widely regarded as a traitor, having deserted from the army of Napoleon Bonaparte just three days before the Battle of Waterloo. General de Bourmont was no great soldier, so his desertion in 1815 made very little difference to either side, but his action had not been forgotten, and if any dirty job came up in the French Army in the 1830s, General de Bourmont usually got it.

His unenviable role in North Africa charged him with 1) collecting plants and fossils; 2) collecting 60 fine camels; and 3) capturing Algiers. De Bourmont duly executed these tasks, but the first news to reach him after his army entered Algiers on 5 July 1830 was that yet another French revolution had swept the Bourbon king, Charles X, from his throne and into exile in England, taking with him any prospect of preferment for the luckless general.

Charles X, heir of the Bourbons, had been replaced by Louis-Philippe, scion of the Orleanists, and Louis-Philippe directed his minister of war, Marshal Soult, a veteran of the Napoleonic Wars, to rid France of foreigners, and indeed of any restless spirit, French or foreign, who might hanker after a fresh dose of revolution and support any party seeking to put Louis-Philippes's crown in jeopardy. As a step to this end, Marshal Soult amended the law of 9 March 1831, the law that created the Legion, adding a clause which stated that the Legion 'should not be employed in the metropolitan territory of this kingdom'. That clause created a problem, for if this new legion were not to serve in France, where could it go?

The answer was close at hand, a night's sail across the Mediterranean, in the half-conquered territory south of the city of Algiers. Hussein, the evicted Bey of Algiers, was a pirate and slave dealer, leader and supplier to those roving Barbary corsairs that had preyed on the coastal people of the Mediterranean for centuries. The bey was now in hiding but his people were up in arms and fresh glory seemed to beckon in their subjection.

Besides, the French had lost most of their colonies to the British, either in the Seven Years War of 1757–64, or during the Napoleonic Wars. Now the time had come for a fresh burst of empire-building, in Africa, and especially along the North African shore, or in the Far East, where the French East India Company had lost out to the British in the Indian sub-continent, and not least in Central Africa, which was largely unexplored but promised rich bounties to those who could seize it. These lands were known to be perilous, places where soldiers died in quantity, usually from disease rather than enemy action; far better, then, if soldiers must die for France in these remote and dangerous places, that the soldiers should not actually be French citizens, with mothers who were liable to complain or demonstrate in the streets at such a sacrifice. For such a purpose the Foreign Legion was the perfect tool.

The Foreign Legion has never been exclusively foreign. All the officers were French, at least to begin with, though most of the NCOs were and still are foreign, men then driven to the Legion by a fondness for soldiering or some personal or national disaster. Those who, according to the story books, 'join the Legion to forget' are probably very few, as the Legion is no place for romantic souls and, certainly until recent years, most legionnaires ended up in the ranks from necessity, though it has been alleged that a fair number join to escape their wives, or their debts. Many, however, were refugees.

Over the decades since its creation, every war or political upheaval in Europe has added a fresh quantity of recruits to the Legion ranks; in the present century, the aftermath of the Great War and the Second World War saw many Germans joining, and a similar influx arrived after the end of the Spanish Civil War in 1939 and after the Hungarian uprising of 1956. After any crisis in human affairs those with nowhere to go and willing to soldier can find a home in the Legion. There has also been a steady supply of recruits from nations with a long history of mercenary warfare, like the Swiss and the Germans, though the British, who are relentlessly warlike and have at times made up 10 per cent of Legion numbers, are noted in the Legion histories both for their fighting ability *and* their fondness for desertion.

(In this book, incidentally, there will be no mention of people 'escaping' from the Legion. All legionnaires are volunteers and soldiers who volunteer to serve and then run are *deserters*, nothing more. The Legion accepts the fact that men will desert and varies the punishment for captured deserters according to the circumstances. In Algeria in the period 1950–60, the Legion offered a bounty of 200 francs for any Legion deserter captured and returned by the Arabs, and the man might then serve a few weeks in prison before returning to his unit. If he deserted *with his arms*, however, the punishment would be much longer and much harder – beginning with a terrible beating at the hands of the Legion NCOs.)

In the first months of the Legion's existence, recruitment was brisk and desertion almost unknown. Volunteers flocked to join, as an alternative to starvation, expulsion or constant harassment by the police. Recruits could be of any age, from 16 to 60, and, according to one account, any medical examination was at best cursory. If a man could walk and carry a musket there was a place for him, and if he chose to desert, that was one way of eliminating the unsuitable – though any deserter caught was sent to a punishment battalion, where life could be very hard indeed. But then life was hard everywhere in Europe at that time, and by December 1831 the first commander of the Légion Etrangère, a Swiss officer, Colonel Stoffel, who had served in the armies of Napoleon Bonaparte, was able to tell Marshal Soult that he had sent no less than five battalions of legionnaires – some 3,000 men – to the war in what we may for convenience call Algeria, though the name was not coined until much later.

These first battalions, and the two that were to follow, were mustered on national lines, one battalion containing Frenchmen (though masquerading as Belgians), another full of Swiss, most of them Swiss soldiers who had previously served in the now-disbanded Hohenloe royalist regiment. The third battalion was composed of Italians. The sixth and seventh battalions were composed of Belgians and Poles, and it was some years before the idea of 'national' battalions was dropped and the men were deliberately mixed up within the battalions, partly through recruiting difficulties, mainly to create, in place of national rivalries, a new loyalty – to the Legion.

The next commander of the Legion, a Belgian officer named Baron Boegard, was soon replaced by a French officer and a veteran of the Grande Armèe, Colonel Bernelle. It was soon put about that the actual commander of the Legion was the Colonel's wife, Madame Bernelle, a formidable lady who ruled her husband with a rod of iron, had a liking for handsome young men, and used the legionnaires as unpaid, unfed staff in her new Algerian mansion. One of the men thus employed was Achille Bazaine, then a sergeant in the Legion, but a man destined to become a marshal of France during the Franco-Prussian War of 1870–1. Bernelle – or Madame Bernelle – did introduce a few additions to the Legion order of battle, forming an artillery unit, a few squadrons of lancers for reconnaissance duties and a force of sappers for use in the many sieges that the conquest and pacification of Algeria seemed to involve.

This multinational Legion force was duly despatched to Algiers, where they were soon engaged in fighting that grew more bitter as the months passed. Nor were the men ideally dressed, equipped or trained for service in North Africa. They wore thick serge tunics and trousers, boots that disintegrated after a few miles across the mountains, and carried the same weapons, muzzle-loading muskets and long bayonets, that the Grande Armée had carried less than twenty years before. Their opponents, the tribesmen of the coast and hinterland, were better clad for the climate, better armed and avid for war. They also had a nasty habit of handing over any captured prisoner to their women, who would compete to see just how much they could make a man suffer before he finally screamed his way to death, then bombarded any surviving comrades with a shower of severed heads and testicles. War in Algeria was hard at the start, and as the months went by it got harder.

The Legion still managed to do well in the guerrilla fighting that marked its first campaign, and a year after its foundation the 1st (Swiss) and 3rd (German) Battalions of the Legion were in action, storming the ramparts of a fortified village called the Maison Carrée, a few miles from Algiers. This sign of loyalty so impressed King Louis-Philippe that he sent the Legion their first colours, a battle ensign bearing the words 'From the King of the French to the Foreign Legion'.

This colour was carried into battle for the first time outside the walls of the city of Oran on 11 November 1832, when the Emir Abd-el-Kader, a man who was to become a famous leader in the long Algerian struggle against the French, appeared outside the city with a small army of 3,000 mounted tribesmen. The Legion had just been permitted to form élite 'light infantry' companies, armed with rifles and employed in a scouting role, and grenadier companies, used in storming fortified positions, where grenades were highly effective, and these companies were soon briskly engaged with Abd-el-Kader's horse.

The French were too wily to risk being cooped up within the city while more Arabs flocked to el-Kader's banner, and marched out to give battle on the stony slopes of the Jebel Tarafouine. The Arab tactic was a massed cavalry charge by sword and spear-armed horsemen, which swept down on the 4th Battalion of the Legion, a body composed of Spaniards, most of whom had first experienced war in Spain in Britain's Peninsular Army, under General Lord Wellington.

These were men who had fought cavalry before, and they greeted the Arabs by forming square and blasting the Arabs from their saddles with musketry fire or, once the charge had been stopped, by slipping out to rove among the disordered horse, stabbing the men and horses with bayonets, or forming groups to haul individual Arab warriors from the saddle and stabbing them to death. This was hard, brutal, hand-to-hand fighting. These ex-*guerrillero* legionnaires were very good at it and the Arabs had no taste for it at all. Within a short while they had drawn off from the defiant ranks of the outnumbered legionnaires and that night Abd-el-Kader stopped his attack on Oran and withdrew to the mountains.

The conquest of Algeria was to take years of constant fighting against a stubborn foe, and the Legion was in it from the first, but their task of pacification was not restricted to military duties alone. The French used the Legion for any task at hand, and if they were not needed for fighting they could be used as labour. The 2nd Battalion of the Legion was ordered to build a road from Douera to Bouffarick, across terrible country where the mountains were thick with tribesmen and the swamps droning with malarial mosquitoes. This was a task in which men would surely die, in war or from disease, and so the Legion was committed. This pattern, of fighting, working and dying, was to form part of the Legion experience.

The men had no training in this work and no special

tools, just shovels and pickaxes, but the ranks of the Legion have always contained men of many talents. Given any such task, some men were found with engineering experience, and they took charge, planned the route and organised the work. The 60-kilometre road was built by the Swiss legionnaires in two months, in between fighting off the encroaching tribesmen and watching men die from malaria. It was a magnificent road, and from that time on, when the Legion was not fighting, it was labouring on roads, building ports or digging tunnels. Leave was unheard of and training was of the practical kind; when a man joined the Legion he learned to soldier quickly or he died.

In 1833, the Legion began to clear the Arab tribesmen away from the coast and by June of that year they had assaulted and taken the small port of Arzew, which fell to the Spanish battalion, and the town of Mostaganem, which was promptly besieged by the dauntless Abd-el-Kader. Abd-el-Kader was to remain a thorn in the side of the French for years, and in June 1835 two battalions of the Legion, the 5th and 7th, made up of Italian and Polish legionnaires, force-marched from Oran to rescue a column of French troops which el-Kader's Arabs had surrounded in the Macta salt marshes and was on the point of massacring before the legionnaires came swarming to the rescue.

This was the Legion's last action in Algeria, at least for a while. In 1834 the French began peace talks with Abd-el-Kader, which led to the Treaty of Tafna and a peace that lasted for six years until, enraged with the growing number of French settlers who were now pouring into Algeria and helping themselves to Arab land, Abd-el-Kader raised an army of 60,000 warriors and swept down on the coastal plains, burning French farms and slaughtering any settler he could find. All that lay in the future and is outside the scope of the Legion story. For the moment there was peace in Algeria and no employment for the Legion who, by the law of 1831, could not serve in France. They had done good work for France in these

Algerian wars, for little reward and few thanks, but now they were not wanted by the French at all. France had a new problem, in the troublesome peninsula of Spain, and it occurred to King Louis-Philippe that in Spain he might solve two problems with one simple action.

He gave the Foreign Legion – officers, men, arms and equipment – to Queen Marie-Cristina of Spain, for service in her Carlist wars. The Legion was shipped to Spain and Louis-Philippe forgot about them – at least for a while.

Spanish wars are always cruel and usually complicated, and so it was with these Carlist wars. The late King of Spain, Ferdinand VII, a reluctant ally of Napoleon during the late wars, died in 1833, leaving the throne to his daughter Isabella but with his wife Marie-Cristina as regent. This did not suit the dead king's brother, Don Carlos, who wanted to be regent, or better still king, and he raised a rebellion in the north, around the Basque provinces and in Catalonia. Marie-Cristina appealed for help to Spain's former ally, Great Britain, and the first force to arrive was a body of men from Britain, 12,000 ex-soldiers and wastrels who became known as the 'Spanish-British Legion', a force composed of soldiers who, as the saying went, 'left their country for their country's good'.

This British force was shipped to San Sebastian in the Basque country and waited there, drinking, brawling and catching the pox, while a French force was shipped to Barcelona. This was the now 8,000-strong French Foreign Legion, Algerian veterans and new recruits from France, mustered in five battalions and shipped off to Spain without any attempt at consultation, on the understanding that Marie-Cristina would pay them and supply them with food and ammunition. In anticipation of this the legionnaires all acquired a wine bottle and leather cartridge pouches which they wore slung about their waists; as a result of this fashion the local people came to call them the 'leather bellies'. This force arrived in July 1835 and soon discovered exactly what they were up against, struggling against a hard-fighting foe in a desolate, waterless, rugged terrain. If the war in Algeria had been harsh and cruel, the war in Spain was every bit as bad and reached new depths of cruelty as the local people, who had an in-built antipathy to foreigners, turned on the newly arrived legionnaires.

In September 1835, for example, a Legion outpost was overrun by a large force of Carlists and 30 legionnaires were taken prisoner. The Carlists knew that the legionnaires were 'mercenaries' and offered them a large sum of money to change sides; the legionnaires refused. Why they did so is unknown, but the suggestion that they should then fight against their former comrades may have been the cause. Perhaps the Legion *esprit de corps*, which was to prove so valuable in difficult times, was already taking effect. Whatever the reason, the legionnaires' refusal to desert to the enemy brought upon them a dreadful fate.

The 30 legionnaires were taken into the village square and blinded with nails and hot irons. They were then stripped naked and dragged from village to village, across country and through cactus thickets, roped behind the tails of horses. Finally, after days of this torture, they were shot. Word of this atrocity soon got back to the Legion, spread by the Carlists in anticipation of the fact that the Legion would now be afraid to meet them in the field.

The opposite happened. From that time on the Legion never surrendered, fought to the last man and the last cartridge, and took no prisoners. Torture is not usually a Legion vice, but they shot any Carlist prisoner who fell into their hands, including the wounded, and burned any village sheltering Carlist troops. Atrocity begat atrocity. For their part, the Carlists shot, blinded, burned, nailed to barn doors or buried alive any legionnaire they captured, from either the French or the British contingents.

Colonel Bernelle had been appointed a field marshal by Queen Marie-Cristina and he used that rank to carry out some far-reaching reforms in the Legion. The first of these, which was to affect the composition of the Legion to this day, was a mixing up of national battalions. Not only was it proving impossible to find enough Poles or Italians to keep their national battalions up to strength, but Bernelle believed that the separation of nationalities actually did the Legion harm, increasing rivalry and dissension and preventing the building of *esprit de corps*. He also believed that from the moment a man joined the Legion his nationality did not matter; he was no longer a Pole or a Spaniard, he was a legionnaire.

Colonel Bernelle also found that the Legion needed to be more than a pure infantry force if it was to be fully effective. He therefore formed an artillery unit, equipped with field guns, an engineer unit, where the technical skills of the legionnaires were mustered to direct such tasks as road-building, and a cavalry unit, the latter mainly drawn from the disbanded Polish battalion, which had contained a large number of former Polish lancers. The sappers of Colonel Bernelle's engineering unit became a part of the Legion establishment and Legion sappers, in their white aprons, still lead the Legion's ceremonial parades. The bulk of the Legion remained and still remains a 'heavy infantry' unit, but it was now a much more balanced and formidable force, and it needed to be so, for the Carlist War in Spain was hotting up.

At the Battle of Zubiri in August 1836, the Legion gunners went into action for the first time, beating back a series of assaults by Carlist infantry, though by the time the battle was over the Legion's 3rd and 4th infantry battalions had lost more than 500 men killed and wounded, and most of the wounded would die later, for the Spanish made no effort to look after them. The same can be said of the entire Legion; the Spanish had taken over the Legion from the French and with it the notion that the legionnaires were expendable. They were in the Legion to fight and die and need not be fed or clothed or supplied with anything other than ammunition.

Colonel Bernelle demanded that Queen Marie-Cristina honour the commitment made when the Legion was taken over – that the men should be paid, fed and clothed – but her reaction was to dismiss her 'Field Marshal' and appoint a new officer to the command of the Legion, a Major Lebau, another Napleonic hero, a man who shambled about the Legion lines, his belt adorned with a curved Turkish sabre.

In spite of his dramatic appearance, Colonel Lebau was not the man to command the Legion. He was a retiring, intellectual officer and the men – thin, ragged, multilingual and heavily armed, more like brigands than regular soldiers – appeared to intimidate him. Colonel Lebau did not last long, barely three months, before he was in turn replaced with Colonel Conrad, who had already served as an officer in the Legion, where he had won the admiration of all ranks by refusing to take any orders from Madame Bernelle. Conrad was the paradigm of the Legion officer, a man who led from the front in any attack, a product of the French Military Academy at St Cyr from which he had graduated in 1808 in time to take part in some of the most gruelling campaigns of the Napoleonic Wars.

Colonel Conrad did his best for his new command but the situation did not improve. The Legion was reduced to a scarecrow force, clad in rags, shoeless in bitter weather, without money to buy food or supplies. In spite of the fate usually meted out to any French soldier who fell into Spanish hands, desertion became a problem and, perhaps to increase their security during their flight, the men deserted in quantity, whole companies disappearing at the same time, many deserting for the better pay on offer in the army of Don Carlos. The men also died in quantities from malaria and other diseases, but the fighting went on, with a particularly ferocious encounter at Huesca, on the southern slopes of the Pyrenees, in May 1837, when the Legion were hurled into battle by the Spanish general to shouts of 'The Legion forward . . . the Legion forward!'

Street fighting eats up infantry and so it was here. The Carlists had been taken by surprise but they had a good defensive position in a town well supplied with narrow streets and stone walls, and they were soon up and armed and taking the advancing legionnaires in the flank. The Spanish troops failed to come up in support, the Spanish general who had ordered the attack was killed, chaos reigned, and by the time the Legion could be extricated more than 500 precious soldiers, including 28 officers, had been killed or wounded. The Legion could not afford such losses as it had no means of obtaining reinforcements.

One man who did well in these Carlist wars was the former Sergeant Bazaine, now a commissioned officer and a protégé of Colonel Conrad. Between 1836 and 1837 the Legion fought more than 100 separate engagements, large and small, and at one of these, the Battle of Barbastro in June 1837, a battle fought a few weeks after the shambles at Huesca, Colonel Conrad was killed at the head of his men while the Legion were engaging a Carlist legion, formed by Don Carlos from French deserters, including men from the Legion.

In this bitter battle, where legionnaire fought legionnaire, 'the men recognised former comrades in the opposing ranks, called out to them by name or nickname and charged at them with the bayonet, killing their former friends in hot blood or cold for no prisoners were taken', according to a German officer serving with the Carlist Army, who witnessed this engagement. The fury of the Carlist charge broke the lines of Marie-Cristina's army, and it was while he was attempting to rally the soldiers and launch a counter-attack that Colonel Conrad was shot from his horse. After the battle, Captain Bazaine took command of the weary legionnaires and took them off to Saragossa.

The Legion had been without reinforcements for more than two years and had shrunk from seven battalions totalling over 8,000 men to a single battalion by the time the Carlist war ended in victory for Queen Marie-Cristina. Even then the remaining legionnaires got no thanks and little comfort. The survivors retired to Pamplona, on the south side of the Pyrenees, and stayed there, living on local charity or on what work they could find until word came that the survivors could return to France, where another Legion formation had been formed and would welcome more men. Still carrying their now tattered regimental flags and with muskets shining, all that remained to indicate that this was a fighting force, the last of the 'Old Legion', old in experience though established for just six years, marched back over the Roncesvalles pass into France.

2

THE NEW LEGION, 1837–49

*'You have become soldiers in order to die, and I am
sending you where you will die . . .'*

General François de Negrièr, Légion Etrangère

While the Old Legion had been fighting and dying in
Algeria and Spain, a new Legion had been formed in
France. That flow of refugees which had prompted the
formation of the first Legion had not ceased and that
influx, plus the demand of French generals in Algeria for
more troops, prompted the formation of a second Legion,
which was put together in 1835 and sent to North Africa
in 1836, where it was joined later by remnants of the 'old'
Legion from Spain. These mercenary formations, if unusual in most European armies, were quite common in
French history, which may be the reason why France
adopted this method of dealing with its refugee
problem.

The French had been employing mercenary forces since
the Middle Ages, when the kings of France had body-
guards of Scottish archers, and the later Bourbons had
engaged a Swiss Guard, and the first of these new mercenary forces, the old Légion Etrangère, now fighting in
Spain, had already proved itself useful. Perhaps sending
the old Legion to waste itself in Spain had been a mistake,
but there were still plenty of foreigners in France and the
ranks of the 'new' Legion filled up quickly . . . and then

came a renewal of the former problem. Where should this Legion serve if it could not remain in France?

By the terms of the law that authorised its formation, the Legion was not allowed to serve in France or enlist Frenchmen into the ranks. The latter provision had never been strictly enforced and the Legion has always contained a high proportion of Frenchmen, but it was the rule in 1837, and one that applied for many years afterwards, that any Frenchman enlisting in the Legion had to enter as a Swiss or a Belgian, a ruse employed by many early recruits without official encouragement. It had also been accepted by the French Government that in the tumultuous political climate of Europe in the 1830s many men joined the Legion either because they had nowhere else to go, or because they were being actively sought by police or political forces in their native countries and needed somewhere to hide.

Provided none of their actions took place in France or posed a threat to the French Government, the Legion did not care, but it became accepted that men joining the Legion could, and usually did, take another name, which they retained until their term of service was over. This became so much the Legion custom that even volunteers with nothing to hide took a false name on enlistment.

The other provision, prohibiting the deployment of the Legion in France, *was* strictly enforced, at least until the Legion was needed to fight for France in Europe, but there was no lack of volunteers for Legion service in African or tropical hell-holes. The Legion soon found it necessary to maintain recruitment centres in Paris and the principal French towns, as well as a depot at Fort St Jean in Marseilles, where Legion volunteers could be collected for shipment to Algeria or whatever battle front required their services. Wherever they were recruited, the men were shipped out of France as quickly as possible and sent to learn their business at Legion depots in North Africa. This was convenient, for the war against the Arabs in Algeria had not ceased and this new Legion force, so unwelcome in metropolitan France, was soon to prove itself on the former Legion battlefields in North Africa.

The 'New' Legion was slightly better organised that its illustrious predecessor, and certain physical and mental qualities were insisted upon in a would-be legionnaire. He must be between 16 and 42 years old, though no birth certificates were required; young boys and old men certainly joined the new Legion, and served it well. A volunteer must be at least 1.28 metres tall, but need not be otherwise robust, for it was soon discovered that small, slim men could often outmarch the big, broad-shouldered kind.

He must be free of any obvious disease, like syphilis or tuberculosis, but if he was not otherwise physically fit, no matter. Many Legion recruits joined in the early stages of malnutrition or starvation, and a few weeks on good Legion rations – for the food was good, even if the treatment was harsh – soon built them up again. The Legion also rejected those men who, on closer inspection during the early weeks of training, were seen to be obvious psychopaths or were otherwise mentally unbalanced.

This 'New Legion', consisting initially of two battalions, was shipped to Algiers in January 1837, before the 'Old' Legion had tottered back from Spain, and took part in the French Army's second attempt to capture the town of Constantine in 1838. Constantine, a city of the powerful Kabyle tribe, east of Oran, was more of a fortress than a town, occupying a rocky peak, the innermost fortress of the city, the citadel, being equipped with a resolute garrison who in turn were equipped with plenty of heavy cannon which commanded the approaches. Constantine was clearly a tough nut to crack. Moreover, the Kabyle commander in Constantine was the Emir Hadj Achmed, a resolute, ferocious man and a good soldier. The emir was a typical Arab potentate, with several harsh characteristics, unusual even in that time and place. He was notably cruel. For example, having acquired a troop of dancing girls, who were obliged to dance naked before his court, he decided that lesser men should not look upon their beauty and had all his musicians blinded with hot irons. In that state, they were still obliged to play before the court.

By 1837 the French had decided to occupy and colonise Algeria and the capture of Constantine was a major step towards the subjugation of that country. It took several months for the French Army to fight its way as far as Constantine and it was not until 9 October 1837 that the siege actually began. The French had sent a large expedition, led by General Damremont, and containing a 500-strong 'marching battalion', *battalion de marche*, of the French Foreign Legion, formed from the cream of the two battalions then in the country.

The climate of North Africa is not always benign and the weather that autumn was terrible, with rain and snow flurries soaking and chilling the besiegers as they dug their trenches and set up their camp. After three days of battering the walls of Constantine with light field artillery it was apparent that the only way to get into the citadel was by infantry assault. This was bound to cost a lot of lives, and since French lives were valuable and the legionnaires were expendable, the Legion was chosen to lead the 'forlorn hope', the advance contingent in the first assault on the city walls.

By now General Damremont had already been killed, hit by a sniper's bullet, and the emir was already certain that he could defeat the besiegers and drive them away. In a defiant message to the French he said, 'If you run out of gunpowder we shall let you have some of ours and if you run out of bread we shall share our supplies with you . . . but as long as one of us remains alive, you will not take Constantine.'

The French were equally determined to take it and the new commander, General Valee, a skilled gunner, ordered the artillery to concentrate on one spot and somehow create a breach in the walls. This was done by 12 October, and on the following morning, just after dawn, the Legion attacked, carrying the breach in the face of murderous fire and making a lodgement beyond the walls. The man leading the Legion assault was Captain Achille St Arnaud, a man who, though a French officer and a graduate of St Cyr, was a typical legionnaire, having applied for a posting to the Legion to escape his creditors and the outraged husband of his mistress. St Arnaud was the first to scale the tumbled stonework of the breach, and on the top, waving his sword, he rallied his followers with words the Legion would remember . . . '*A moi, La Légion!!*' His men, leaping over their dead, rushed up after him and carried the breach. The struggle for Constantine had, however, only begun.

'The Turks [Arabs] handled themselves with great courage,' wrote St Arnaud later. 'They fired and we advanced, killing them while they were reloading and our bayonets did not leave one alive . . . we did not take prisoners.'

It then took all day, a day of continuous street fighting, for the Legion to reach the citadel, a day of hand-to-hand combat, bayonet against sword and dagger, with constant musketry fire cutting into the attackers from the rooftops, but at last, as dusk fell, the Legion broke into the citadel and put the defenders to the bayonet. The last enemy flag was torn from its Arab owner by Sergeant Major Doze of the Legion and hangs today in the Invalides in Paris. The Legion was made famous by their actions at the taking of Constantine but the cost of fame, as always, was very high. Of the 500 legionnaires who had marched on the city, less than 50 marched back to Algiers.

The capture of Constantine must have been a blow to the Algerians but their former leader, Abd-el-Kader, was now back in the field, having rejected the Treaty of Tafna, and apparently undaunted by this defeat. His Arab horsemen and well-armed musketeers continued to ambush and attack the French convoys and garrisons, and there were a number of battles and small-scale engagements, many involving the Legion, which, by the end of 1838, with the welcome arrival of the 'old' Legion contingent from Spain, had risen to a strength of three battalions, about 2,000 men.

The Legion was entrusted with the defence of Algiers, but when there were no Arabs in the vicinity the men were not given any rest but employed in civilian pacification tasks, building roads and tunnels, preparing the way for a long-lasting French occupation. One of the roads they built across Algeria, and one that still remains, though under a different name, was known as the Chaussée de la Légion – the Legion's Road. These public works and labouring tasks, especially road-building, were to occupy the Legion in times of peace until they left North Africa for ever in the 1960s.

In 1840 the newly raised 4th Battalion of the Legion was besieged by Abd-el-Kader's forces in the town of Miliana. This siege lasted for four months, and although the legionnaires beat off any Arab assault with comparative ease – though taking losses in the process – this siege introduced them to a new enemy of the North African wars, *le cafard* – a form of madness brought on by stress and constant fear. A *cafard* is, literally, a small black beetle, and the sensations of *le cafard*, which induce a deep, even suicidal depression, were said to be similar to having black beetles running about inside one's head. Under the influence of *le cafard* men in Miliana attacked their comrades, made suicidal assaults on the Arab siege lines, seeking death, hanged or shot themselves, or sank into catatonic stupors. When the town was relieved in October 1840, less than a third of the 4th Battalion were totally sane, but given rest and a few weeks of normal barrack life, most of those affected recovered and returned to normal duty. *Le cafard*, however, never quite went away, constantly stalking men serving in lonely outposts, and we shall hear of it again. The story of the siege of Miliana, with *le cafard* within and the Arabs outside, remains a Legion legend.

Miliana had been a French outpost in the Aures Mountains which el-Kader had destroyed in 1840, soon after tearing up the Treaty of Tafna. The French wished to rebuild this outpost and the task was given to a force of 1,000 men, half of them from the Legion, among them Captain Bazaine, a future marshal of France. The Legion had managed to rebuild the walls and dig out the well when Abd-el-Kader reappeared with his entire army and brought the French and the legionnaires under siege. Before the siege settled down riders were sent to warn other outposts of what was happening, returning with the news that the Miliana garrison would have to hold on – perhaps for weeks – until a relief force could be mustered, and it may have been this dire news which induced *le cafard*.

In fact, four months went by before relief arrived, four months of starvation and bloodshed, with rations running low and Arab attacks by day and night taking a steady toll of the garrison. Those who attempted to escape were inevitably captured and tortured to death before the walls, their screams and the sight of their sufferings adding to the defenders' torments. Eventually, the active members of the garrison were down to about 300 men, so here, as elsewhere in this long and terrible war, dead men were propped up in the embrasures to give the impression that the fort was still fully manned. While the attacks were in progress, *le cafard* disappeared, but when the besiegers just stayed out in their trenches, rarely seen but always there, men's nerves began to fray and the affliction re-appeared.

Finally, four months after the siege began, a relief column arrived, to find just 300 men left from the original 1,200. Most of those standing in the embrasures bore untreated wounds. The Arabs, who had lost many men attempting to overwhelm this outpost, finally withdrew, and the garrison of the fort came out from behind their walls and formed up to greet the newcomers with a guard of honour, thus establishing a Legion tradition that endures to this day. One of the men leading the relief was Colonel Marie-Patrice MacMahon, a man descended from one of the Scots soldiers who had fought for the Stuarts and Bonnie Prince Charlie, a man who would become a marshal of France.

By 1841 the Legion was large enough to form two regiments, each of three battalions, the 1st Régiment Etranger, which was based in Algiers, and the 2nd Régiment Etranger, which was based at the port of Bone. It was now clear that the Legion was too useful to be disbanded and needed a permanent home, a depot where recruits could be introduced to Legion ways and trained in soldiering and the Legion's harsh *esprit de corps*.

This Legion training was always brutal. P. C. Wren's sadistic Sergeant-Major Lajaune, the villain of *Beau Geste* who greeted his recruits with the welcoming words 'Here we make soldiers out of scum like you', though a fictional creation, is not that far removed from the truth. The 3rd Battalion of the 1st Regiment were sent to build a depot in the little Arab town of Sidi Bel Abbès, about 60 miles south of Oran.

When the 3rd Battalion arrived at Sidi Bel Abbès there was nothing there but a squalid Arab settlement, named after a local religious hermit, and a well, supporting an impoverished population of fewer than 500. Within a few years, as the Legion built its barracks and began to settle in, more Arabs arrived, to open shops and brothels catering for the needs of these strange, fierce soldiers, and the population of Sidi Bel Abbès rose to several thousands. The Legion was given no assistance in building its depot, but the 3rd Battalion, a typical Legion unit, produced three former architects to draw up the plans, plus a quantity of skilled stonemasons, carpenters and bricklayers who willingly took up their former trades and rapidly taught their skills to others.

This, too, is typical of the Legion. There are tales of men stepping from the ranks to tend the wounded and turning out to be former surgeons, and on one famous occasion, when the priest due to conduct church parade failed to arrive, a legionnaire came forward to take the service, declaring that as a former bishop, who had never been unfrocked, he was still qualified to do so. His offer was accepted, and all the legionnaires, officers and men, took communion at his hands.

Working under the direction of their own experts, the legionnaires produced a barracks which – one suspects to the considerable annoyance of the French high command

– was far better than anything else in the French Army, so well designed that it remained in use for another 130 years, until the Legion left Algeria. Around these barracks a large town grew up, chiefly to cater to the legionnaires, and if at first their wants were few and their pockets empty, it still managed to fill up with bars and brothels. Later on, as legionnaires left the service, married and retired, many of them settled in the town, farms were established to supply the barracks with fresh provisions, and a whole community, largely legionnaires and ex-legionnaires, grew up around the town.

These barracks, La Caserne de la Légion, later the Quartier Vienot, became the Legion depot, but even the time of construction was far from peaceful. Apart from building barracks and training recruits, the Legion was constantly forced to send out pacification patrols into the surrounding countryside, and find parties to build roads and chase roving bands of Arab horse, raiding local villages on the orders of Abd-el-Kader. These local actions were useful in getting the Legion volunteers used to the conditions they would meet when their training was complete.

By 1840, a routine had been established for processing Legion recruits, and with Abd-el-Kader on the rampage again, more recruits were urgently needed. After acceptance a man was kept at the recruiting centre until he could be sent, under guard, with other recruits to Fort St Jean in Marseilles. He would not be allowed to leave the fort, for fear of desertion, his civilian clothes would be taken away and sold, and the usual recruit garb, the blue uniform of a French infantry soldier, would be issued in its place. When enough men had been mustered to make a draft of troops, the men would be shipped, still under guard, to Algiers, and then marched or sent by train to Sidi Bel Abbès.

Here the Legion draft – *les bleus* – would be examined a little more carefully, and those most obviously unsuited, ill or insane were sent back to France. There were very few of these for the early Legion was not fussy. If a man could stand on parade and fire a musket in the field, the Legion would take him, and turn him into a soldier. That preliminary cull completed, the men were marched to the infantry training centre at Mascara and put through four months of the most rugged – not to say hellish – basic training in existence. Most of this training was left to the senior NCOs and corporals, who were nothing if not harsh with the recruits.

Failure to understand a command in French – even if the new recruit did not speak the language – resulted in a blow or some severe punishment – imprisonment in cold cells, hours of pack drill under the blistering sun. As a result, though, men learned French – or at least the words of command – and the elements of drill and musketry very quickly. What took longer to learn were the Legion standards in the field, especially the ability to march long distances under heavy loads. Marches began in the first week, starting with a march of 24 kilometres, but this distance was rapidly extended. The final test was 50 kilometres a day – carrying 45 kilograms of kit, across mountainous terrain and on terrible roads. The time allowed for this was eight hours, no more. No one fell out and anyone who collapsed was simply tied to the back of a wagon and dragged along until he staggered to his feet again.

There was a reason for this: any man who fell out and got left behind would be found and murdered by the local Arabs . . . so no one was allowed to fall out. On arrival at the final campsite, the legionnaires had to establish a camp, dig trenches and build defensive walls. Then they would stand guard and next day at dawn they pulled on their boots, on to blistered, bloody feet, and did it all over again. After some months of such training the Legionnaire recruit, now a trained soldier, left to join his regiment, and take part in the war of pacification. 'March or Die' – '*Marchez ou Crevez*', literally 'march or croak' – became one of the many unofficial mottos of the Legion, and one that wise legionnaires took to heart.

In the 1840s the Legion developed a new method of

combating the enemy, a method they would retain in various forms throughout the endless Algerian wars – the flying column. It was clearly necessary to run down the roving Arab bands and the ponderous French punitive expeditions were too slow to do this in a terrain that was almost entirely without roads. The Legion bought mules, stripped its stock of supplies down to the three essentials of water, food and ammunition, and began to chase the Arabs deep into the mountains, the 'flying columns' proving fast enough to catch even the best-mounted Arab force and bring it to battle. Fortified outposts were established as patrol bases and roads were constructed to link these bases together, slowly strangling Abd-el-Kader's forces in a network of fortifications.

While the 1st Regiment was building its depot and fighting around Sidi Bel Abbès, the 2nd Regiment was made responsible for similar tasks from its base at Bone, especially in controlling Arab activity and raiding from the Kabyle Mountains, and pacifying the country south towards the endless sand seas of the Sahara and the Aures Mountains. A few years later, here in the Aures Mountains in March 1844, the 2nd Regiment earned their regimental colour when they carried the Kabyle stronghold of M'Chounech by assault.

The Legion force sent to reduce M'Chounech was led by Colonel MacMahon, who had two battalions of the 2nd Regiment under his command, and when the experienced legionnaires saw M'Chounech they knew at once that they had a stiff fight on their hands, for the Arabs had fortified the village, which occupied a naturally strong defensive site on a hilltop, with a trench system and stone sangars. This was a small-scale rerun of the Constantine attack, for the Legion artillery could make no impression on the stone and mud walls of the village and the rifle fire from the defenders commanded all approaches. The French infantry and the legionnaires assaulted the village across open ground, putting in attack after attack, carpeting the ground before the walls with their dead, all to no avail.

There was only one way to do this and only one force in the field that day to do it. The position must be carried by an assault that pressed on regardless of casualties, and that was the Legion's task. MacMahon and his second-in-command, Major Espinasse, put themselves at the head of their legionnaires and led them at the trot, towards the one small breach in the walls. Men fell, bullets flew, the Arabs stood in the breach waving their swords to welcome the attackers, but the Legion did not falter.

The two officers got to the breach first, hacked a path to the top, and in the manner of Captain St Armand summoned their men with the cry of '*A moi La Légion!*' On came the Legion, clawing their way up the boulder-strewn slope already littered with Legion dead. A strong force of tribesmen had mustered to defend the breach but nothing could stop that terrible infantry and the Legion broke through, to carry the walls and overrun the town.

The final Legion attack was seen by a French noble-man, the Duc d' Aumale, who carried news of this exploit to his father, King Louis-Philippe. The award of a regimental colour to the 2nd Regiment was the result of his glowing report.

Meanwhile, Algeria had received a new governor-general, an army officer, General Thomas Bugeaud. Bugeaud was a considerable soldier, who had served in Napoleon's famous Imperial Guard, that force of whom their commander said, when summoned to surrender at Waterloo, 'The Guard knows how to die, but not how to surrender.' General Bugeaud, who eventually became a duke and a marshal of France, was a product of that splendid company, and he found the Algerian war – and the Foreign Legion – exactly to his taste.

Bugeaud's first task was to carry the war to the enemy. To do this he had to get his battalions out of their defensive positions in the towns along the coast, where they were simply hanging on to what they had, and set them to staking out fresh ground in the interior which French settlers could then farm. Bugeaud ordered all the French regimental commanders to form 'flying columns', in the Legion fashion, composite units with cavalry, artillery, infantry and supply elements, then get out into the countryside – the *bled* – and hunt the Arabs down. Supply depots – one of them being Sidi Bel Abbès – were established in the hinterland, and the pace of pacification speeded up, though not without considerable opposition from the local tribes, who raided constantly from their bases in the Aures and Kabyle Mountains.

Savage action against the Chaua tribesmen of the Aures Mountains in 1844 did not contain them for long, and they were soon on the rampage again, raiding coastal villages and Legion convoys, doing macabre work with their knives on any prisoners or French wounded who fell into their hands. The cost was high, but the French were gradually winning the struggle and gained a great psychological victory in 1847 when, worn out with years of fighting, Abd-el-Kader finally surrendered.

After suffering various defeats in Algeria, he had established himself and his army in Morocco, and used that as a raiding base for his attacks into Algeria until General Bugeaud decided to ignore the existence of the frontier, take an army into Morocco and root out Abd-el-Kader once and for all. Bugeaud occupied the Moroccan border town of Oujda but a great international outcry and protests in Paris soon forced him to withdraw. Fortunately for Bugeaud, this withdrawal had the benefit of encouraging Abd-el-Kader to follow Bugeaud back into Algeria where el-Kader and his army were defeated at the Battle of Oued Isly in August 1844. El-Kader's fortunes never recovered from this defeat and three years later he laid down his arms.

Abd-el-Kader had become a hero to the French of the Métropolitain, so his captivity was light and probably most pleasant, for the French let him take his wives and concubines with him into exile, and he installed them in the beautiful château at Amboise on the River Loire, where he soon became very popular with the local people and attracted a crowd of admiring visitors. He was later awarded the Légion d' Honneur and retired in old age to

Damascus in Syria, where he died in bed, aged 75, surrounded by beautiful women, an unlikely end for a desert warrior.

The surrender of Abd-el-Kader did not end the struggle in North Africa, for Algeria contained many warlike tribes and new leaders constantly arose to defy the French invaders. Two years after Abd-el-Kader gave up the struggle, another major pacification was called for, and it led the Legion to one of their most famous battles in the long struggle to conquer Algeria, the fight for the oasis at Zaacha in 1849.

This fresh outbreak of violence in Algeria came as a great surprise to the population of metropolitan France who assumed, not unnaturally, that with the surrender of Abd-el-Kader the pacification phase of their conquest of Algeria was over. All that remained was to build more roads and farm out the fertile parts of the country to an ever-larger quantity of European settlers. These, the '*pieds noirs*', or '*colons*', from a number of European countries, Italy and Spain as well as France, were starting to arrive in Algiers in increasing numbers, but the next phase of settlement could not begin until the tribesmen had been crushed . . . and the men for that task were already there, in the Foreign Legion.

In over 100 years of shared experience in Algeria the Legion and the *colons* never really got on; the *colons* regarded the legionnaires as little better than dangerous animals, who had to be kept in their place, well away from decent men and women, and the Legion regarded the *colons*, with thinly veiled contempt, as civilians. Even so, a campaign was a campaign and the campaign against the next tribal leader to arise, Sheikh Bou Zain of Zaacha, proved a hard campaign indeed.

Zaacha was a large oasis. Oases are not always the small, palm-fringed pools of cinematic imagining. Many are very large, and extremely fertile, where crops are raised and irrigated with canals or underground sluices. They can also contain many villages and even small towns, supporting a population of several thousand. Such a place was Zaacha, in the south of Algeria near Biskra, where the sheikh supported a force of some 6,000 fighting men, none of whom had any intention of being evicted from their homes by European intruders.

The French administration might well have left Zaacha alone but General Bugeaud had recently died and the new governor-general was anxious to proceed with colonisation. In addition, Sheikh Bou Zain of Zaacha had the habit of leading his men north to raid along the coast. A punitive attack seemed called for and if, as a result, the European *colons* acquired that fertile oasis, so much the better. The task was handed to the 2nd Regiment of the Legion, who sent a small force of 500 men, commanded by Major Gaillard de St Germain. He led them to disaster.

The campaign got off to a very bad start in July 1849 when Major St Germain attacked the oasis without adequate reconnaissance and was savagely repulsed, losing 32 men killed and over 100 wounded in less than an hour of savage fighting. The defences and fighters in Zaacha were far tougher and more numerous than the Legion had been led to expect, and a second assault, with artillery preparation, was clearly going to be necessary. Before that could happen another tribal chief, Sidi el Afidt, encouraged by the Legion defeat at Zaacha, mustered a force of some 4,000 well-armed tribesmen and took the field, capturing the village of Seriana and fortifying it. Major St Germain had his reputation to recover, and he was therefore charged with driving the Arabs from Seriana. Taking the remnants of his battalion, St Germain attacked Seriana with about 300 men. The result was another defeat. The legionnaires were outnumbered by ten to one and stood no chance when the Arabs came out from behind their walls and surrounded them; not for the first or last time in Algeria, a Legion unit stood and fought and died to the last man.

These reverses could not continue, or the entire Arab population, so recently quiescent, would take up arms. The 2nd Regiment had caused this situation and they must put it right, whatever the cost. An expedition, largely composed of legionnaires from both regiments, marched again on Zaacha, knowing that this time they must not fail. Their commander, General Herbillon, told them that much quite bluntly. 'We must take the fortress at any cost. Die if you must, but abandon all thoughts of ever returning until you take Zaacha.'

The siege of the oasis began in October 1849 and lasted for nearly two months, for the Arabs defended their homes bravely, and contested every foot of ground. Bayonet charges were repulsed, sniping was constant, any legionnaire who was wounded and not recovered by his comrades was swiftly submerged in a shrieking cloud of Arab women and cut to pieces. Captured legionnaires were tied up to be eaten alive by starving dogs or tied high in the palms for use as targets. Eventually the Legion began to reduce the oasis to a wilderness, destroying houses and water courses as they advanced into it, chopping down the date palms, employing the worst kind of 'scorched earth' policy, killing anyone, man, woman or child, who stood against them.

This fighting continued, on and off, until the end of November 1849, when the Legion took the last stronghold in Zaacha at the point of the bayonet. A few surviving Arabs were marched away into brief captivity, but Sheikh Bou Zain and his son, captured in the final assault, were killed on the following day and their severed heads sent about the country as a warning to other tribesmen thinking of taking up arms against the French.

So the wars in Algeria continued, and were to continue, in their various ways, for decades, until the Legion finally left Algeria in 1962. These Algerian wars were to provide a constant backdrop to the Legion's actions in other wars, but it was in Algeria that the legend of the Legion began to take shape. That legend and the truth that underpins it should now be examined, before proceeding with this story.

3

THE LEGEND OF THE LEGION, 1850–54

'The dogs bark at night when the Legion passes by'

Colonist saying, Algeria, 1848

At this point, with two decades of Legion fighting described and Algeria at least partially at peace, it would be as well to take a closer look at this famous fighting force and discover exactly what it is that makes the Legion different from other élite units. Legends surround the Legion, attributing various reasons for its military success and superb reputation, but these legends sometime obscure the more brilliant and exciting truth.

The Legion is a mercenary force. That at least is the theory and the technical definition of a unit in which men serve a nation other than their own for pay. However, as this book will reveal, pay is rarely the motivation for the Legion soldier, and anyway, in the glory days of the Legion's history, a legionnaire's pay was very low. To find a reason for the Legion's reputation we must look elsewhere, for money is not the answer.

Fierce discipline, harsh training, a commitment to fight to the last round and the last man – and then charge with the bayonet, to *'faire Camerone'* or 'do a Camerone' as the Legion calls it – are all part of the reason, but the basic explanation more probably lies in the quality of the recruits, in the training they receive – which, though undoubtedly hard, is still based on sensible military principles – in the officers and NCOs who lead legionnaires in battle and, most of all, in the establishment of that most elusive yet most essential of all military assets, *esprit de corps*.

The French Foreign Legion is one of the world's most famous fighting forces, one that ranks with the Royal Marine Commandos, the United States Marine Corps, the Brigade of Guards or the Brigade of Gurkhas. It is no accident that all the units have tremendous *esprit de corps*, a feeling, a belief, even a conviction, that they are special and that their hard-won reputation must be maintained at all costs, even, if need be, to the death.

This may sound melodramatic, especially to civilian ears, but it happens to be true. The military annals are full of instances where a regiment has been driven on by a reminder of what it is, what it stands for and what it must do, whatever the cost in lives. This characteristic is not confined to the Foreign Legion, or indeed to any so-called or self-styled 'élite' unit.

To give one example of what unit pride – *esprit de corps* – can do, during the breakout from Tobruk in 1942 the Highland infantry of the Black Watch were caught by German machine guns and driven to ground by terrible fire. They were pinned down, taking heavy casualties and unable to move, when their adjutant, though already wounded, got to his feet, among a storm of machine gun fire, and cried out, 'Isn't this the Black Watch? Then come on.' The adjutant was killed within seconds, but the survivors of the battalion got up and carried the German position at the point of the bayonet.

And yet, even when compared with other famous regiments, the Foreign Legion remains somewhat apart, somewhat different, and *la différence* is more than one of degree. There are many élite units, at least one in every army, famous for their prowess on the battlefield, but the French Foreign Legion also has the reputation of providing a refuge for hard men fallen on hard times.

This was true even before Madame Louise de Ramée,

better known as the writer Ouida, wrote her legionnaire novel *Under Two Flags*, back in 1866. Madame Ouida failed to get her facts right and her hero, who rejoices in the distinctly unheroic name of Bertie Cecil, is said to serve in the Spanish–French cavalry, which the good lady took to be the same thing as the formidable Légion Etrangère. *Under Two Flags* is a lively read, but the picture it presents of life in the Legion is ludicrous.

The question that has to be asked and answered, therefore, is why do men join the Légion Etrangère, when most nations have élite units in their armies that will suit a willing volunteer perfectly well, however anxious he might be for the military life and even for the hard training and strict discipline found in any élite unit, provided, of course, there is also the prospect of action.

To obtain the answer to that question it would be necessary to question some of the 10,000 legionnaires currently in service and digest some 10,000 different responses. A slightly smaller sample reveals that part of the attraction of the Legion lies in its legendary – but well-founded – reputation as a tough fighting force. Perhaps this has always been the case, for there are always men who want to serve in a tough, firmly disciplined, hard-fighting unit. There are also men who for some personal, even emotional, reason want to make a fresh start and feel that five years in the Foreign Legion, perhaps under a false name, will wipe the slate clean. Then there are men who want to prove themselves, who need a challenge and feel – for some reason – that wearing the *képi blanc* will meet that need.

That said, legionnaires are not supermen. They are superb soldiers but they put their trousers on one leg at a time, like most other soldiers. And yet the difference is there, and the only way to put a finger on the difference is to examine the Legion and so discover exactly what makes this fighting force so different and so formidable.

Separating legend from reality in the 166-year-long story of the Légion Etrangère is one of the aims of this book and poses the first difficulty, for in the case of the

Foreign Legion, truth and legend are curiously inter-twined. There is at least a scrap of truth in every story, however far-fetched. This being so, it might be as well to begin this story with a few facts.

The Legion is a 'mercenary force' in that the men who join it are not native Frenchmen and are paid to serve the French Government and fight in French wars. Pay, in itself, is not why they join, for until quite recently legion-naires were very badly paid. Legion pay in the last century was a *sou* a day, about ten cents, just enough, if carefully hoarded, to provide enough rough red wine to get drunk on and perhaps pay for a short visit to the regimental brothel once a month. Therefore the usual sneer made about mercenary soldiers, that they fight other people's wars for money, can hardly apply here. Though modern legionnaires are well paid – and those in the Legion parachute regiment, the 2nd Régiment Etranger Para-chutiste (REP), even very well paid – this was not the case in the past. Whatever motivated the Legion soldier, it was certainly not money.

In the early days, when the Legion was establishing its fearsome reputation, it was a refuge for the dispossessed, for political refugees, for the stateless and the homeless and the man on the run from some minor crime. It offered a kind of sanctuary for men of all nations, and at one time or another more than 80 nations have served in the Legion, though some national contingents usually pre-dominate. The Swiss and Germans have a long tradition of Legion service, partly because both have a tradition of serving in mercenary units and their men enjoy soldiering. Other than the Legion, the only foreign force available to the Swiss is the Papal Guard in Rome, which has a purely ceremonial function and is armed and dressed as in the sixteenth century ... no place for the modern fighting man.

Germany has lost two great wars in the present century and was highly unstable until united by Bismarck in the last century, so the tradition of joining the Legion was well established in Germany quite early on in the Legion's history, and still continues. Within the Legion the various nationalities have established certain reputations. The Swiss and Germans are good legionnaires and well disciplined, though German NCOs are said to be harsh to the point of brutality and have to be watched. The Spanish are terrors with the women, fight in barracks and are brave to the point of foolhardiness in battle. The Italians enjoy soldiering, as do the Poles and the Hungarians, and all three nationalities are noted for supporting the girls in the Legion brothels, where, incidentally, part of the money paid to the girls is diverted into Legion funds and is used to buy comforts for the men and their families.

The British are known as good soldiers but they tend to be insubordinate, and they also have a tendency to desert. On the other hand, when things get difficult in action and the section leaders are killed or wounded, it is likely to be a British legionnaire who takes charge and gets the job done. British legionnaires were never very common in the early days of the Legion but their numbers have increased and now – in 1997 – Britain usually supplies about ten per cent of the Legion intake. As for the Americans, a number of ex-Vietnam veterans joined the Legion in the 1970s and did very well in the 2nd REP but, as a rule, Americans do not take well to Legion life, though some of the most famous Legion recruits, like the composer Cole Porter and the Great War poet Alan Seeger, were both Americans.

And then, increasingly, there are the French. Many old legionnaires disapprove of the fact that French citizens can now openly join the Legion. This is a curious reaction, for Frenchmen have always made up a significant part of the Legion strength, though obliged by the law to enlist as foreigners, usually Swiss or Belgians; even so their true identity was no big secret. The difference today is that the Legion now openly recruits Frenchmen and they can keep their own names and national identity. Perhaps that does make a difference, makes the Legion in some way more 'ordinary', more a part of the established French military machine, and not as special as it was when everyone took a false name on joining – or even a false nationality.

Legend also has it that anyone can join the Legion, even those with a criminal past, and the Legion will protect them. That is true, but only up to a point. In 1931 the French Government passed a law that enabled the Legion flatly to deny the existence of any legionnaire, unless the legionnaire himself gave permission for such disclosure. Anyone breaching this confidentiality is still liable to prosecution, but his protection from investigation is not absolute today. The truth is that the degree protection depends on the crime.

Even in the early days murderers and paedophiles would not be welcome in the Legion, though petty theft, fraud and minor convictions for assault would not – and do not – ban a man from the Legion's ranks. Men who might be wanted as petty or political criminals in their native lands, and republican fugitives from the rough justice meted out in Franco's Spain after the Spanish Civil War, certainly found shelter in the Legion, as did a number of Hungarian and Czech patriots after the attempt to overthrow the Soviet communist domination of their native countries led to the risings of 1956 and 1968. After World War II a good number of German soldiers, even from the notorious SS divisions, were able to join the Legion – but only after checking had shown that they were not wanted for war crimes. Those who were so guilty were handed over to their pursuers and justice took its course.

After the Algerian War of 1954–63, things changed. France was no longer willing to offer protection to anyone who asked for it, however willing they were to serve, and any foreigner joining the Legion today will be carefully vetted by the Deuxième Bureau, the French Security Service. If the Deuxième Bureau are not satisfied they will inform Interpol, and those wanted for serious crimes – murder, for example – will not only not be permitted to join, but will be arrested and extradited to their own countries.

And yet, as with all matters concerning the Legion, it is

not quite that clear-cut. In the majority of cases an enlisted legionnaire is protected by the Legion. The Legion may treat its men harshly but it prevents anyone else from doing so. If his wife, ex-wife, debtors or even the police come looking for him, the Legion will most probably deny that such a man is serving in its ranks – which is another reason why the old custom of joining the Legion under a false name still continues – it offers the Legion, and the legionnaire, 'deniability'. In return for this protection, the Legion expects, even demands, total loyalty from the legionnaire.

So the first plank in the establishment of a first-class regiment is established. The men who join it are all *volunteers* and, as they used to say in the Royal Marines, 'one volunteer is worth three pressed men', a saying as true today as when it was first coined in the days of sail. Having joined, the man must be trained, and since the Legion training is known to be harsh, the idea of it will certainly thin the ranks of potential volunteers.

The actual training endured by legionnaires was – and is – no harder than in any other comparable unit in any army, but the standards of performance expected at the end of that training are high, and the legionnaire recruit, the *bleu*, so called because in the early days volunteers arrived at the training depot in blue French infantry uniforms, has to cope with the problem of language and the rapid inculcation of discipline and Legion *esprit de corps*.

The language of the Legion is French – though a great many German words seem to form part of Legion slang – and the recruit who cannot swiftly pick up at least the words of command and simple orders in French will have a much harder time than the native French speaker. The training is in the hands of the NCOs, and since they will have to live, work and fight with these men after training they have every incentive to turn out tough, resolute fighting men. A kick or a blow would reinforce a command, or be used instead of one, if the recruit was not performing well, and a kick up the pants is probably still in use today, though any NCO abusing his men will soon be deprived of his stripes. Many legionnaires smile when the question of brutality is raised by an outsider and reply that as long as a man is prepared to try hard and do his *devoir* – his duty – he has nothing to fear in the Legion. Drill, relentless inspections, many in the *tenue de campagne*, the full service marching order, and a high standard of musketry are all part of the training. But, above all, the legionnaire must learn to march.

Many of the modern élite units – with the exception of the Brigade of Guards – can trace their origins to light infantry or amphibious assault troops. Not so the Legion, which has always been a 'heavy' infantry formation. The legionnaire was a foot soldier *par excellence*, and his marching ability was, and still is, even in these days of helicopter transport, quite incredible, up to 64 kilometres a day in full kit, over any kind of terrain. Other units can do this but the legionnaires can do it day after day, for weeks if necessary, and fight a battle at the end of it. Part of the secret of such performance is belief in the ability to do it, and such a belief is not built up easily. Legionnaires start marching in the first week of training, progressing to ever longer marches as their training goes on, though their feet are blistered and bleeding.

Disciplinary punishments are hard but fair, and not quite as hard as legend would have it. Legend tells of men being buried up to their necks in sand, or staked out in the sun, or whipped senseless, and from time to time these and other such things may have happened in the past, but rarely. Flogging was never employed in the armies of the French republic, though the British flogged their soldiers until their backs were raw until well into the Victorian age, and were still inflicting Field Punishment No. 1 – tying a man to a wagon wheel and leaving him there all day – as recently as the Great War of 1914–18.

The most notorious of Legion disciplinary punishments was the *crapaudine* in which a soldier was put into a prone position, with his wrists and ankles lashed together behind his back. Within a few minutes cramp began to cause pain

43

and a few hours of this treatment caused agony. Other men might be put into Arab grain silos, shut up in the dark, unable to stand or lie straight, and left there without water, sometimes for days. This punishment was abolished before the Great War, but even in the 1960s legionnaires under punishment were being ordered to dig a shallow trench and sleep in it, on the stones, without blankets in freezing weather. The *crapaudine* was abolished in 1920 and replaced by imprisonment in the barrack cells, pack drill, or a combination of the two.

Sleeping in the cells, denied all contact with one's fellows, a stoppage of pay, and turning out twice a day to be shunted about the barrack square, carrying a pack filled with 20 kilograms of stones, was gauged a sufficient deterrent. As late as the 1960s this last punishment, *la pelote*, was employed on recalcitrant legionnaires for up to three hours at a time. The prisoner stripped to the waist and heaved on a stone-filled sack, fitted with wire shoulder straps. He then put on a steel helmet with the padding removed. Thus burdened, he was bustled about the parade ground, urged on with slashes from a rope's end, ordered to hurl himself to the ground and crawl for 50 or 100 metres across the stony ground before getting up to run on again. This process was repeated, sometimes for hours.

This was brutality that barely stopped short of torture, and though many of these punishments were actually forbidden by the French military code, they happened quite often in the Legion, especially to deserters. Today the discipline of the Legion is no different to that found in other élite units: in other words, hard, enforced, but fair. A man who knows how to soldier and sticks to the rules will get on perfectly well in the Legion, and if he feels himself victimised by an NCO he always has the opportunity, out of working hours, of challenging the NCO to a private fight in some corner of the barracks . . . though since no one gets to be an NCO instructor in the French Foreign Legion without being able to take care of himself, this must be seen as a last resort.

The inculcation of discipline is largely left to the NCOs, for at least in the early days of training a legionnaire will not see much of his officers. That said, Legion officers are the pick of the French Army crop. When it is considered that the Legion is generally – if incorrectly – regarded as a refuge for petty criminal misfits, it is surprising to note that becoming an officer in the Légion Etrangère is considered the height of honour for any graduate of St Cyr, the French military academy – equivalent, perhaps, to getting a posting to the SAS.

So great is the honour, and so high the demand, that only the first ten or so graduate cadets are even considered for such a posting, and in any year only about six actually get to join the Legion. Officers in the French Army believe that it is an honour to serve in the Legion and one of the much-prized honours of any French general is to be appointed an honorary legionnaire – not an honorary officer, but an ordinary legionnaire or NCO, wearer of the *képi blanc*. This honour is not given lightly. General de Gaulle was weighed down with national and international honours but he never became an honorary legionnaire, because the Legion did not like him – or he the Legion.

If becoming an officer in the Légion Etrangère is not easy, staying alive in the Legion during wartime or on campaign must be equally difficult. Legion officers, even commanding officers, are expected to lead from the front, and the attrition among the battalion and company officers is notably high. It has been said, without irony, that the way for an officer to make his name in the Legion is to get himself killed. Legion officers are brave men – and expected to be brave in a regiment where bravery is taken for granted – and they are not noted for being unduly careful with the lives of their men.

It was a famous Legion officer, Colonel Negrier, who told his men in 1883 that they had enlisted to die in battle and he would take them where they could do so, and that sentiment has remained with the Legion ever since. In spite of this prodigality, the devotion of the legionnaire to his officers, and of the officers to the men, is marked, provided the officer leads from the front and shares the everyday dangers faced by his men in action.

The Legion has a mystique. The Legion creates that mystique and part of the job of that mystique is to imbue the new legionnaire with the Legion spirit . . . and the Legion rules. The Legion fights, but does not retreat. The Legion dies, but does not surrender. The Legion lives, but does not leave its dead on the battlefield. At the end of the twentieth century there is something awesome about a force that deliberately sets out to teach its soldiers that death in battle is expected of them – if that is the price of maintaining the Legion mystique and the hard-fighting Legion tradition.

This attitude is not for show, or often on show, but it is there and the Legion does not attempt to conceal the fact. The Legion has been compared with the medieval military orders, like the Knights Templar or the Knights of Santiago, warriors who dedicated themselves to fighting and dying in the name of Christendom and by that vow became the backbone of the crusading armies. It is not likely that too many legionnaires believe in God – but they believe in the Legion.

The Legion never rests. In other armies, when there is no war to fight, the men spend their time on exercises or in sport. The Legion exercises constantly to keep its skills sharp, but it does not seem very interested in sport, though in recent years Legion teams have done well in marathons and other physical challenges. Mostly, though, the legionnaires work, building roads or improving their barracks. Nor does discipline relax, and punishments for lapses are severe, even in peacetime, though perhaps less severe than they used to be. Legionnaire Simon Murray recalls that in 1960, in the Legion punishment camp at Colomb-Bechar, at the height of the Algerian War, 'the day began at 0430 hours followed by inspection at 0600 hours, followed by a barrack inspection. This is followed by hard labour swinging a pick or shovel or with a hammer bashing stones, under the Saharan sun. Endless inspections punctuate the day; there are no recreation facilities, no cinema, no association with other prisoners.

The brutality is indescribable and the punishments severe
. . . and this goes on for month after month, with nothing
except the sweat of labour in the terrible heat.'

By learning the story of Legion 'last stands', and especially the story of Camerone, a legionnaire learns that
the Legion fights and dies, but does not surrender –
at least until every man is wounded and all hope is gone.
The legionnaire is taken to see the Monument aux Morts,
formerly at Sidi Bel Abbès and now at Aubagne, and
learns what it means to join that company. He sees the
wooden hand of Captain Danjou, sees the Legion flag,
torn to pieces and hidden after the battle at Dien Bien
Phu to keep it from the hands of the Vietminh, then
brought back to Algeria and carefully sewn back together.

He learns the Legion songs, especially the famous
'Boudin', a slow, impressive march, which extols the
attractions of *boudin*, a blood sausage, of which, for some
reason, there is never a portion for the Belgians. Eventually, after a few weeks, the recruits are presented with their
képi blanc, the cherished and distinctive white cap of the
Légion Etrangère, which is presented at an evening ceremony, by the light of torches or a bonfire, and to the
singing of Legion songs. The adoption of the *képi blanc* is
of quite recent date. During their time in North Africa at
the end of the last century, legionnaires were issued with
khaki cap covers, as a form of camouflage. In time the sun
bleached these khaki covers white and so – as is the way
with soldiers – a white cap cover became the mark of the
'old sweat', the experienced, veteran soldier, and thus
highly prized. Gradually the white *képi* cover crept into
semi-official use, but it was not until as recently as 1939
that it became the Legion's official headdress, when the
Legion detachment wearing the *képi blanc* swept down the
Champs-Elysées in the 14 July parade.

The new legionnaire learns this and more. He learns the
Legion motto, not '*Honneur et Patrie*' as in the French
regiments, but '*Honneur et Fidélité*', 'Honour and Loyalty',
and that the old motto of the Legion, '*Valeur et Discipline*',
is worth remembering as well.

He learns other things – to hold his liquor and to enjoy the benefits of the Legion regimental brothels. The Legion understands that men need women, and here as in other things it caters for demand. The brothel area in Sidi Bel Abbès – the Village Nègre – was one of the largest in North Africa, crammed with women and girls from around the Mediterranean shore; a surprising number of former whores married legionnaires and settled down to a life of total respectability when his – and her – service was over. Though more discreetly, at least among those units based in France, the Legion still maintains its brothels (the BMC, the Bordel Militaire de Campagne) and these brothels accompany the Legion battalions on campaign.

He learns, or absorbs, the fact that although he has joined one of the most demanding professions in the world, that of the legionnaire, he is not alone. Neither is he stateless; he has a new home, a new loyalty, a new country. Meet a legionnaire at Calvi or Aubagne and ask him what country he is from and he may tell you, but that said he will usually add, 'But now the Legion is my country.'

'*Legio patria nostra*.' To the legionnaires that phrase – 'The Legion Is Our Country' – is a not just an unofficial motto, carved in a Legion memorial, but a daily fact of life, the final link that binds him to his unit during his years of service and very often for the rest of his life. Loyalty to the Legion is essential, the binding ingredient in the mixture that makes up the legionnaire. At this point, at last, it is possible to separate legend from reality and see why the Legion has always exercised an attraction for generations of fighting men. Put all the points listed here into a frame and a picture emerges.

The first point, surely, is that every man in it is a volunteer. Secondly, every volunteer has quite deliberately cut his ties with his homeland. Once a man joins the Legion, the Legion is his home – *Legio patria nostra* – and to that home, as to his native land, he gives love and loyalty. Once in the Legion a man can look only to the Legion for support and justice, and signs a contract to which he will be held for at least five years. For its part of the contract, the Legion will supply all a man needs: uniform, weapons, food, pay – decent pay in the 1990s – a regulated brothel for his physical needs, even a retirement home if he serves until he is old and has nowhere else to go. It is an honourable contract and one fair to both sides.

The legionnaires may not feel any particular love or respect for France. Indeed, it has been said that many legionnaires actually detest France. But the Legion is different, even if it is now part of the French Army and carried in the Army List. As for the French, they respect the Legion and cheer it mightily on parade, but their admiration is qualified; after all, it is hardly a matter of national pride that you pay men of other nations to fight your battles. Nobody really *likes* the Legion or legionnaires, and quite a lot of people are actually afraid of them. Many pretty girls enjoy a summer fling with a legionnaire in Provence or Corsica, but it is not something they would want their mother to know about.

The legionnaire therefore is a man apart – but a part of the Legion. Having looked at various aspects of Legion history and tradition it is apparent that the Foreign Legion has created something unique among mercenary forces: a sense of pride – *esprit de corps* – and that, and that alone, is what provides the special ingredient. It is, after all, something special to be a legionnaire, and no one can or would deny it.

The Legion makes a tremendous and highly successful effort to implant in every legionnaire that spirit, that *esprit de corps*, that grasp of Legion rules and traditions which, when welded to hard training and good leadership, makes the Legion such a formidable fighting machine.

This, then, is the legend of the Legion, simply a set of rules and traditions, built up over 150 years and jealously maintained because they work on the field of battle. The inculcation of these rules and traditions begins the moment a man joins the Legion and never really stops. The end result is to create a force in which it is an honour to serve – and a regiment worth dying for.

4

THE LEGION IN THE WARS: THE CRIMEA, ITALIAN AND FRANCO-PRUSSIAN WARS, 1854–71

'Packs off . . . Forward the Legion!'

Colonel de Chabrière, Magenta, Italy, 1859

The stories and campaigns covered in the first chapters of this book should not be taken as an indication that Foreign Legion battalions were used only in last stands and frontier wars. The Legion was not a 'special force' but a conventional infantry unit, trained to fight in a conventional fashion – but to fight to the death. It has to be admitted that the French tended to regard Legion units as expendable, and sent them to places where the risk of death and disaster was exceptionally high, knowing that if a Legion unit were wiped out or suffered heavy casualties there would be few protests from the citizens of France, whose own sons were not involved.

In the first few decades of their existence, therefore, the legionnaires had evolved into shock troops *par excellence*, heavy infantry who could be used like a battering ram in the assault, or as the forlorn hope in storming some well-defended breach. They had, however, taken a pride in this role, in being noted as fearless troops, men who could tackle any dirty job and frequently pull it off. If a man wanted action and glory – though most actions led to death and wounds and precious little glory – let him join the Foreign Legion ... and that reputation spread throughout the French Army.

Young officers graduating from the French Military Academy at St Cyr were already taking an interest in this superb fighting unit, knowing that the path of duty was the way to promotion, as well as glory. It would take a few more decades before service in the Legion would become so prized that only the first few graduates earned a right to that appointment, but already the cream of the French officer corps were applying for a Legion posting, knowing that if a war came France's way, the Legion was sure to be sent to it – and wars were very common in the middle decades of the nineteenth century.

Europe in this period was not the Europe we know today. Germany and Italy were simply geographical descriptions, not states or political entities. Italy was a collection of small principalities – including the Vatican and the Papal States – as well as smaller city states, and it needed foreign wars and the influence of Garibaldi to forge the modern Italy. Likewise Germany, where the many and various states, though all under the influence of Prussia, the strongest and most aggressive state in Europe, still retained much of their independence and autonomy.

Saxony and Bavaria were kingdoms, as was Prussia, and there were over 100 lesser states and electorates between the Rhine and the Polish frontier. To bind these together into a German 'empire' or reich, the Chancellor of Prussia, Prince von Bismarck, wanted a war, and the Franco-Prussian War was the result of his actions, but before he got it, there were other wars to fight, beginning with the war in the Crimea, where two old adversaries of Napoleonic times, France and Britain, found themselves fighting side by side, aiding Turkey to stave off the advance of Czarist Russia.

The Russians had always wanted a warm-water port, and in 1853 they seized the city of Constantinople, modern Istanbul, then, as now, the capital city of the Turkish Empire. The Turkish Empire of the Ottomans was then starting its permanent decline, and the Sultan of Turkey and his government were unable to evict the Russians unaided. They therefore called for assistance from the French and British, neither of whom had any intention of letting Russia have a seafront on the Mediterranean. An expeditionary force of British and French troops was duly raised and sent to fight in the Crimea, east of the Dardanelles, the French corps being designated as the Armée de l' Orient. This force contained two Legion regiments, the 1st and 2nd Régiments Etrangers, which sailed from Oran to the Crimea in September 1854, landing a few weeks later, just in time for the Battle of the Alma and the onset of the terrible Crimean winter.

These two Legion regiments, now designated the Foreign Brigade, were sent into action on the Alma on 5 November 1854, when they successfully repulsed a Russian attack on the Alma heights and drove the enemy off with loss, though suffering over 100 casualties. The campaign was then virtually suspended for the winter; the troops went into quarters, usually hovels or unheated tents, in which poor food, an indifference to sanitation and a lack of proper clothing combined with enemy action and bitter cold to decimate their ranks before the coming of spring.

The Legion, here as elsewhere, was denied the rest given to other units, but was principally employed at the siege of Sebastopol. The task of the legionnaires was to sap, or dig trenches towards the city walls, digging by day and night under a constant barrage of mortar shells, and forced to stay on guard each night to prevent Russian parties destroying the trenches they had constructed with such labour during the day. These Russian night attacks were often delivered with considerable force, such as the one on the night of 5 November when 53 legionnaires were killed or wounded before the Russians were chased back behind the walls of Sebastopol. These sorties by the defenders went on throughout the winter and left a large number of frozen bodies between the lines, bodies that began to decompose and stink when spring finally returned to the Crimea.

This six-month siege culminated in an all-out assault by all the Allied forces on 1 May 1855, after the city had been pounded for days by artillery. The initial bombardment, though it lasted for days, did not damage the defences adequately or cow the Russian defenders who met the Legion assault, by six élite companies drawn from both regiments, with a storm of fire, killing or wounding over 100 men, including the colonel of the 1st Battalion, Colonel Vienot, who was leading the Legion assault, sword in hand. To this day the Quartier Vienot, the Legion barracks at Aubagne, recalls the gallant colonel and his final exploit.

Vienot's men seized one of the outer bastions of Sebastopol and they hung on there until 22 May, when they took part in yet another assault on the city walls, making a diversionary attack to cover the main assault and losing another 200 men in the process. Meanwhile the rest of the Foreign Brigade were taking part in the main assault, a battle that went on for two days before the French commanders called it off. This assault having failed, the Legion remained in the siege lines before Sebastopol until the Russians decided to turn them out with a counter-offensive on 18 June, which cost the British and French forces no less than 6,000 men killed and wounded. Many of the wounded were succoured in the new hospital, established at Scutari, just across the Sea of Marmara from Constantinople, by an English gentlewoman, Miss Florence Nightingale.

The siege of Sebastopol went on throughout the summer, with assault following assault, and nothing to show for them but more casualties. Then, on 8 September 1855, the Legion again spearheaded an assault, with the 'forlorn hope' – a body of picked men leading the charge – carrying scaling ladders and grenades. They also carried beams and had their sappers along in the front line, for while the riflemen took and held the breaches it was the task of the sappers to build scaffolding and bridges to get the rest of the troops across the breach and into the city.

Losses were very high, especially among the leading Legion companies, but the city was stormed and after a day or two of street fighting the Russians started to evacuate. It was not until French troops captured the Malakoff battery that Sebastopol fell and the post of Commander of the Sebastopol was given to General Bazine, who had served with the Old Legion in Spain. He summoned the Legion Brigade to occupy the city they had done so much to conquer, and the men moved in from their vermin-infested siege lines with great relief, looting the city and hunting along the docks for firewood and stores.

The Crimean War went on until March 1856 when a peace treaty was signed, and as a reward for their efforts in this bitter campaign Louis Napoleon offered the legionnaires immediate French citizenship and transfer to any French regiment of their choice; over 1,700 legionnaires had been killed or wounded in the Crimea, but few of the survivors accepted either of Louis Napoleon's offers.

The war was a pointless affair but it did mark the establishment of the Legion as a regular force, and here for the first time they fought against regular troops in a European war rather than against native irregulars in colonial campaigns. More of these wars were to follow but, for the moment, there was, as always, the problem of Algeria.

The Legion Brigade returned to Algeria and marched back to Sidi Bel Abbès in July 1856, trudging out of the city to the sound of their new march, a march that some years later, in 1870, was to be given words and become better known as 'Le Boudin'. At Sidi Bel Abbès the returning legionnaires, who were, as usual, drawn from a score of nations, heard that by decree of the Emperor Napoleon III a new or Second Foreign Legion was to be formed, composed of Swiss legionnaires, who would be distinguished from other legionnaires by wearing a green rifleman's uniform. This was yet another attempt to tinker with that *Legio patria nostra* notion that bound the Legion together. The damage was exacerbated this time when, after the Swiss veterans had been transferred to this new legion, the Swiss Regiment was then designated the 1st Régiment Etranger and the rest of the Crimea Legion Brigade as the 2nd RE.

However, the legionnaires had little time to fret over this insult for there was more trouble brewing in Algeria, at no great distance from Sidi Bel Abbès, where the Arabs of the Kabyle Mountains were up in arms.

The 'pacification' of Algeria never really stopped in all the years of the French colonial occupation. The French had now been at it for over twenty years and still the local Arabs rose up against them, most noticeably whenever the Legion was otherwise engaged, and so it was here. Now that the Legion had returned they were given a few weeks to re-equip after the Crimea and sent out again in punitive columns, aiming to find the strongholds of Kabyle resistance and stamp it out once and for all. Three Legion battalions were committed to the campaign of 1856 and they slowly converged on the centre of Arab resistance, on the Ischeriden ridge.

The force sent against the Kabyle was commanded by Marshal Randon with General MacMahon, who had French Army troops as well as legionnaires under his orders, commanding a division. The Kabyle ridge was held by at least 4,000 Arab tribesmen, who had built stone sangars and were well supplied with rifles and ammunition. MacMahon was not the sort of general who believed in probing a position to see what he was up against. He called up his artillery to fire a short bombardment and his next move was to send two French infantry regiments against the ridge, hoping to take the Arab position with the bayonet.

The Arabs waited for the advancing French battalions, crack troops from the Zouves and the 54 Régiment de Ligne, holding their fire until the French battalions were within a few yards of their positions then greeting them with a storm of rifle fire. Then the Arabs charged down on their disordered ranks with sword and dagger, driving the French soldiers back in some disorder, many of their wounded being left on the slope where they were slaughtered slowly by Arab knives.

MacMahon then quickly sent two battalions – about 2,000 men – of the 2nd Régiment Etranger, most of them Crimea veterans, to assault the ridge, not even giving them time to take off their greatcoats, the men marching out to the sound of 'Le Boudin', the first time it had been played in action. The legionnaires were determined to show the other units present what legionnaires could do, and they went into the attack without firing a shot, their rifles on their shoulders, led by Major Paul Magrin, the commander of the 2nd RE, riding on his horse.

The battalions endured scalding fire as they advanced up the hill, but waited until they were less than 100 metres from the crest before they halted, presented their weapons, fired one crashing volley into the shrieking Arabs dancing along the crest and then charged at them with the bayonet. The Arabs promptly fled.

'It was the men in the *"grandes capotes"* [greatcoats] who made us run,' said one captured Kabyle fighter. 'We drove off the first attack but when the *"grandes capotes"* came on and on against us, without firing a shot as they came, that was too much and we lost our nerve.'

Within half an hour of the first note of 'Le Boudin', the crest of Ischeriden had been cleared and a new battle honour would later be embroidered on the colours of the 2nd Régiment. Decorations flowed on the officers and men, and when one young officer, Captain Mariotti, was receiving his medal from Marshal Randon, the marshal, while praising his bravery, told him that he would not live long if he continued to behave in such a foolhardy manner.

'That is not quite correct, sir,' replied the captain. 'I was taking no risks for my legionnaires were behind me.'

The 1850s were an active decade for the Legion, and they still had another campaign to fight before the decade ended. It is fair to say that Napoleon III, the new Emperor of the French, was a meddling monarch. He was the nephew of the great Emperor Napoleon and therefore perhaps over-anxious to gain a little of the military glory so abundantly bestowed on his famous relative. As a result, he was keen to involve his army, if not his actual person, in far-flung campaigns, like the ones in the Crimea just described and the one in Mexico which will be described in the next chapter. In 1859 he found another battleground, rather closer to home, in Italy, where his mighty forebear had first won military glory and had indeed, if only for a time, been King of Italy.

Now a new king, Victor Emmanuel, currently King of Sardinia, Piedmont and various other Italian provinces and Count or Comte of Nice, a county that was destined not to form part of France for many more years, had decided to make a bid for the sovereignty of Italy, an ambition in which he was encouraged by his chancellor, the wily Cavour.

Victor Emmanuel had already obtained possession of a large part of Italy and the *carbonari*, the local patriots, supported him, so Italy was in the process of uniting. Unfortunately, the efforts of Italian patriots to unite their country were hampered by the Austrians, who occupied half the peninsula and were eager to take over the other half and add another dimension to the currently forming Austro-Hungarian Empire. The *carbonari* were stout fighters but no match for the entire Austrian Army, so they applied to France for assistance, offering Napoleon III the lordship of Nice and Savoy in return if the French troops were victorious.

Both these territories lay on the French side of the Alps and were prizes worth having, and here, as formerly in Spain, the French were anxious to get involved if the losses among French manpower were kept to the minimum. The answer to that problem, yet again, was the Légion Etrangère.

In the spring of 1859 the 1st Régiment Etranger was shipped to Corsica and devoted itself to training recruits and bringing its companies up to full strength. Meanwhile the 2nd Régiment Etranger was shipped to Marseilles, leaving one battalion behind to garrison Sidi Bel Abbès and keep the peace in Algeria. In May the two regiments were formed as a brigade in a division of General Mac-Mahon's corps and sent to Genoa in Italy, to take part in the Italian campaign.

The Austrians were less than happy to find a French army aiding the *carbonari* in what the Austrians were choosing to regard as a private war, and their first reaction was to send their field army marching towards Genoa and drive the French into the sea. The two armies met on 2 June 1859 outside the town of Magenta, close to the city of Milan on the plain of Lombardy. Magenta is a wine town, full of well-stocked cellars, and the surrounding countryside is draped with vines and the walls of vineyards, which make it perfect for a defensive battle.

At first the Austrians seemed to be getting the better of the engagement. A French cavalry charge was repulsed by heavy rifle fire and the French Army looked like faltering when Colonel de Chabrière of the Legion drew his sword and gave his famous command, 'Off packs . . . forward the Legion!'

The bayonet has always been a favourite weapon of the Legion, and so it was here. The legionnaires threw off their heavy packs, formed line, fired one blistering volley into the faces of the Austrian infantry and charged with the bayonet, leaping over walls and vines to close with the enemy. Within a few minutes the Austrian front line collapsed and a general rout began, though Colonel de Chabrière, leading the charge, was mortally wounded in the moment of victory.

General MacMahon, watching this spirited attack, turned to his aide-de-camp and said, '*Voici la Légion. L'affaire est dans le sac.*' ('There goes the Legion . . . the battle is in the bag.') The Legion then drove the Austrians out of the little town of Magenta after some ferocious house-to-house fighting down the streets, their fervour increased, or so it was alleged, by an eagerness to get into the wine cellars and among the casks. Next day, some legionnaires were indeed found dead of drink, floating drowned in the wine vats. Legion discipline broke down in Magenta after the battle, and it is recorded that on the following day it was possible to walk from one end of the town to the other, stepping on the corpses of the dead, or the drunken bodies of Legion soldiers.

Milan was liberated on the following day, 7 June, and the two Legion regiments, taking with them the dying Colonel de Chabrière, headed the march into the city. Colonel de Chabrière, one of fifteen Legion officers killed at Magenta, died on 29 June, five days after the 2nd RE had played a significant part in winning the battle at Solferino.

Solferino was a much fiercer battle than Magenta and the sufferings of the wounded so shocked a Swiss writer, Jean-Henri Dunant, that a few years later, in 1862, he founded the Red Cross movement in Geneva. The losses so horrified Napoleon III that a week after the battle he concluded an armistice with the Austrians, bringing this campaign to a close.

In exactly three weeks, between 4 and 25 June, the French had lost 12,000 men, the Austrians some 13,000 and the Italians about 5,000, so that some 30,000 men were killed or maimed to eject the Austrians from Lombardy. There was also a dawning realisation in Paris that the foundation of a united Italy would create another, possibly competing kingdom on France's southern doorstep, and so, having aided Victor Emmanuel and Cavour to capture Lombardy, the French forces withdrew.

The Legion attempted to make good some of its losses by recruiting in Italy, and such was their reputation after Magenta and Solferino that hundreds of Italians flocked to join. This enthusiasm soon passed, and by the time the Legion reached Genoa, there to embark on their ships for Algeria, most of their new recruits had thought better of their decision and deserted.

The Legion, which had lost many good men in this brief, violent campaign, did receive a signal honour in return. Napoleon III decided to celebrate the freeing of

Lombardy with a victory parade in Paris, and by common consent of the French veterans the Legion regiments – regiments that were not even supposed to be in France – led the way down the Champs-Elysées, their band playing 'Le Boudin'. Moreover, the emperor listened to the advice of veteran Legion officers and disbanded the 'Second Legion' of Swiss, reforming the old regiments and allowing the battalions to mix up the nationalities as before. All in all, it was a happy and united Legion that disembarked at Oran and set out down the old familiar path to Sidi bel Abbès and home.

The main campaign in the 1860s was the one in Mexico, a campaign noted for the engagement at Camerone, but in 1870 a much larger war broke out on the Continent between France and Germany, the Franco-Prussian War of 1870–1, a war that was to pose some particular problems for the men of the Foreign Legion.

Throughout its history the Legion has always contained a large number of German soldiers. The Germans are good soldiering stock, but until 1870 the nation we now call Germany was fragmented into a score of states which squabbled among themselves, each squabble providing a new supply of recruits for the Legion. One of the reasons for this Franco-Prussian war, a conflict into which Napoleon III blundered almost by accident, was to provide the Prussian chancellor, Otto von Bismarck, with the political means to unite these German principalities, binding them together in the face of a common foe – France – and so form a united German nation dominated by Prussia and with the Prussian king, Wilhelm I, as Kaiser – or Emperor – of Germany.

To succeed in that ambition was Bismarck's problem, but as a cunning and astute politician he found no difficulty in persuading the French to declare war on Prussia, at a time when his forces were ready and able to defeat any force the French could put in the field. The Prussian Army tested its strength against the much larger Austrian Army in 1866 and defeated the Austrians utterly at the Battle of Sadowa. To defeat the Prussians the French must put all their forces in the field, and that included the formidable, hard-fighting Légion Etrangère. The problem for the Legion was rather more complex: could those German legionnaires who made up the backbone of the force be relied upon to fight against their compatriots in the Prussian Army?

No one, not even the legionnaires, could be quite sure of that. The motto *Legio patria nostra* was fine when fighting Arabs or savages or other nationalities, but would a German legionnaire really fire on the colours of a Prussian battalion if he saw them advancing to the attack?

In the end, a simple solution was hit upon. The German legionnaires would form a separate all-German Legion regiment, solely for the duration of the Franco-Prussian conflict, and remain in Algeria where there was, as always, plenty of fighting to do. Their numbers would be made up by recruiting all those Francophile foreigners in Paris now clamouring to fight for France, and forming these into a new unit, the 5th Foreign Battalion. One of the volunteers for this force was a Legionnaire Kara, who turned out on closer inspection to be Prince Karageorgivic, a prince who eventually became King of Serbia. The 5th was one of the most international of all the Legion battalions, with men from nearly 40 nations serving in its ranks, all united in hatred of Prussian arrogance and militarism which they saw, rightly, as a threat to the peace of Europe.

This new battalion, with more enthusiasm than training, was formed at Tours in September 1870, under the command of Major Arago. It was then flung against the advancing Prussians at the village of Bel Aire-les-Aides, outside Orleans, in October 1870, and almost destroyed in its first battle. Major Arago was soon killed, and most of the new legionnaires were killed, wounded or captured, though not without putting up a tremendous fight that greatly impressed the Bavarian troops hurled against them. One legionnaire, a skilled hunter and marksman, is reported to have killed 80 Bavarian troops on the road near Aides, but his accuracy was not enough to stem the enemy advance.

The 5th Battalion fought until it was crushed and swept aside, over 800 men being killed or wounded. The survivors were sent to one or other of the two regular Legion battalions recently arrived from Algeria – the rule about the Legion not serving in France never stood in the way of military necessity – and France was in a parlous state by now, her armies pounded by Prussian artillery using guns with unheard-of power, her infantry shot down in quantity by the skilled and highly disciplined Prussian troops.

As for France's generals, they were completely outclassed by their Prussian counterparts. The generals included several who had served with or commanded battalions of the Legion, like Field Marshal MacMahon or General Bazaine, that fearless officer, who on this occasion was so stunned by the rapid Prussian advance and the power of her army that he allowed his forces to be shut up in Metz where they stayed, impotent, until the war was over and France defeated. In fact the Franco-Prussian War of 1870–1 was effectively over before Bazaine led his army into Metz. Following the defeat at Sedan where Napoleon III was captured, the French fell back on Paris, which the Prussians were soon besieging, pounding the city with their heavy guns.

The small Legion brigade fought on outside the city, skirmishing with the Prussians throughout the winter of 1870 until an armistice was signed in January 1871. Then they were called into Paris and employed to crush the Commune, that group of liberal citizens who attempted to take hold of the government after Napoleon III had been forced to abdicate and gone into exile.

During the last weeks of the war the Legion had formed part of the Armée de l'Est, a small army of about 60,000 men that was charged with cutting the Prussian supply lines from Germany. This force duly marched east towards the Rhine, but winter came hard and early in 1870–1 and the Armée de l'Est could make little progress on frozen tracks and icy roads.

The Legion, as usual, led the advance, and even

managed to recapture the city of Montbeliard in the Jura massif, but the defeat at Sedan and the capture of Napoleon III meant that the Prussians had gained a clear victory. France had been outmatched and defeated and the Prussians could dictate terms, harsh terms that would lead, eventually, to the Great War of 1914–18. Among other concessions, and the payment of huge reparations, the defeated French were obliged to cede the two rich Rhine-side provinces of Alsace and Lorraine to Bismarck's newly established German Reich – Germany. France had been defeated in battle and humbled at the conference table, and the resentment went deep.

In June 1871, the remnants of the Legion regiments that had fought in France returned to Sidi Bel Abbès to rejoin their German comrades and reform their regiments yet again, this time into two regiments, each of five battalions. Many of the new recruits were ex-soldiers, a significant number of them men who had deserted from other armies, even from units of the French Army. Provided they could soldier, the Legion did not care where they came from, and they were soon absorbed in the ranks of the Legion battalions.

Together, these battalions set about the old Legion tasks, fighting recalcitrant Arab tribesmen inspired by this massive French defeat, building roads across the barren parts of the country, and taking part in more colonial expeditions as France, sadly reduced at home, attempted to claim territory beyond the seas or dabble again in foreign adventures by supporting a European attempt to interfere in the affairs of Mexico.

5

MEXICO AND CAMERONE, 1863–67

'These are not men, but devils'

Colonel Milan, Commander of the Mexican
Forces, Camerone, Mexico, 1873

Fighting forces need action. In 1863 the Legion was back in Algeria, carrying on with the seemingly endless task of pacification and public works, their time divided between fighting the Arabs in the *bled* and building roads across the country to nail down the territory and provide a pathway for the ever-increasing number of settlers, *colons*, now arriving from metropolitan France. It was hard and useful work, but in Legion eyes it hardly counted as real war, the sort of work they had enlisted for.

Then came the prospect of something larger, more serious, in the troubled country of Mexico, which was then in the grip of civil war. The revolutionaries under Benito Juarez – the Juaristas – were currently winning the war, and Mexico had recently cancelled her vast debts to several European nations, including France, citing the revolution as a reason for refusing payment.

This unilateral action infuriated Napoleon III, Emperor of the French, and since the Mexican conservatives, the main group fighting Juarez, had declared that they needed a new leader, a figurehead to unite the nation behind them, Napoleon decided to provide one in the person of his young nephew, the Archduke Maximilian of Austria. Maximilian would be provided with a small French army, go to Mexico and thrash Juarez. Then he would become Emperor of Mexico and repay those outstanding debts to France. It all seemed so simple, and it was all to go so tragically wrong.

The French contingent went to Mexico as part of a multinational force, with troops from Spain and the United Kingdom, and this force landed at Veracruz, on the Atlantic coast, in January 1862. Before long, the British and Spanish governments realised that the Mexicans would fight to the death rather than accept foreign domination, and saw no point in sending troops to aid a further extension of French power. They therefore pulled out. The French, however, chose to stay on, and soon had as much war as they could handle, for the Mexicans were not only doughty fighters, they were also well armed with repeating rifles and Colt revolvers, far superior weapons to those of the French, who were armed with rifled Minies, single-shot muskets.

The Legion took no part in the first expeditionary force, a fact that caused a considerable amount of *angst* in the messes of Sidi Bel Abbès. In fact, the Legion may have been fortunate at this time, for the French Government almost decided to give the Legion to Maximilian, lock, stock and rifle barrel, as Louis-Philippe had once given the 'Old Legion' to Spain. The Legion was used to leading the way in France's wars, and the younger officers had only joined because life in the Legion offered the possibility – even the certainty – of action. Therefore, without telling their superior officers, the junior officers sent a direct petition to the Emperor Napoleon asking permission to attend the war in Mexico.

There was a considerable outcry at such impertinence, so much so that the commanding officer of the Legion, Colonel Butet, was sacked from his command. An officer obeys orders and serves where he is ordered to serve, and all the young officers were summoned to Legion headquarters for a severe official dressing-down. That done, these chastened young men were then warmly – but unofficially – congratulated on their initiative and duly rewarded when the Legion was ordered to send a detachment to Mexico, with the utmost despatch.

It should not be thought that the entire Legion were anxious to be committed to this foreign war. It contained plenty of wily old soldiers who had long since ceased volunteering for anything, and word was already abroad that the war in Mexico could not be won and was causing considerable casualties. Nor was the war popular in France, where the majority of the population were unable to understand why the French Army was involved there at all. Desertion soared, in the French Army and in the Legion, but the decision had been made and the Legion prepared to embark.

The Legion formed a '*régiment de marche*', a picked force of men drawn from all the Legion regiments. This force, 2,000 strong, was then formed into two battalions, each of seven rifle companies plus a headquarters company, and sailed from North Africa on 10 February, arriving at Veracruz on the Atlantic coast of Mexico six weeks later, on 28 March 1863, under their new commander, Colonel Jeanningros.

By now the situation in Mexico had deteriorated. The entire Mexican nation was up in arms and the Juaristas were on the rampage, intent on driving Maximilian and his mercenaries out of their country. Then there were the Americans, lurking just across the Rio Bravo del Norte – a river better known outside Mexico as the Rio Grande. The Monroe Doctrine of 1833, in which President Monroe had declared the Americas a no-go zone for the European powers, was not yet 30 years old, and the United States meant to maintain every clause of that uncompromising declaration.

The terms of the doctrine – that the Europeans would not be permitted to establish colonies in the Americas or interfere in Latin American affairs – did not, of course, apply to the United States. The USA interfered constantly in Latin American affairs – as it still does – and as recently as the 1840s had finished a war with Mexico by annexing Texas, California and large parts of Arizona and New Mexico. The French had attempted to undermine the doctrine by declaring that their 'involvement' in Mexico was to prevent further US expansion and to restore to the Mexicans some form of democratic government, but the Mexicans were not deceived. They wanted the French to leave, and if they would not leave willingly they would be forced out.

Napoleon III and the 'Emperor' Maximilian were convinced that their European army could thrash any number of Mexican irregulars and neither man was worried by United States displeasure or by the possibility of American involvement in their scheme. In 1863, the Americans were involved in their Civil War – the War between the States – which was then at its height, with the Battle of Gettysburg taking place that July, and had enough on their hands at home to prevent their becoming involved in the affairs of another country. The French calculated that they could beat Juarez and take over Mexico before the Americans were able to interfere, but it was not to work out like that.

Maximilian's more immediate problem was with the Juaristas, who were cutting up his troops and blocking the main road from Veracruz, the country's main Atlantic port, to Mexico City. Up this road came all his munitions and supplies, and it was vital to keep this road open, so when the Legion battalions arrived at Veracruz, opening the road, and keeping it open, was the first task they were given.

This order was a great disappointment to the firebrands of the Legion. The young officers expected that they would be sent inland at once to carry out an assault on the Juarista stronghold of Puebla which the French expeditionary force was currently besieging. Instead, they were assigned to guard Veracruz and had to provide escorts for the slow-moving mule and oxen convoys being sent up to Puebla.

The legionnaires soon found out that this role, if boring, was not without its dangers. Not only was the countryside infested with Juaristas, it was swarming with mosquitoes and blackfly. Veracruz lies on the jungle-clad, swampy, humid coastal plain of Mexico, well below the high and breezy uplands at 1,800 metres which contain Mexico City. Even today Veracruz is not a health resort, and in the middle decades of the nineteenth century it was an unsanitary pest-hole. The sea is full of sharks which make bathing hazardous, the countryside is flat, scrub-covered and swampy in the rains, and the air hums after dark with swarms of mosquitoes. Disease began to decimate the Legion battalions before a shot was fired, and by the end of 1863 more than 800 legionnaires had died from fever alone.

Malaria, cholera, yellow fever, the *vomito negro*, swiftly put half the regiment in hospital and a lot of good men in their graves before orders came to Colonel Jeanningros to take the expedition payroll, some three million gold francs, up the road to Puebla, a difficult and dangerous task for which his forces were barely adequate.

The Legion had already seen some action and scored some small victories. In April 1863, soon after arriving, a company of the Legion had been attacked by a strong force of Juaristas led by General Antonio Diez, a local guerrilla leader and mayor of the town of Jalapa. Diez's horsemen had been harassing the road for weeks, shooting and putting to the sabre any workers trying to improve it, but the Legion infantry formed line when his horsemen swept down on them and blew the Mexicans from the saddle with volleys of well-aimed rifle fire. They then got among the dismayed Mexicans with the bayonet and Lieutenant Milson, the company commander, killed Diez with his sword. This was before disease began to stalk the ranks of the Legion, but when the order came to provide an escort for the payroll Colonel Jeanningros was hard put to find the men or the officers.

The hinterland behind Veracruz is rugged, inhospitable country, and in 1863 the natural enemies of terrain, climate and mosquitoes were reinforced by the warlike

Juarista horsemen who sniped at French convoys, ambushed patrols and put any French soldier who fell into their hands to various unpleasant kinds of death: hanging, shooting, staking them out in the sun, dragging their naked prisoners through cactus clumps on the ends of lariats. With all this in prospect the Legion mustered whatever men it could for the convoy escort, but all they could find was 62 men of the 3rd Company of the 2nd Battalion of the Régiment Etranger, which was also the duty company and charged with guard and escort work. All the company officers were down with fever and so the man appointed to command the escort was a Captain Jean Danjou, a member of the headquarters staff and the adjutant of the *battalion de marche*.

Two other headquarters officers then came forward as well: Second Lieutenant Maudet, the regimental colour bearer, and Second Lieutenant Vilain, the regimental paymaster. Since the convoy was to carry the regimental pay and fresh funds for the entire force – enough money to make several men millionaires – perhaps Second Lieutenant Vilain felt he should go along to keep an eye on it.

The US frontier was not all that far away if a man had a good horse, and with these legionnaires you never knew ... with three million francs to spend a man could live very well, even in Texas, and a large number of legionnaires had already deserted and left the hazards of Mexico for the hardly less hazardous Texan frontier. The company task was to meet the convoy and escort it on its way to Puebla, and Captain Danjou and his officers were determined to complete that task, whatever the odds.

All these legionnaires, officers and men, had seen service in Italy, Algeria or the Crimea. Captain Danjou, who was just 35, a slim man with a receding hairline and a drooping moustache, had served in the Crimea and lost his left hand in Algeria when an overcharged musket exploded. The captain's shattered hand had been amputated and replaced with a reticulated wooden one, with which he managed very well, and like his junior officers he had seen recent combat and was anxious for more. Early on the morning of 30 April 1863 he led his force, just three officers and 62 legionnaires, out of Veracruz and into Legion history.

The company left Veracruz at 0100 hours on the morning of 30 April, hoping to reach Palo Verde soon after sun-up. The local Juarista commander, Colonel Millan, whose intelligence network in Veracruz was extremely good, had already heard about this convoy and was preparing to ambush it, taking a force of about 2,000 men and 800 horses and the rest on foot to attack the French escort.

Danjou's men passed through the Legion outposts outside Veracruz where one outpost commander, alarmed by the small numbers Danjou was taking on this dangerous mission, offered him another platoon of 30 men, a reinforcement that Danjou refused. At dawn, which came at about 0500 hours Danjou halted his men and ordered them to fall out and brew coffee, posting sentries while they did so. This was a fortunate order, for as the men were sipping coffee in the chilly dawn the sentries ran in to report that a large force of Juaristas was approaching.

The Legion company swiftly formed square in the scrub and drove off the first Mexican charge, but more cavalry were coming up and they could not stay long in the open. Danjou therefore looked around for a place to make a stand and led his men swiftly to a dusty little hamlet nearby, a place called Camerone, where the arrival of the legionnaires was greeted with a blast of rifle fire from some Mexican sentries. In this withdrawal to the village, Danjou lost sixteen men, who were cut off and shot down by the Mexicans, so he had less than 50 men to defend his final position, in the farmhouse of the Hacienda de la Trinidad, which occupies a small rise about a hundred yards east of the village.

A record of the fight at Camerone was written after the battle by Corporal Louis Maine, one of the survivors: 'As far as we could see the enemy had neither infantry or artillery and we were sure that we could defend ourselves against cavalry for a long time. Carbines without bayonets cannot dislodge a company of the Legion behind walls.'

The Mexican outposts were swiftly driven away and the legionnaires set about preparing the farmhouse for defence, occupying the rooms, knocking loopholes in the adobe wall around the farmyard and scrambling up to vantage points in windows and on roofs. They also attempted to barricade the entrances to the courtyard by pulling carts across the single entrance and barring all the gaps between the house and the barns. Sergeant Morziki, a Polish legionnaire, clambered up on the roof and shouted down to his commander that the surrounding scrub was 'full of sombreros, as far as the eye can see'. He was ordered down and got back to his position under the lee of the barns just in time, for the Mexican cavalry came roaring into the attack, rifles and pistols blazing, leaping their horses over the hastily erected barricades.

They were soon driven out with a blast of musketry that emptied many saddles, but when they rode off into the scrub they took with them the mules which carried all the legionnaires' food and water and the reserve ammunition. The legionnaires faced a brigade of Mexicans and had only the ammunition in their pouches – about 60 rounds a man.

Danjou had two choices, neither of them good. He could attempt a break-out and head up the road towards the convoy, hoping to get away in the scrub and find ammunition when he got to the convoy, or he could stand and fight where he was. For an officer of the Legion that was no choice at all, and he elected to occupy the building and defy the Mexicans, hoping that while they were busy with his men, the convoy would get away. Clearly, as long as the Mexicans were attacking him, the convoy and its valuable cargo were safe, so their job now was to hang on as long as possible. The battle began and lasted, with mounting fury, for most of the day.

Corporal Maine again: 'We held the enemy at a distance but it was difficult as our bullets were becoming exhausted, but we had sworn to fight to the last round and that we were ready to do.'

By nine in the morning it was already very hot and the

71

legionnaires were feeling the shortage of water, but by conserving their ammunition and firing only when the Mexicans got close, they were still holding out and killing plenty of the enemy. Colonel Millan sent in a man with a white flag to ask for their surrender but this proposal was rejected by Danjou and his men, the legionnaires assuring their commander that they intended to fight to the last man and the last round if need be – quite apart from the fact that, as all of them knew, French or legionnaire prisoners in Mexican hands did not seem to live long or die easily.

So the battle went on, hour after hour of charge and counter-charge, of cavalry galloping into the farmyard and sweeping out again, of a constant barrage of fire from Mexican riflemen hidden in the bush around the out-buildings, and steadily creeping closer. The legionnaires were dug in and fighting hard, but at around 1100 hours, Captain Danjou was killed by a single shot from a Mexican sniper while he was walking about the courtyard of the central farmhouse, cheering his men on.

About the time he was killed, or just as the news of his death reached the legionnaires, a fresh contingent of Mexican infantry arrived, three more battalions to re-inforce an enemy that already outnumbered the defenders by 30 to one. Having given the legionnaires time to absorb this fact, Colonel Millan once again asked them to surrender. The men remembered their promise to their captain and replied, briefly, '*Merde!*'

By noon, the company has lost about half its strength and the Mexicans had managed to infiltrate the farmhouse. As they crept ever closer so the Legion casualties increased, and at about two in the afternoon Lieutenant Vilain was killed. When Lieutenant Maudet called the roll of his new command, he found he had just twelve unwounded legion-naires and a handful of walking wounded, but all of them still full of fight. The situation was desperate, for the Mexicans had set fire to some of the buildings, and smoke and flames were steadily driving the legionnaires out of the main house and into the outbuildings.

Still they fought, making every shot tell, and so it went on until at around 1700 hours, when Colonel Millan, whose own losses in tackling this hornet's nest were not inconsiderable, again called on the legionnaires to surrender. There was no reply. The legionnaires had gone too far to back down now and the firing continued, but slowly, for their ammunition was almost spent, and they were able to maintain resistance only by salvaging what cartridges they could from the pouches and pockets of the dead and wounded – and at last even that scanty supply dried up.

The firing stopped on the French side and gradually died out on the Mexican side too, as men came out of cover or rose from their firing positions, to gaze at the bullet-pocked walls of Camerone and wonder what would happen next. They did not have long to wait.

Lieutenant Maudet had five men left, Corporal Louis Maine and four legionnaires – Leonhard, Wenzel, Constantine and Catteau. As the Mexicans watched, wondering, these six emerged from their positions, came out of cover, and formed an assault line. They then fixed bayonets and, firing their last rounds as they advanced, they charged out upon the Mexican Army.

The Mexican soldiers were so amazed that the legionnaires were upon them before they opened fire and shot them down. Maudet was hit twice and mortally wounded. Legionnaire Catteau threw himself in front of his officer and was killed instantly; nineteen bullet wounds were counted in his body after the battle. Leonhard also died but Maine, Wenzel and Constantine, though all wounded, were overpowered and disarmed by the Mexicans and led away, three survivors from among the 65 men who had marched into Camerone that morning.

The final tally of survivors was a little higher. Of the entire company, two officers and 22 legionnaires, about a third, were dead. One officer and 27 men were mortally wounded and died later in captivity. Just twelve, all wounded, were taken into captivity and treated well by the Mexicans, all eventually returning to France. When the last three were offered their lives by Colonel Millan, they told him that they would only surrender if they could keep their weapons and tend to their wounded comrades. Though Colonel Millan had lost nearly 500 men, killed or wounded, at Camerone, he was full of admiration for the Legion's stand, saying, 'I can refuse nothing to soldiers like you.'

Eventually, before the Legion left Mexico, a monument was erected at Camerone – where it still stands – to the memory of this epic fight, a monument replaced in 1892 and now inscribed with these words:

Ils furent ici moins de soixante opposés à toute une Armée; sa masse les écrasa. La vie, plutôt que le courage, abandonna ces soldats français. Avril 30, 1863

'Here fewer than sixty men stood against an entire army. Numbers overwhelmed them but life, rather than courage, forsook these soldiers of France.'

This memorial, which was erected with the permission of the Mexican Government, is not entirely accurate. The soldiers who died at Camerone were legionnaires and came from Italy, Germany, Poland and Spain, as well as France . . . but why quibble? All French Army companies in Mexico were ordered to halt and present arms when passing Camerone and the ashes of the Legion dead, gathered into a chalice shaped like a Mexican eagle, were sent back to Sidi Bel Abbès. A company of the Legion had fought a great battle at Camerone and the entire French Army was proud of them.

The fighting in Mexico was to continue for years after Camerone, and from 1865, with the end of the Civil War, the struggle was to intensify, with the US Government openly supporting Juarez and many ex-Confederate soldiers, unhappy with the outcome of the 'War between the States', crossing the Rio Grande to aid the Mexican people in their war against a foreign invader. Much of this war was a guerrilla war, of the kind the Legion was well used to after Algeria, but there were pitched battles, and at least one terrible defeat in a battle not unlike Camerone.

74

In February 1866, Major Brian, commander of the 3rd Legion Battalion, heard that a band of Mexicans had camped at a farmhouse called Santa Isabella near the town of Parras, close to the US border. Brian was under orders to withdraw towards Mexico City, but the chance of a final fight with the Juaristas was too good to miss. Accompanied by six officers and about 200 legionnaires, he set out on a night march to Santa Isabella, and marched straight into a trap. The Mexicans were waiting for them, and in the first volley of rifle fire Major Brian and half his men were shot down, killed or wounded.

His second-in-command, Captaine Moulinier, crazy with courage, refused to break off the action, which would anyway have meant leaving the wounded behind, and put in one attack after another against the Mexican positions. These positions were well defended and Moulinier's actions were quite hopeless but he persisted, until every man in the company was dead or wounded, except one man who escaped back to Parras to tell the tale. As for the wounded there was no repeat here of the mercy and kindness shown by Colonel Millan at Camerone. The Legion dead were dragged into a pile and burnt and the wounded were shot.

Chasing mounted guerrilla fighters on foot can never be successful, and in 1866 the *battalion de marche* formed a cavalry squadron of 60 men, chosen largely from legionnaires who had at some time served in cavalry regiments. This was more a body of mounted infantry than a proper cavalry force, and when the squadron was surrounded by a large number of Mexicans at Parral in October 1866, they left their horses, took cover in the scrub and, skirmishing forward, drove the Mexicans away, beating off seven Mexican cavalry charges in the process. Even so, it was very clear to all the legionnaires that this was a pointless, hopeless war, and one that was causing them considerable losses for no appreciable gain.

Perhaps it was in an attempt to get some return for their efforts that the legionnaires pillaged the town of Mier in August 1866. The inhabitants had fled as the French troops entered and the soldiers were able to spend a profitable day, looting the houses and drinking the bars dry, while Juarista fighters sniped at them from the hills around the town. One Legionnaire records that he picked up, 'gold and silver, about 800 francs worth, plus a pair of excellent duelling pistols and a fine clock which I sold for a good price in Monterrey . . . several of my comrades picked up a fortune.'

Following this profitable excursion in Mier, some 90 legionnaires, their finances taken care off, picked up horses, lit out for Texas, and never returned. Those who stayed with the colours finished looting the town, loaded their booty into wagons and drove it back to Monterrey, taking no heed of the Mexicans they were supposed to be chasing away.

Three Legion battalions were eventually involved in the Mexico campaign, and in the course of that fruitless war the Legion lost nearly 2,000 men and a few thousand more wounded . . . and all the Legion had to show for it was a small monument in a dusty village on the road to Veracruz and an undying tradition. On balance they probably thought that a fair exchange.

It was not until 1866 that Napoleon III finally decided to call off this futile attempt to foist a foreign ruler on the Mexican people, and then only because he became worried when the newly emerging power of Prussia erupted on the European scene by defeating the Austrian Army at Sadowa, a defeat that made the French Emperor wonder, correctly, where the Prussians would strike next. The Franco-Prussian War of 1870 was already looming and the time had come to call his fighting men home. The last legionnaires sailed from Mexico in February 1867, bringing with them the men of Camerone. The 'Emperor' Maximilian would have done well to leave with them but he elected to stay with his adopted people, convinced to the very end that they would support him. Instead the Juaristas took him, put him against a wall at Queretaro and shot him.

When the Legion left Mexico they took with them a

strange memento. When the convoy eventually reached Camerone they found nothing there but a smoking ruin and a pile of dead, but rooting about among the ruins the legionnaires came on the wooden hand of Captain Danjou. They took it back with them to Sidi Bel Abbès and placed it in their chapel and museum where countless legionnaires and visitors have looked at it and heard again the story of the gallant captain and the epic Legion stand at Camerone. The hand can still be seen today, in the museum at Aubagne, from where it is taken out every year for the annual Camerone parade on 30 April.

Camerone remains the battle that defines the Legion spirit. When all seems lost, and the enemy are everywhere, when ammunition is low and the wounded are crying out for aid and there is no apparent option but surrender, the Legion remembers its past and the great fight at Camerone. The story is drummed into them as recruits and repeated every year at the Camerone Day memorial services and celebrations, rituals held wherever the Legion is posted, even in the middle of a battle. The Legion does not surrender, ever. When the ammunition has gone, the rule is to 'faire Camerone' and go out on the enemy with the bayonet.

Men who will fight like that make a formidable foe, and the Legion have so fought in a score of actions since Captain Danjou laid down the rules of engagement in a dirty Mexican village more than a hundred years ago.

Napoleon III ordered that the word Camerone should be inscribed on Legion battle flags, but the memory of princes is notoriously short. When Corporal Louis Maine was presented to him at a parade in 1869 the emperor had forgotten all about Camerone and had to be reminded of the battle, but at last he turned and said to the corporal: 'Of course, you are a member of the 3rd Company.'

Corporal Maine shook his head. 'The 3rd Company is no more, Sire,' he replied, 'but while it existed there were only good soldiers in it.'

6

COLONIAL WARS: INDO-CHINA, DAHOMEY, MADAGASCAR, 1871–1914

'We have fought here for a thousand years – and we shall fight for another thousand if need be'

Vietnamese saying, 1883

The end of the Franco-Prussian War of 1870–1 found France somewhat reduced in size, having lost her valuable eastern provinces of Alsace and Lorraine, but determined to compensate for these losses by expanding her colonial empire in North Africa and the Far East. The latter half of the nineteenth century was the great era of colonial expansion for all the European powers, a time when the Dutch, Belgians and French began to compete for overseas territory with the long-established colonial powers, the Portuguese and the British.

In the 40 years between the ending of the Franco-Prussian War and the outbreak of the Great War of 1914–18 – a war which the armistice of 1871 had done so much to bring about – the Legion was almost constantly in action, in Africa and the Far East or the Indian Ocean. These were small affairs compared with the two big wars that preceded and followed them, but some of the effects were to be far-reaching – especially France's involvement in Indo-China, a name which to the French colonialists meant the three countries of Laos, Cambodia and, ominously, Vietnam. From the moment the Legion arrived in Tonkin in November 1883, they were marching down a road that led them inexorably to Dien Bien Phu.

And yet, that said, Indo-China soon became as much of a home to the Legion as the stony deserts and mountains of Algeria, with Saigon as another Sidi Bel Abbès – not a Legion town perhaps, but a far more popular posting. In the warm scented air of Indo-China the Legion relaxed a little, and that fierce, relentless discipline that caused so much misery in North Africa wilted a little in the tropical heat. There was fighting in Indo-China and plenty of it, but there were also plenty of complaisant women, and beautiful women at that, many of them more than willing to take up with and care for a serving legionnaire. Every legionnaire had his *congais*, his Vietnamese mistress, who travelled about with her man wherever he was posted, and the practice continued until the Legion – and the French – left Indo-China for ever in 1955.

After the ending of the Franco-Prussian War in 1871 the Legion, now a five-battalion force, returned to Algeria, where it spent a large part of the next ten years on public works duties, building roads and ports, and expanding their much-loved and much-altered depot at Sidi Bel Abbès. Sidi Bel Abbès was now a substantial town, a large part of it given over to the Village Nègre, a sprawling district of bars and brothels, teeming with whores of every colour and many nations. The Village Nègre was the scene of many riots and massive fist and knife fights, especially on pay day, when the legionnaires settled scores with their enemies within the ranks or took on one of the other units that had the temerity to trespass in a Legion town. At such times Sidi Bel Abbès took on the appearance and atmosphere of any Wild West cattle town, a place where a man needed to keep his wits about him and be handy with his fists or a knife.

When matters got out of control, as they did from time to time, the disturbances were quickly quelled by the

Legion NCOs, and those guilty of excessive behaviour – like stabbing a comrade or brawling with a corporal – were further subdued by a week or so in the Legion prison, with plenty of *pelote* to keep them busy, or sent for a spell in one of the much-feared Battalions d'Afrique, (Bat d'Af), the French Army punishment battalions, where life could be hard, even for a legionnaire.

During this postwar period the Legion also acquired a new commanding officer, Colonel François de Negrier, who was to become one of the most popular commanding officers in Legion history. De Negrier did not court popularity and was said to be particularly severe with drunks and the undisciplined, but provided the men stayed sober and obeyed orders he looked after them. 'We did what he told us to do, without hesitation. We were his Legion and he counted on us. We had to prove that we were worthy of his esteem and his affection,' is one comment on this remarkable officer.

De Negrier took command of the Legion at Sidi Bel Abbès in 1881, having previously commanded a battalion of the Chausseurs d'Afrique. De Negrier respected the legionnaires because they liked to fight and the legionnaires took to him because he was an efficient, innovative officer, who studied his men and acted to address their problems, though he was a stern commander. It was de Negrier who told his men bluntly, 'You have become soldiers in order to die and I shall send you where you can die', a statement that still adorns Legion walls. De Negrier commanded the Legion for only two years but his actions were far-reaching. His first order, one which instantly won many stone-hard hearts, was to take the Legion off labour duties and turn it back into a fighting force. The downside of this was a return to long marches, dress parades, drill and spit and polish, but at least they felt like soldiers again.

De Negrier also founded the 'Mounted Companies', two legionnaires to one mule, units that were to prove so useful in the wars in Morocco and which in 1882 gave the Legion its famous 'flaming grenade' badge which it carries to this day. Grenadiers were the élite troops in many armies – hence the Grenadier Guards – so the often despised legionnaires took this badge as a signal honour. De Negrier led the Legion in the campaign against the Bou Amama rebels in Algeria in 1881, and he managed to find a fresh field for Legion employment when, having been promoted to brigadier general and sent to Indo-China, he sent for a Legion *battalion de marche* of 600 picked legionnaires to form part of his brigade in the Courbet expedition to Indo-China in 1883.

'Tonkin', as it was then called, a territory now part of North Vietnam, had been under some form of French Army occupation since the 1850s. The French sent troops there after French missionaries had been first imprisoned and then beheaded by the local ruler. This provided the excuse for intervention, and after a short campaign the French ended up occupying half the country.

The Legion had not been sent there in the first decades of French rule; their involvement began in 1883 when the Emperor of Annam – a region best imagined as South Vietnam – sent a message from his capital at Hue, invoking French aid against military incursions from China and help in suppressing the large and powerful warlords and pirates – known as the Black Flags – who were turning his 'empire' into a battlefield.

Here was a classic situation for the Legion and its French masters; a war that promised hard fighting without any political justification but with the prospect of further colonial gains as the price of assistance – pure intervention, but that was not something that bothered any European power at the end of the nineteenth century. The 1st Battalion of the Legion duly disembarked at Haiphong – later the main port of North Vietnam – on 8 November 1883, as the vanguard of an expeditionary force commanded by Admiral Courbet. This force consisted of several warships and some 5,000 French infantry and marines as well as the Legion *battalion de marche*, barely enough for such a large and difficult task.

Courbet had to fight on two fronts, against the Black

Flags and the Chinese Army, and he elected to take on the Black Flags first, sending the Legion battalion to attack the two Black Flag strongholds at Son Tay and Bac Ninh. The 1st Battalion took Son Tay in short order, advancing with the bayonet to storm the defences which were briefly manned by over 20,000 Black Flags. The hero of this action was Legionnaire Minaert, a man who, in spite of heavy fire and the weight of his equipment, shinned up the first scaling ladder pressed against the walls of the fortress and held the top of the ladder until his comrades could climb up to his aid. It is said that during this engagement Minaert, a Belgian, encouraged his comrades with shouts of '*Vive La Légion!*' and '*Vive Belgique!*' When Admiral Courbet pinned the Médalille Militaire on Minaert's chest after the battle he told him, 'If you had thought to add "*Vive la France!*" this would be the Légion d'Honneur!'

In 1884, after the 2nd Battalion Etranger arrived, the newly formed Legion brigade marched to join the French forces besieging Bac Ninh, an altogether tougher proposition. De Negrier recalled the actions of Minaert at Son Tay and declared that 'The honour of being the first into Bac Ninh belongs to the Legion.'

Since the defences of Bac Ninh were very formidable and strongly held there was not a great deal of competition for this honour, and the Legion was therefore accorded the rather dubious prize of leading the assault on the Bac Ninh citadel, which fell after more hard fighting on 12 March 1884. Then followed a disaster. Following the fall of Bac Ninh, the Chinese elected to recognise the French claim to a protectorate in Amman, and agreed to evacuate the province.

Just how sincere they were in making this agreement was revealed just three months later, in June 1884, when a 600-strong French column was ambushed by Chinese forces on the border close to the town of Lang Son – a place we shall hear of again – and massacred to the last man, the wounded and prisoners being beheaded by the Chinese and their heads piled up before the town. It gradually transpired that the Chinese had sent an army of some 20,000 men into Tonkin, and the two Legion battalions were soon hard at work trying to evict it. There was a hard-fought engagement at Bang Bo, just across the Chinese border, in 1885, followed by a major battle at Lang Son, where a French and Legion force numbering around 2,200 men was attacked by ten times that number of well-armed Chinese regulars. The Legion took up a defensive position on high ground and formed square as the Chinese troops – blowing bugles as they were to do in the Korean War of 1950–3 – made a mass infantry assault on their position.

The Legion infantry and their supporting artillery greeted the Chinese formations with heavy fire and short charges with the bayonet, which soon littered the slopes of the hill with Chinese dead. Brigadier de Negrier was hit by a bullet in the chest, and handed over to his second-in-command, Lieutenant-Colonel Herbinger, who conducted a skilful withdrawal from this position and got back to the south with the majority of his command. The French Government were on the point of regarding this battle as a defeat when the Chinese Army packed up its wounded and retired across the frontier.

These assaults and battles showed the Legion's mettle in the assault, but a year later some of the Legion were given a chance to *faire Camerone* – fight to the last man – when two companies of legionnaires, the 1st and 2nd of the 1st Régiment Etranger, formed the garrison of an old fortress at Tuyen Quang in North Vietnam. Tuyen Quang was a formidable outpost, a brick-built fortress with two encircling walls, but the garrison was small, just 590 men, half of them legionnaires, not enough to man the defences adequately if the place was besieged.

In 1885 the fort was besieged by a large enemy force estimated at over 20,000 men, all hand-picked troops from the Chinese Army, a highly trained and professional force which soon had the legionnaires closely beset. The Chinese first invested the fort, cut off all communications and surrounded it with trenches and artillery positions.

They then started to sap towards the walls, digging tunnels to mine beneath the defence lines and opening a heavy artillery barrage in an attempt to breach the walls.

After a three-day bombardment, the first assault, by 3,000 Chinese infantry, came in on 26 January. This first assault was repulsed but further Chinese troops were then committed, the struggle concentrating on a legionnaire outpost commanded by a platoon NCO, Sergeant Leber – a German legionnaire. Leber and his men held the outpost for three days and nights before falling back to Tuyen Quang and gained precious time for the defenders to strengthen the main position.

Having failed with their initial assault, the Chinese kept up the sniping and bombardment, while moving their trenches closer to the walls (sapping) and digging more mines under the walls. Tunnelling (mining) was met with counter-mines and a number of skirmishes were fought between the tunnel rats of Tuyen Quang, far beneath the ground. On 11 February, one of the miners, Legionnaire Vaury, took a swing with his pick only to see the wall he was aiming at collapse, revealing a very surprised Chinese soldier, who was not too surprised to fire a shot at Vaury before vanishing back up the Chinese tunnel. Vaury received a flesh wound and was in hospital when, later that day, another tunnel reached the walls of the fort and a breach was blown. As the mine went off, throwing the defenders caught in the blast high in the air, a mass of splintered arms and legs, the Chinese infantry rose from their trenches and saps and rushed the breach created in the walls.

Fortunately, the fort commander, Captain Domine, had anticipated this event and constructed a redoubt inside the main wall, and although there was savage fighting with the bayonet in the breach, the Chinese were once again driven back and the breach was sealed with bamboo stakes. Two days later, another breach was blown in another wall, and this time the Chinese assault troops actually fought their way into the fort, and hung on there for an hour until a counter-attack drove them out again.

So the siege continued for a full month, less than 300

men, most of them wounded, all of them short of food, fighting off an army that vastly outnumbered them. Much of the fighting was hand to hand, with bayonet attack following counter-attack over the gradually crumbling walls. The mining continued and proved the hardest part of the siege, no man knowing when the ground under his feet might erupt into smoke and flame and high-explosive death. Moreover, as the mining war continued, the Chinese got more cunning.

On 22 February, a huge explosion shook the fort at 0600 hours, as a large mine went off under the walls, blowing a gap twenty metres wide. As usual, the expected assault came in, to a fanfare of bugles and, as so often before, the legionnaires counter-attacked with the bayonet and drove the attackers back. However, as they rushed out through the breach, another mine went off, killing or wounding some 40 legionnaires, and then a third mine erupted as their comrades came out to rescue the wounded. A fourth party, undeterred by these three explosions, now came charging through the breach, to drive the Chinese off and retrieve their wounded and their dead – for the Legion does not leave even its dead in the hands of the enemy.

Every Chinese assault was repulsed like this, but the defenders' numbers were dwindling. Another night assault, on 24 February, was hurled back; an assault following a mine explosion under the walls on the 25th was met with the bayonet and again repulsed; and a huge explosion on 28 February which demolished much of the remaining fortification still failed to dislodge the legionnaires from their redoubt.

Time after time, as the debris crashed to the ground and the Chinese infantry rushed forward, the legionnaires rose from the rubble to meet them. Ammunition was getting low but these fights for the breaches could go on for hours before the Chinese fell back, unable to wear down and destroy this terrible infantry. Finally, on 2 March, a full month after the siege began, a relief force, largely composed of a third Legion battalion, finally approached the ruins of Tuyen Quang and the Chinese withdrew, leaving the survivors of the two Legion companies to greet their relief in the now-established Legion tradition, drawn up on parade outside the walls they had held for so long, clothes brushed, muskets glittering and presenting arms. French losses at Tuyen Quang had been high, the Legion alone losing 158 men killed or wounded, including all six of the officers – more than 50 per cent of the defending force.

There was a curious sequel to this action at Tuyen Quang, one worth mentioning because it shows the strong character and long memory of the Legion. During the battle at Tuyen Quang, Captain de Borelli's company captured two black flags from the opposing Chinese forces. After the battle, Captain de Borelli presented these flags to the Legion, on condition that they were never taken to France, since he felt that France had not done enough to help the Legion during the siege. These flags hung in the Legion museum at Sidi Bel Abbès for the next 80 years – but when the Legion had to leave Algeria for France they were taken down and ceremonially burnt on the parade ground.

This campaign, which led to a French takeover of Indo-China, from the Chinese border to the Mekong delta, finally ended on 1 April 1885, when a treaty was signed between the French and the Chinese, but the fighting to pacify the country did not cease. Black Flag bands of pirates and robbers continued to roam the coast and countryside and had to be hunted down, and the warlike Montagnard tribes, which still live in the Central Highlands of Vietnam, the Chinese Nung and the Meo, continued to resist this European intrusion.

In January 1885 the 4th Battalion of the Legion was sent to Formosa to take part in another action against the Chinese, and in a two-month campaign managed to stamp out all Chinese resistance and return to Indo-China, where they began to patrol along the border, and again, inevitably, with General de Negrier no longer around to protect their interests, they were committed to more construction work. Indo-China remained a popular posting but the Legion strength was gradually reduced until by the start of the Great War their contribution to the garrison was down to one battalion, and that was withdrawn in 1919. North Africa was to remain the principal field of Legion activity, but there were other expeditions in the dying years of the nineteenth century, notably to the West African country of Dahomey – now Benin – in 1892.

The French had been trading along the West African shore and probing into Central Africa for many years without any major trouble, finding that certain French goods, like wine and brandy, were easily exchanged for ebony and timber. The trade was small but highly profitable, and matters only began to go awry after the French defeat in 1871 when the Germans, who had always been jealous of French and British colonial expansion, began to interfere in Dahomey, telling the local king, Behanzin, that France had been conquered and no longer existed as a separate state after the Franco-Prussian War and the time had come to forge fresh allegiances with the Prussians.

Behanzin was a total savage, a man addicted to bloodshed, a king who held an annual ceremony at which 500 people were beheaded in the centre of his capital, Abomey, and their skulls used to decorate the wall and roofs of the huts. For all his savagery, Behanzin was a powerful monarch, maintaining an army of 10,000 warriors and a corps of 2,000 female fighters, women who supposedly gave rise to the legend of the Amazons. Behanzin was always looking for ways to improve his army, as the Europeans encroached on his territory a little more each year, and what he needed now was firepower.

The Germans therefore backed up their suggestions with supplies of arms, including breech-loading Mauser rifles and teams of instructors to train the Dahomey warriors in their use. Thus equipped, Behanzin looked around for people to conquer, and his eyes fell on the French coastal trading ports and settlements, where more brandy and European goods were on hand for the asking, if the man asking for them was armed.

In fact, the French, having got rid of their Emperor, Napoleon III, had recovered very quickly from the Franco-Prussian War and, apart from vowing to retake Alsace and Lorraine as soon as possible, were more than eager to protect their trading interests in Africa or anywhere else. When their traders, who were normally occupied in buying timber and suppressing the slave trade, asked for protection, a French expeditionary force was rapidly formed and sent to their assistance.

The 1892 expedition to Dahomey consisted of 4,000 men under Colonel Dodds, a force that included a *battalion de marche* of 800 foreign legionnaires commanded by Major Faroux. The Legion was given the prime task of the expedition: to seize Behanzin's capital, Abomey, force Behanzin to negotiate the surrender of his rifles, expel the Germans, and therefore be sufficiently cowed to leave the French traders alone. This was a considerable task, to take over and dominate an entire country with just 4,000 men, and it was anticipated that the force would suffer the usual attrition from tropical diseases. This was the terrible, fever-haunted Bight of Benin, which sailors had been warned about for generations:

Beware, Beware, the Bight of Benin,
Where few come out, though many go in

However, undaunted by the probable cost, the expedition sailed from Toulon in midsummer and was soon off the Dahomey coast.

The legionnaires landed at the main port of Benin, Cotonou, on 26 August 1892, and set off through jungle and swamp towards Abomey. There were no roads, the tracks were soon poached out and turned into swamps as the army passed, and the air hummed with malarial mosquitoes and a thousand other stinging and biting insects. Every afternoon a deluge of tropical rain swept down, drenched the legionnaires and turned the paths into slippery quagmires. It was a hard country to soldier in, and the troops, clad in the thick woollen tunics and breeches then considered proper for warfare, whatever the climate, and heavily laden with the full *tenue de campagne*, suffered considerably as they hacked their way through the jungle.

Men were already falling sick when, on the night of 18 September, after a terrible march of 60 miles, the Legion camped at Dogba on the banks of the Oueme river, entrenching themselves behind thorn defences, with the river guarding one flank and the thorn hedges guarding the other three. They anticipated an attack but, even so, when the attack came it was a complete surprise.

At dawn, without any warning, the jungle suddenly swarmed with Dahomey warriors, including large numbers of the famous Amazons – the female warriors – all stark naked, except for a skirt of human skulls and necklaces of human teeth, but armed with spears and hatchets, relentlessly brave and very anxious to get to close quarters with the European soldiers, where their numbers and edged weapons could tell.

The legionnaires who faced the Dahomey warriors in battle remembered the Amazon women as the fiercest and most fearless of them all, the warriors mustered in well-drilled companies of 300 or more, the officers wearing a white headdress but otherwise as naked as the rest, all with shaved heads and teeth filed into points; a fearsome sight. These women could march long distances in this jungle terrain, and outfight any man, especially a man who was unused to fighting women and was therefore often cut down before he recovered from the shock caused by their appearance. The legionnaires swiftly got over their surprise and shot the Amazons down as fast as they could, as a matter of necessity, for these warrior women closed upon them slashing with axes and sharp swords.

This was a wild attack, in great strength, for the bulk of Behanzin's army was here, and the warriors swiftly swarmed over the thorn barricades and were in among the legionnaires, striking out with spear and hatchet, cutting men down with every blow. Nor were they without support, for their German instructors had done their work well. Those Dahomey warriors armed with rifles climbed trees and brought the French camp under heavy fire, and the fate of the entire *battalion de marche* lay in the balance until the Legion rallied and resorted to its favourite and most effective weapon – the bayonet.

Forming companies amid the swarm of shrieking warriors, the Legion counter-attacked, once, twice, three times, then a fourth, slashing and stabbing at their opponents in the thick bush, pausing to shoot the Dahomey snipers down from the trees, matching the bayonet against the spear. No quarter was given on either side in a hand-to-hand battle that lasted a full two hours before the Dahomey warriors had had enough and withdrew into the jungle. The Legion lost 100 men, killed or wounded, including the commander of the *battalion de marche*, Major Feroux. The Dahomians lost about 800, including many of the Amazons, who fought with particular ferocity and had to be shot or bayoneted, or clubbed to death with rifle butts, for they would not surrender.

The march continued, with the legionnaires alternating their leadership of the column with a contingent of the Senegalese infantry who formed part of the expeditionary force. It was the Senegalese's turn to hack a path through the jungle when, on 4 October, the advance guard was attacked and overwhelmed by another fierce attack which came sweeping out of the forest, the Amazons and warriors getting among the Senegalese infantry before they could get off more than a single volley. The legionnaires pushed their counter-attack home over the dismembered bodies of the Senegalese soldiers and the skirmishing went on for most of the day, with groups of Amazons making isolated attacks all down the length of the French column.

The Legion still had a long way to go, through more terrible country, before they reached Abomey, and as they battled forward for another two weeks they were harassed every step of the way by Dahomian and Amazon warriors. Finally, on 17 November, two full months after stepping ashore, the French expedition marched into Abomey, where they found all the huts in flames and King Behanzin a fugitive, hiding somewhere in the jungle. The legionnaires marched into the city along streets paved with human skulls and found that other skulls had been used as drinking tankards. Skeletons were found wedged into mud walls as household ornaments, and skulls adorned the royal throne. Abomey was a fearful place, an African Golgotha, and the legionnaires were not sorry to leave and march back to the coast, leaving many good men behind and taking others so sick of fever they looked likely to die.

The *battalion de marche* had now lost some 50 per cent of its strength, mostly from disease, and was down to less than 400 men, but they did get one fascinating trophy from the blazing city, the king's ceremonial sunshade which was fringed with human jawbones, which they took back to Sidi Bel Abbès. The expedition might be considered a success, for King Behanzin had fled and the French traders were secure, but the cost had been high.

More than half the 800-strong Legion battalion that landed in Dahomey in September stayed behind, dead of wounds or disease, when the Legion sailed back to Algeria. This was a brief stay before another expedition loomed and a fresh *battalion de marche* was formed in 1895 for another colonial expedition to the island of Madagascar in the Indian Ocean.

The Legion's involvement in tropical Africa was by no means over, however. It was to fight many other small-scale battles in the region, many concerned with the on-going task of stamping out the slave trade. In 1892 the Legion deployed a mounted company in Senegal and marched against the slavers around Kayes and the famous town of Timbuktu, where a hundred legionnaires and a few hundred Senegalese levies were attacked by over a thousand well-armed slavers. These were eventually beaten off in a counter-attack led by that stalwart Belgian legionnaire, Sergeant Minnaert, the hero of Son Tay, who had signed on after Indo-China for another term in the Legion.

Madagascar is a large island off the east coast of Africa, with an unfortunate history of tyranny and misrule. The fourth-largest island in the world, the size of California and containing some of the rarest wildlife on this planet, it was ruled at the end of the last century by a half-mad woman, Queen Ranavola, who had abrogated a trade and friendship treaty with France and begun to imprison and ill-treat French residents. This was at the height of imperialism and the result was inevitable. An expeditionary force of 20,000 men was organised under General Duchene, including an equally inevitable *battalion de marche* of the Légion Etrangère, and it landed on the Madagascar coast on 23 April 1895.

These expeditions followed a fixed, almost predictable pattern. As in Dahomey, the expedition's first task was to capture the capital, Antananarivo, which lies on the high plateau of Madagascar, 400 kilometres from the sea. Here lay the first problem for Madagascar had no roads; even today, 100 years later, Madagascar has only 800 kilometres of road, but building roads was a normal task for the legionnaires, and if no road existed from the coast to Tana the Legion would simply build one.

This they did, fighting and road-building for nearly three months until they climbed out of the mountains and rainforest and arrived on the central plateau. By now the expedition and the Legion battalion had lost a great many men, the vast majority to malaria and yellow fever, hardly any in combat and more were falling sick every day. If it went on like this the expedition would be dead of disease before the campaign, so clearly something had to be done. General Duchene, the commander, therefore formed the 1,500 fittest men into a light column, with the Legion in the vanguard as usual, and ordered them to march hard on Tana, defeat the Hova army and overthrow Queen Ranavola.

'March or die,' he told them – not, as people have said since, a heartless order. If Tana fell the war would end and the soldiers could be removed to places where they could recover. So march they must and march they did,

30 miles a day with full pack, ammunition and weapons, to arrive at Tana five days later, where the Hovas, the Malagasy Army, drawn up to defend the capital, surrendered without a fight. The French had dragged a battery of artillery all the way from the coast and the gunners did not intend to end the campaign without firing at least one shot. One shell was duly despatched and exploded harmlessly against the wall of the queen's palace, the only artillery shot of the entire campaign.

The casualties of the Madagascar expedition were still high. Of the 21,000 men despatched, just 20 were killed in action, but a further 5,700 – 25 per cent of the force – died of malarial fever. One French regiment, the 200th Infanterie de Ligne, was almost wiped out by malaria, losing over 90 per cent of its men to this disease. The French stayed in Madagascar until the Second World War, and French – or Legion – influence hangs over the country to this day.

All these little wars and expeditionary campaigns did not detract from the continuing pacification of Algeria, which went on steadily as the French expanded their control from the coast south towards the Sahara and east and west towards Morocco and Tunisia. Each step of the way had first to be cleared and secured by troops, usually from the Legion, and then held down by roads and railways which were normally built by the legionnaires in what time could be spared from fighting. One way or another the legionnaires were kept occupied. Then, in the second decade of the new century, came the Great War of 1914–18, a war that would mark Europe for a generation and cause millions of deaths. In this cataclysm the Legion would play an honourable part, but as the European nations slid steadily towards disaster in the summer of 1914 the prospect of another European war was causing a great many problems for the Legion and for the legionnaires.

7

THE LEGION IN MOROCCO, 1870–1914

*'It is clearly necessary to teach these fanatical
Moroccans a lesson they will not forget in a hurry'*

Editorial, *L'Illustration*, Paris, 1903

The Great War was a watershed in Legion affairs, a time when the Legion became engaged in the most terrible of wars. Before that, though, its problems expanded in North Africa, where the usual degree of insurrection was compounded by the fact that the Algerian rebels – or freedom fighters – were making increasing use of the sanctuary offered by the Moroccan frontier, and the tribes were being stirred up by agents of the German Kaiser.

The defeat of France in the Franco-Prussian War of 1870–1 inevitably produced repercussions in North Africa. The tribes in Algeria soon realised that France was preoccupied with European problems, and the reduction of French garrisons during that conflict made it much easier to carry out attacks on French settlements, ambush convoys and plan larger insurrections. Moreover, German agents were soon at work, during and after the war, inciting the tribes with offers of money and arms to rise up against their colonial masters and throw the French *colons* into the sea. As a result, revolt was soon simmering in various parts of Algeria, and it came to the boil in the spring of 1871 with a major rising in the Kabyle mountains and along the always turbulent Moroccan frontier.

94

At first this took the form of sniping at Legion outposts and the ambushing of patrols and supply convoys. As this activity grew, Legion resources with which to contain the growing tide of violence became severely stretched, but fortunately the Arabs, encouraged by their successes in this guerrilla war, then abandoned it for an all-out rising, led by a dissident *marabout* and sheikh, Ben Hunza, who, after some weeks of skirmishing, attacked a large French force at Mangourah on 17 April 1871. The French and Legion infantry were badly outnumbered but they had recently been rearmed with a new, accurate, breech-loading rifle, the '*chassepot*', and having formed square, their rapid volleys and aimed fire at long range soon decimated the oncoming Arab tribesmen. Ben Hunza kept up the attacks for most of the day and withdrew only when the ground before the Legion squares was heaped with dead men and horses.

It was ten years before the Algerian tribes again tried their arms against the Legion, in 1881 when yet another tribal mystic, Bou Amama, called for a *jihad* – or holy war – against the Christians. He sent disciples around the tribes, urging the warriors to take up arms, and the Legion – hearing of this activity – sent out patrols to intercept and arrest the disciples as they travelled about the country. This led to a Legion officer being murdered in an Arab village by a crowd incited by one of Bou Amama's followers. This murder infuriated the Legion, which began to send punitive columns about the country seeking out recalcitrant tribesmen. The first major attack came in May 1881 when a large Arab force attacked a Legion infantry column.

This column, escorting a supply train, also contained a squadron of the Chasseurs d'Afrique, crack Zouave infantry, and some Arab irregulars called '*goums*'. As always in these Algerian conflicts, the French were heavily outnumbered, the first attack on the column coming from an estimated 4,000 tribesmen, who came charging down from the hills, urged on by the ululations of their women on the ridge above. This attack by the Arab foot-soldiers fell on the Legion vanguard, which broke the Arab charge, though a large number of tribesmen literally leapt into the Legion ranks, bounding over the men in the first line to plunge into the heart of the Legion square, where they were spitted on bayonets, cut down with sword slashes, or felled by blows from rifle butts.

While this hand-to-hand fighting was going on at the head of the column, the Arab horse appeared and charged in on the rearguard – at which point the *goums* deserted and went over to the Arab side, turning back to join in the attack on the French. The Chasseurs d'Afrique were wiped out in this new attack and much of the column was captured, the drivers and escorts being hauled from the wagons to have their throats cut, but the Zouaves and the legionnaires battled on, back to back in some cases, and slowly fought their way out of the ambush position. Once free of their shrieking, sword-slashing opponents, they formed square, and as at Mangourah, shot down a large quantity of tribesmen, who braved the *chassepot* volleys to press home their attacks with great resolution. In a very real sense the Arab bravery was their undoing, for by meeting the French in open battle they became vulnerable to the full firepower of modern weapons. Bou Amama had lost several hundreds of his best men before he saw that the attack was pointless and called his warriors off.

This battle, so profitable in booty, so costly in lives, convinced Bou Amama that ambushing, sniping and other forms of guerrilla warfare would be more effective than all-out battle where his tribesmen engaged the French and Legion infantry in close combat. The campaign therefore developed into a series of night raids and small-scale attacks on French patrols and outposts, the Arabs drawing off as soon as the French mustered enough men to give them a drubbing. Guerrilla warfare, where the advantages of surprise and mobility rest with the attacker, has always been effective against large conventional forces and was effective here until the new commander of the Foreign Legion – a man who has already appeared in this book, Colonel de Negrier – found a way to give his troops the means to strike back swiftly at their Arab attackers. This new method took the form of partially mounted troops, the Mounted Companies, or *Compagnies Montées*.

It is worth restating the fact already noted, that Legion prowess and reputation were based on its performance as a 'heavy infantry' force, organised on conventional lines and, at least in equipment and role, much like any other infantry regiment or battalion in the French Army of the period. The difference lay in the quality and training of the men and the Legion's peculiar insistence that it would rather fight and die than merely fight and run away to fight another day. Mobility was not a Legion asset. The officers had horses but there was, as yet, no Legion cavalry, and though the legionnaires were prodigious marchers, able to march 40 to 80 kilometres a day for weeks on end – as they still can today – an infantry force lacking mobility is always at a certain disadvantage in a guerrilla campaign.

One obvious answer might have been to raise a cavalry detachment, but cavalry forces required men who could both ride and care for horses, and such skills are not easily acquired. Anyway, horses require such quantities of fodder, especially grain, that a full supply train is needed to support them – which tends to limit the mobility cavalry are alleged to supply. Colonel de Negrier pondered this problem for some while before coming up with the idea of the mounted companies.

It might have been more accurate to call them the 'half-mounted companies', for the mounted companies were based on the idea of two men – *and one mule*. Mules, half-horse, half-donkey, are amazing animals. Cantankerous but full of character, the mule can work either as a draught animal, pulling a wagon, or as a steed, carrying a man all day and even managing a gallop when required; many experienced cavalry soldiers came to prefer a mule for campaigning rather than some temperamental, full-blooded Arab charger. Mules do not need horse fodder or issues of grain; they can live and thrive on almost anything and have no great need of water, a particular bonus in the arid countryside of Algeria and Morocco.

Since mules are largely self-sufficient, no great skill is needed to look after them, though they have to be carefully loaded for fear of saddle and harness galls, ulcers caused by the chafing of poorly fitted equipment. The legionnaires soon learned this skill and became very fond – in an undemonstrative, Legion kind of way – of their four-footed friends, kindred spirits who were not unlike the legionnaires themselves – short on beauty but capable of getting the job done. Hardy, hard-working, capable of carrying heavy loads for long distances, the mule was the means by which Colonel Negrier and his legionnaires broke the Arab revolt.

Negrier formed one *compagnie montée* in each regiment, later expanding this to one in each battalion while the Legion was on campaign. The principle was that one man rode the mule while the other legionnaire walked or trotted alongside, the men changing over every hour. The man on foot loaded his equipment onto the mule and kept only his rifle and ammunition and, thus freed from the crushing weight of the *tenue de campagne*, he was able to keep up with the faster pace. Thanks to their mules, the Legion companies were able to pursue the Arab raiders, run them down and bring them to battle. The *compagnies montées* became the élite units of the Legion and remained in service until after the Great War, long after the advent of aircraft and motor transport should have made them obsolescent. They stayed in use because they were effective.

Even so, one of the steps to pacification was the installation of civilian economic facilities, like roads and railways, and the Legion, as ever, was always building roads when there was no enemy around – and not infrequently when the enemy might be over the next ridge and it was advisable to keep a loaded rifle propped against the wheelbarrow. This road-building task brought on one of the first mounted company actions, when a large Arab force attacked a Legion mounted company that was part of a French force surveying a route to the Figuig oasis in the Sahara in 1882.

The mounted company was escorting the surveying party when they ran into some Arab shepherds with a flock of 2,000 sheep. Shots were exchanged and the Arabs fled, leaving their sheep behind, only to return with a force of some 2,500 tribesmen, 1,000 of them mounted and all heavily armed, part of Bou Amama's army for whom the sheep had been intended as provisions. The Legion party of some 300 men was soon closely beset and began a slow retreat across the desert, their commander, Captain de Castries, sending a galloper back to the Legion command post, requesting assistance.

De Castries led his men to a low plateau jutting up from the desert floor, intending to occupy the high ground and make a stand. On the way, a part of his force, including the *compagnie montée*, was cut off and surrounded by hundreds of Arabs, who succeeded in killing seventeen legionnaires and Lieutenant Massone, the company commander, before the company fought its way clear. The Arabs had already occupied the crest of the plateau and it was necessary to take the hill at the point of the bayonet before the Arabs were driven off and the legionnaires could pile up the stones to make low-walled sangars, dig shallow trenches, and prepare to fight for their lives. Meanwhile, the baggage animals, carrying most of the ammunition, had been captured or had bolted and another officer, Captain Barbier, had been killed, fighting furiously in a press of the enemy, falling with nine bullets and seven sword wounds in his body.

The Arabs continued to assault the hill and by mid-afternoon, with water and ammunition getting low, de Castries decided to fight his way out in the direction of the expected relief force, and at dusk that evening the break-out began. Fighting off repeated Arab attacks, the remains of de Castries' force marched off across the desert, greatly relieved when the Arab attacks gradually petered out, discovering the reason when Colonel de Negrier appeared out of the night with a strong Legion force.

De Negrier had hoped to catch Bou Amama while he

was engaged in the attempt to wipe out de Castries' force, but the Arab was far too wily to be caught like that; having killed 50 legionnaires and wounded another 27, he broke off the action. These totals, the wounded being half as many as the dead, are another reminder of the grisly fate of legionnaires in these campaigns. In any European battle, the wounded might be expected to outnumber the dead by three to one or more, but in these Arab wars a wounded man was instantly marked down for slaughter, and unless his comrades were quick off the mark he would be dragged away for mutilation and death.

After two years of fighting, Bou Amama gave up the struggle in Algeria and withdrew across the frontier to the safety of Morocco. Eventually, though it was not Bou Amama's doing, the Legion came after him, determined to put a stop to these cross-border raids once and for all.

By the mid-1880s the French had been in Algeria for 50 years and could fairly claim to have pacified the country. The Arab tribes did not like the French and were always prone to revolt, but even they were getting used to the French way of life, sending their children to French schools and accepting that a European-imposed peace was a marginal improvement on constant tribal wars. There were, however, two remaining problems – the southern frontier and the border with Morocco.

On the southern frontier lay the Sahara desert and the warlike Tuareg tribes, while the country beyond the Moroccan frontier was a refuge for Algerian tribal dissidents and a haven for large Moroccan raiding parties – *harkas* – whose activities needed constant curbing. The French needed to do something about Morocco but could not invade or annex that country without provoking a storm of protest among the other European nations, especially Spain, which also had greedy eyes on that potential colony, just across the Straits of Gibraltar.

The French therefore decided to begin with the pacification of Sahara and sent roving columns to explore the region and plant the French flag in any territory not occupied or contested by any other European power.

After an outpost had been set up – usually by the Legion – a road would be built, also by the Legion, to link this outpost with some Algerian outpost further north, and so, slowly, the French advanced into the Sahara and towards the humid depths of equatorial Africa.

By 1900, the Legion had advanced and built a road as far as Salah on the northern edge of the sand sea. Then, having crushed the local tribes, recruiting many of the warriors into French service with offers of pay and rifles, the Legion expanded French power across the Sahara towards Timimoun and Goura. During this exploration and subjection period, the Legion demonstrated yet again its amazing ability to march. In the summer of 1900, the two REI marched for over 1,250 miles across the 'Erg', the sandy, stony wastes of the Sahara, from Geryville in the north as far south as the Goura, returning to base in rags, many of the men barefoot, their boots destroyed by the march across a stark, arid wilderness. This was the first time the 'Great Erg' of the Sahara had been crossed on foot; only one man fell out and only seven reported sick when the march was over.

The Sahara extends along the Algerian frontier and stretches west to run beyond that of Morocco, and the Moroccan tribes soon became concerned by this fresh French expansion, which they saw as an attempt to outflank their eastern frontier and curb their raiding activities. When the French started to plot the route for a railway that would head into the Sahara but run close to the Moroccan frontier, the tribes decided to take action and began to raid the line, pulling up track and attacking survey parties and the construction teams. This activity brought on a major engagement when a large Moroccan force crossed the Algerian frontier and attacked a huge camel train bringing supplies to the survey teams.

This camel train – which comprised some 4,000 animals – had reached the Igli oasis and unloaded some of its supplies before half the column, escorted by a Legion *compagnie montée*, marched on towards El Moungar. On the way the column was attacked by 500 mounted Moroccan tribesmen, who swept down on the camel train, killed ten legionnaires and wounded eight, losing 100 of their own men before breaking off the engagement, but driving away a large number of camels. This attack marked the start of a long series of cross-border attacks by the Moroccans, which eventually forced the Legion to build a series of *Beau Geste*-style forts along the Algerian side of the frontier, to occupy the oasis of Taghit and maintain regular patrols between these positions.

This failed to do more than limit Moroccan incursions, and in 1903 the Legion made a punitive strike across the Moroccan frontier to take and destroy the Moroccan citadel called the Kasr-el-Azoudj in the heart of the Bechar oasis.

A desert is only a desert because it lacks water, and where water exists the desert blooms into fertility, and so it was here. Many Saharan oases cover dozens or scores of square kilometres and support a population running into thousands, farmers who produce plenty of food and cash crops by installing irrigation canals and *birs* (wells) from which water from an underground reservoir reaches the fields and the date palm plantations. The Bechar oasis was just such a place, and the Kasr was the central fortress or citadel, set in the midst of the fields and date palm plantations.

The Legion took a large force equipped with field artillery to destroy the Moroccan force at Bechar, but found to their dismay that the mud walls of the Kasr were extremely resistant to shellfire, the explosions doing no more than making some of the mud fly, leaving the main structure intact. Their attack therefore dissolved into a frantic, hand-to-hand infantry battle, fought out by small parties in the narrow lanes and small-walled fields, between the legionnaires and swarms of Arab warriors.

This battle lasted all day, and though it ended in a Legion victory the Moroccans were not subdued. They retaliated with a tit-for-tat assault on the Algerian oasis of Taghit in August 1903, sending an 8,000-strong *harka* to destroy the French camp and kill all the soldiers it contained. In spite of their numbers, and the fact that the tribesmen had brought along their women and children to observe the battle, this *harka* got to Taghit without being detected and attacked the French lines at midday on 17 August, hoping to catch the soldiers either stunned by the heat or deep in a siesta.

The *harka* succeeded in overrunning an outpost held by a company of *goums* and occupied a long ridge that overlooked the Legion positions within the oasis, which they then brought under heavy fire. This harassing fire went on for most of the night, and at dawn the weary garrison was subjected to the first of a series of assaults, which went on all day, wave after wave of tribesmen sweeping off the ridge and into the oasis, in bands 3,000 to 5,000 strong, urged on by the screams and cries of their women dancing on the crest of the ridge. It must have been a strange, barbaric, frightening experience, but the legionnaires were not the sort of soldiers to be discomforted by such tactics. They laid out their ammunition on the parapet of their fort and in the surrounding trenches, and methodically shot down every tribesman that strayed into their sights. Moroccan casualties for the day were later estimated at over 1,000 men, killed or wounded . . . and the cost to the Legion was a slight wound to just one soldier.

The *harka* drew off to lick its wounds but it did not disband or return to Morocco. Two weeks later a *compagnie montée* platoon ran into this *harka* again and was soon surrounded by Moroccan tribesmen eager to avenge their losses at Taghit. The platoon officers were killed in the first exchange of fire and the platoon, just 50 men, commanded by an NCO, Sergeant Tisserand, who had already been wounded three times, prepared for the fight of their lives. They had no opportunity to dig a defensive position and were in the open desert, so they formed a rough square, took what cover there was available and prepared to fight it out. By dusk, twenty had been killed but the 30 left were still full of fight, beating off attacks that grew in intensity as their numbers shrank.

It could not go on for their position was untenable, but just as they were about to be overwhelmed a Legion patrol was seen, coming up fast from a distant ridge. There were only a score of legionnaires in the patrol, but their headlong approach concealed that fact and the dust they were kicking up hinted at a larger force. Having fought so hard against so few, the thought of fighting more legionnaires was too much for the *harka*, which broke off the action and withdrew across the Moroccan frontier.

This constant border bickering and the frequent battles kept the Moroccan situation in the headlines of the Paris newspapers, where questions were soon being asked about what, if anything, was or could be done to curb the attacks of the Moroccan tribes. Not wishing to get involved in further expansion along the turbulent North African shore, but anxious to show that they were doing *something*, the French Government recalled an experienced officer, Colonel Hubert Lyautey, to duty. Lyautey had been dismissed from active duty for daring to question the entire thrust of French colonial policy, and sending him to deal with the Moroccan situation was regarded in Parisian political circles as a touch of genius. If he succeeded they could take the credit; if he failed, he could take the blame.

Lyautey was to spend the next 25 years in Morocco and Algeria, and his name would eventually be resurrected as the architect of those countries' development into modern states. When he arrived in Algeria – he was promoted general as he stepped off the boat – Morocco was a semi-medieval state, where tribal chieftains did as they pleased and paid no attention whatsoever to the dictates of their nominal overlord, the Sheikh of Morocco, who lived in barbaric splendour in his capital, Fez. Lyautey set out to change all that, and with the help of the Légion Etrangère he succeeded.

Lyautey had already served with the Legion in Madagascar and Tonkin and firmly believed that if the French position in Algeria was to be tenable, then Morocco must either be brought under French control as a protectorate or the tribes totally subdued. As a first step he reorganised his forces into three formations, the tribal *goums*, who were to pursue the Moroccan *harkas* across the frontier and provide intelligence; the French Army were to occupy and maintain large bases in Algeria close to the Moroccan frontier, while the mounted companies and the Legion would provide the heart of the counter-attack forces.

This done, his next task was to stamp out activities emanating from the oasis at Bechar. This probably lay in Moroccan territory – the border had yet to be properly surveyed – and the French Government had told him to leave it alone. Obeying the letter but not the spirit of these orders, Lyautey surrounded Bechar with a string of Legion forts, and had the desert between these strong-points patrolled by reinforced *compagnies montées* of the 2nd and 3rd Regiments.

He also isolated another tribal stronghold, the oasis of Ras el Ain, which definitely lay in Moroccan territory, but using two more *compagnes montées* he first isolated this oasis and then occupied it, telling the government that he had seized control of 'Berguent', a name he made up for inclusion in his despatch. The French Government could not find this place on their maps and allowed Lyautey to retain possession. When Lyautey finally occupied Bechar he told the government he had occupied 'Colomb', after Colonel Colomb who was then in command of the oc-cupying forces, and – such is fate – this place later became – and remains – known as Colomb-Bechar.

In making these necessary moves, Lyautey was taking considerable risks with his career, for the French Govern-ment was quite adamant that there was to be no unprovoked aggression in Morocco. Aggression from Mo-rocco was taking place all the time, in the form of raiding *harkas* and attacks on French outposts in Algeria, but the most that Lyautey could wring out of his masters was permission for 'hot pursuit', which enabled his forces – usually the *compagnies montées* – to chase the raiders back across the frontier.

Morocco was increasingly unstable, and in the end it was internal anarchy, not external aggression, which forced the French Government to modify these stultifying instructions. Basically, the various tribal rulers in Morocco rose up against the sultan, foreign merchants were attacked, robbed and murdered, and by 1906 it became clear to the European powers, including Spain and Germany, that something must be done to restore order to Morocco. The task was devolved to the French, and in 1907 French troops landed on the Atlantic coast and occupied the city of Dar-el-Beida – later called Casablanca – and took over the city of Oujda. While this was happening in the west and north, Lyautey and the Legion were moving up to cross the Saharan border, where a local sheikh and *marabout*, Moulay Hassan, had mustered a huge *harka*, 20,000 strong, to resist them.

Lyautey had formed his forces into three columns, based on Bechar, Berguent and Beni Ounif, and advanced across the Moroccan frontier, determined to find this *harka* and bring it to battle. This did not take long, for Moulay Hassan was itching for a fight and fell directly on the Beni Ounif column at the Menabha oasis on 16 April 1907, the first assault falling on the 24th *Compagnie Montée*, which was commanded by a resourceful Legion officer, Captain Maury.

The attack began in mid-morning when a sudden, heavy and accurate fire fell on the Legion camp from the shade of the oasis palm trees. This was followed, in a pattern that was now becoming familiar, by a violent assault on the picquets, which were quickly overrun, enabling the Arabs to gain possession of the surrounding ridges overlooking the French encampment. It was clearly necessary to regain possession of these ridges, but the first attempt to do so was driven back with loss, the officer in charge of the assault, Lieutenant Coste, being killed. Maury led the second assault in person, and having gained the ridge was attempting to sweep along it when his force was held up by a Moroccan party barricaded into a ruined fort. The legionnaires, their blood up, stormed this fort with the bayonet and killed the defenders to the last man, though Captain Maury was severely wounded in the attack.

The column had lost over 100 men in this short engagement, but the sound of firing brought the other two columns converging on the Menabha oasis, from which the entire force set out next day to track down the *harka*. They followed its tracks to the village of Douiret, the childhood home of Moulay Hassan, and from there to the Denib oasis, which was reached a month later, on 13 May. The *harka* was there in force and the attack, led by the 24th Mounted Company, went in on the following day, after a brief bombardment from the French artillery. Then followed a brief engagement in which yet another 24th Company officer was killed, and the *harka* fell back to the nearby oasis of Bou Denib, with the Légion in hot pursuit.

On the following day this war of movement was resumed, with a further heavy bombardment of the *harka*, which should have been followed by an infantry assault, but as the French columns began to deploy for the attack white flags fluttered from the parapet of the mosque and many Moroccan tribesmen were seen fleeing from the oasis into the dubious shelter of the desert. It appeared that this constant Legion pressure and the not inconsiderable losses had made Moulay Hassan break off his invasion and turn for home.

General Lyautey decided to garrison the Bou Denib oasis and fort and left a force of legionnaires, from the mounted company and the 6th Battalion of the 2nd Régiment Etranger, plus some mounted Spahis, to guard against further attacks. These were not long in coming. Moulay Hassan had seen his forces beaten time and time again by the Legion, but having kept Bou Denib under surveillance for some days, he decided to try again and fall on the oasis with all his power and wipe the garrison out. He mustered a new *harka*, containing no less than 25,000 well-armed and mounted men, and fell on the oasis on 12 August 1907.

By now the garrison had shrunk considerably, and although the commander had sent for reinforcements, none had arrived when the vanguard of the *harka* came swarming in across the desert and put the place under siege. The garrison of the oasis fort comprised 90 men, 40 of them legionnaires under Sergeant Koenig, and with them acting as the bastion of the defences the defenders held out and beat the Moroccans off.

A siege then began and, fortunately, the Moroccans were in no hurry to renew the attack, so it was not until 1 September that their main body was seen advancing towards the fort – by which time the guns of the relief column were in range and directed fire on to the massed ranks of the *harka* as the defenders sallied out on to the open desert and deployed for battle. The odds were still considerable, some 5,000 French and Legion soldiers against the 20,000-plus of the *harka*, but the battle was a massacre, as French artillery and massed rifle fire tore holes in the ranks of the *harka*. Nevertheless, the Moroccans attacked again and again, hurling themselves against the defenders for more than eighteen hours finally pulling back and vanishing into the desert on 7 September.

The skirmish at Bou Denib ended the fighting on the southern border of Morocco, but there was plenty more action taking place elsewhere, especially around the Atlas Mountains and the capital of Morocco, Fez.

As already mentioned, in March 1907 the French had occupied the town of Oujda, the closest Moroccan town to the Algerian frontier, and had sent a naval expedition to take the port of Casablanca – then called Dar-el-Beida – on the Atlantic coast. Under Lyautey, the garrisons of these places now began a programme of pacification using a technique called the *tache d'huile*, the oil spot or stain. The theory was that from these garrison towns the French troops could pacify the surrounding areas, their actions and influence spreading out from the garrisons as a spot of oil gradually spreads across the ground. Many of the local people were tired of the constant tribal wars and the anarchy that went with them, and the French found this task of pacification easier than they had expected, at least for a while.

Lyautey decided to speed up the process by building a military road into the Beni Snassen mountains, a range named after, and the home of, the most recalcitrant Moroccan tribe. The task, inevitably, was given to the Legion, who first surveyed the route, finding a couple of competent surveyors in the ranks, and then set about building the road, beating off attacks from the enraged Beni Snassen tribesmen. This was hard, dangerous work as the example of the 12th Mounted Company clearly shows. The company, then engaged in road-building, was diverted from this task and sent on a fighting patrol to find and punish the Beni Snassen warriors who had been attacking French supply trains.

The company left Oujda at midnight and marched all night, changing places on the mules every hour and making good time, to reach a French supply column by daybreak. Just after dawn there was a brief firefight with some of the Beni Snassen, who drew off when they discovered the company in position, and then the company marched all day with the column, covering 50 kilometres and beating off more attacks before stopping for a brief rest at sunset. They then marched all night, had another fight with the Beni Snassen and – having covered a further 80 kilometres – returned to their camp near Oujda for a short sleep before starting work road-building again at dawn next day . . . and so it went on, week after week of road-building and patrolling, for months at a time.

These border battles during the French incursions into Morocco were not always small affairs. In August 1907, the Beni Snassen sent a force of 4,000 warriors to attack a Legion outpost at Menasseb, a post held by the 11th Mounted Company. The company manned their trenches and in a three-hour battle shot down 300 of the Beni Snassen, for the loss of two legionnaires killed and three wounded. Following this action, Lyautey formed up another four punitive columns and sent them into Beni

Snassen territory. They met no resistance, and everywhere they marched the tribesmen came out, bearing white flags, asking for help in caring for their wounded. The border war, which had kept Algeria turbulent for decades, seemed finally to be over, and the action now switched to the west, where the *tache d'huile* tactics, imposed in the summer of 1907, were starting to take effect in the country round Casablanca.

The origin of French involvement in western Morocco was to be found in a commercial undertaking. Casablanca was an attractive coastal town that could have been a major port but for a large sand bar blocking the entrance to the bay. In 1907 the Sherif of Morocco, Abd-el-Aziz, had commissioned a French dredging company to clear away this sand bar and construct port facilities close to the town. The company imported skilled workers from France and all was going well until part of the port facilities were thought to infringe on the sanctity of a Muslim cemetery. There was a riot, tribesmen from the countryside swept into the town and massacred the French workers, and the townsfolk gave themselves over to an orgy of looting and violence which the sultan seemed unable to contain. The French therefore elected to intervene to protect their own citizens and other foreign nationals in Morocco.

A French cruiser sailed round to Casablanca and anchored off the entrance to the bay before putting marines and fire-fighting parties ashore. The marines occupied the French consulate in the town and fought off the mob for five days before the first military contingent arrived, a brigade of troops containing the 6th Battalion of the 1st Legion Regiment. This brigade put a ring of steel around the town, permitting no one to enter or leave, and soon had the situation under control. A few days later the entire 2nd Regiment of the Legion arrived and it was possible to first beat off, and then pursue, any tribal attacks on the perimeter of the town.

Meanwhile, the government of Morocco – such as it was – had collapsed, with the deposing of Abd-el-Aziz by his brother, Moulay Hafid, who had raised a tribal army and led it against the Court in Fez. Aziz fled to Casablanca to beg for French aid in recapturing his throne, but the French declined to help and Moulay Hafid was duly proclaimed Sultan of Morocco in July 1808.

By the time Moulay Hafid mounted the throne in Fez, the French had gained effective control of his country. There was now an expeditionary force of 15,000 men in Morocco, and they were spreading out gradually from their base in Casablanca, imposing peace and order on the country, but avoiding more than diplomatic contact with Moulay Hafid. So it went on for three years, with the sherifian territory gradually being squeezed between the French coming in from the east and the French spreading out from Casablanca. Within the French-occupied territory, order was imposed, but Moulay Hafid kept to the ways of his ancestors, letting his chieftains and kaids do much as they pleased, provided they served him loyally. Those who chose to revolt were either beheaded, locked in cages for display around the capital, or thrown into his private pit of lions.

Revolt against this savage rule came from the tribesmen around Fez, who began to muster and move against the city in early 1911. By the end of the month, having defeated Moulay Hafid's army, they had the city under siege, and Moulay Hafid implored the French to come and help. A relief column was duly despatched, containing the mounted company of the 2nd Legion Regiment, a company commanded by Captain Rollet, an officer who was to rise to great heights during the Great War and be remembered thereafter as 'The Father of the Legion'. The French reached Fez after a week of furious marching and took over the city. More French troops then arrived and the familiar tasks of pacification began, with the legionnaires yet again employed on the double tasks of fighting off recalcitrant tribesmen and building roads. It took six months to build a military road from Fez to Rabat on the coast, and when that road was opened the French decided that the time was right to declare a protectorate in

Morocco. The other European nations did not demur and the Sultan of Morocco was in no position to complain, so this plan duly went ahead. The people of Morocco, however, did not welcome the protectorate and soon made their feelings clear.

The protectorate was declared on 30 March 1912, and was immediately greeted with riots in the cities and revolts in the countryside. Moulay Hafid was content to rule under French guidance, but his army promptly mutinied and attacked Europeans in Fez, where the troops were swiftly joined by swarms of tribesmen from the countryside. There was a major battle between these tribesmen and the 1st Battalion of the 1st Regiment of the Legion, a battle in which no prisoners were taken on either side, a battle ending, as all these major battles did, with defeat for the tribesmen and victory for the *chassepot*, the machine gun, artillery – and the Legion.

If the French thought that establishing a protectorate in Morocco would end their problems with the Muslim tribesmen of North Africa they were sadly mistaken. If anything, their problems multiplied as they started to move deeper into the country and impose their rule on tribes that had not been subdued in centuries. The Legion spearheaded the task of pacification, but it still proceeded slowly, and while it was in process a far greater problem arose in Europe, with the outbreak of the Great War in July 1914.

8

THE LEGION IN THE GREAT
WAR, 1914–18

*Never more than in this Great War has the Legion
upheld its motto; 'Legio, primus inter pares'*

General Gallieni, 1918

The origins of the Great War are too confused and
complicated for inclusion here. Basically, Germany and
France, at odds since 1871, had each set up a series of
defensive alliances with the other European powers.
France had allied herself with Russia and Great Britain to
form the Entente – though Britain's prime concern was
the neutrality of Belgium – Germany with the Austo-
Hungarian Empire and Turkey to form the Central
Powers. Italy, though linked with Germany and Austria in
the Triple Alliance, at first opted for neutrality and eventually joined the Entente.

When the heir to the Austro-Hungarian Empire, the
Archduke Franz Ferdinand, was assassinated by a Serbian
fanatic at Sarajevo on 1 July 1914, Austria threatened
Serbia, Russia, a protector of Serbia, threatened Austria,
Germany threatened Russia, and so, as these various
alliances were called into play, one country after another
went to war. The last straw came when the German
armies marching on France violated the neutrality of
Belgium and so brought Britain into the war, on 4 August
1914.

France and Germany went to war on 1 August 1914, and as in 1870 this declaration inevitably posed a problem for the Legion: what should be done about the German legionnaires?

The solution of 1871 was invoked again, with the German legionnaires mustered into the 1st Régiment de Marche and left to carry on the border war in Morocco and deal with any trouble in Algeria, while the men in the 2nd Régiment de Marche were sent to fight in France. In fact, the Legion still recruited soldiers from the adversary powers, even during the war; according to Legion records over 3,000 Germans, 1,200 Austrians and nearly 800 Turks joined the Legion between 1914 and 1918, though most of these men saw service in North Africa. These new recruits soon absorbed the Legion philosophy.

'Why are we here?' said one legionnaire. 'Orders, of course. We are professional soldiers. We don't give a damn who we fight or what we fight for. It is our 'métier' – our job. We have nothing else to do, no other object in life, no homes, no wives . . . so a war is welcome.'

As in 1870, Legion numbers were yet again dramatically increased in 1914 by the numerous foreign volunteers who came forward to fight for France and were duly mustered into the ranks of the Legion where they formed the 3rd and 4th Regiments.

During the Great War men from over 100 nations – which then meant almost every nation on earth – came to serve in the Légion Etrangère: Americans, Armenians, Bulgarians, Chinese, Spaniards, Swiss, Turkish . . . all these and dozens more were represented in the Legion ranks and somehow absorbed the Legion ethos and fighting spirit. According to Legion records, over 40,000 foreigners enlisted in the Legion between 1914 and 1918.

These included such people as the US songwriter Cole Porter, and one of the greatest of the Great War poets, the American Alan Seeger, who wrote, prophetically in his case, a memorable poem called 'Rendezvous':

I have a rendezvous with Death
At some disputed barricade . . .

114

Seeger, a graduate of Harvard University, led a group of 60 US volunteers to the Legion recruiting office in Paris in August 1914, marching behind the American flag. He kept his rendezvous during the Battle of the Somme in 1916.

There were enough Italians to form an entire battalion, so these, under command of the grandson of the great Italian patriot Garibaldi, were sent to fight in Italy. As more men joined, new units were formed, and many legionnaires were eventually allowed to transfer to their own national armies – provided those armies were on the side of the Entente. Another Legion battalion was comprised of men from the Paris police force and fire brigades, and the entire volunteer force was stiffened by drafts of non-German legionnaires shipped across from Algeria. Eventually four Legion regiments were formed, each of two battalions.

All this took time. Those countries which blithely went to war in August 1914 all imagined that, like the Franco-Prussian War of 1870–1, this would be a short war, a brief explosion of violence followed by a peace conference and an adjustment of frontiers . . . 'all over by Christmas', in the popular phrase of the time. In every combatant country in Europe, men rushed to the colours in case they should miss the fighting and the fun. It was not to turn out like that and it was not to be funny at all.

By the time the first legionnaires went into action in May 1915, the 450-mile-long western front already lay like an open wound across the face of Europe, running from the North Sea just inside Belgium's frontier, all the way south and east to Switzerland. This western front, a long trench system, was 'a chewed-up terrain full of shell and mine holes, deeply cratered, a place of collapsing dug-outs, crumbling parapets, leaking and scattered sand-bags, tangles of barbed wire, and the shallow beginnings of muddy trenches. There was a terrible smell of shit.'

The first Legion regiment committed was the 2nd/1st – the Second Regiment of the 1st Legion, equivalent to a brigade, which was sent in to make a frontal assault on a

German position at Hill 140, near Neuville St Vaast, a ridge north of Arras. This was a classic Legion engagement, typical of infantry assaults at the time. After a preliminary bombardment, the battalion advanced at dawn, and by nightfall the German 'White works' or *ouvrages blancs* defensive position had fallen, at terrible cost. Almost 3,000 men went 'over the top' that morning. By nightfall, 1,943 officers and men – two-thirds of the force – were dead or wounded, including all three battalion commanders.

That night the Germans counter-attacked and retook the 'White Works', so this terrible sacrifice was all for nothing. It did, however, demonstrate that the new legionnaires, the men recruited for war service just a year before, were every bit as good in the line as the veteran legionnaires recently arrived from Algeria.

Less than a month later, on 16 June 1915, reinforced by fresh drafts, the 2nd/1st attacked again, in the flat, canal-seamed country around Givenchy, north of Vimy Ridge. This time around a quarter of the regiment was lost, for no apparent advantage. Three months later the 2nd/1st took part in the Ferme Navarine action in Champagne, suffering such heavy casualties that the regiment was disbanded and the survivors dispersed among other Legion units.

The Legion had got used to this form of fighting and accepted the inevitable losses stoically in the Legion fashion. One Legion officer, Captain Junot, set the tone for this attack by leaping onto the parapet, in full view of the enemy, and telling his men as they fixed their bayonets for the attack, '*Mes enfants* . . . we are certainly going to die in this attack, but let us resolve to die like gallant men.' Captain Junot and most of his men were killed in the next half-hour. It was also noticeable that the Legion was beginning to get the measure of this new form of warfare – trench warfare – and sent its men into this attack well supplied with grenades and carrying knives for the close combat involved in trench-clearing.

The action at the Ferme Navarine also involved a

British legionnaire, who won the Croix de Guerre and the Médaille Militaire and by such outstanding and well-rewarded a display of gallantry revealed his sad and curious history. Until the retreat from Mons in 1914 this legionnaire, John Elkington, had been a lieutenant-colonel in the British Army, commanding an infantry battalion of the Royal Warwickshire Regiment.

During the retreat, his exhausted battalion had stopped for a rest at St Quintain, and the mayor of the town had persuaded Elkington to surrender his battalion if the Germans arrived, rather than submit the town to the horrors and destruction of street fighting. Worn out by days of marching and fighting, hardly knowing what he was doing, Elkington had agreed and even signed a paper to that effect, but the Germans did not arrive and after a few hours' rest, the battalion marched away.

Somehow, however, the news of Elkington's action got out. He was arrested, tried for cowardice by court martial, cashiered and dismissed from the army in disgrace. He could not go home to face his family with this blot on his honour, so he made his way to Paris and joined the Foreign Legion as a private soldier.

Now he was a decorated hero, and word of his action reached the King of England, George V. A few weeks later a statement in the *London Gazette* announced that His Majesty graciously approved the reinstatement of Lieutenant-Colonel Elkington to his former rank and position in His Majesty's Land Forces, following his gallant service in the French Foreign Legion. As a bonus, the King awarded Elkington the DSO. The Legion has given many men a second chance, but few have taken it so well as Colonel Elkington.

At the Ferme Navarine the 2nd/1st had fought alongside its sister regiment, the 11th/2nd, which also suffered terribly. This regiment had been through a similar mill to the 11th/1st, committed again and again in pointless, expensive assaults against entrenched infantry well supplied with machine guns and supported by artillery. Such were the losses that on 11 November 1915, after the

Ferme Navarine, the two regiments were combined into one, the Régiment de Marche de la Légion Etrangère, the famous RMLE – a regiment of foreigners that was to become, in three short, violent years, the most commended and decorated regiment in the armies of republican France.

The cost of such distinction was high, for the Legion regiment suffered 100 per cent casualties in the Great War. In three years of fighting, 139 officers, 349 NCOs and 3,700 legionnaires of the RMLE would be killed, a number equal to, or exceeding, that of the RMLE at full strength. An American legionnaire, Bennett Doty, recalls the Legion sacrifice in his letters.

'In its first action, charging against uncut wire, the battalion had been almost annihilated. Recruited up to strength again, it had gone on like this for the entire War, depleted almost to nothing time and again – a sort of sacrificial corps, ever at the worst place.' Total Legion casualties in the war are estimated at 31,000 men, some 70 per cent of those enlisted.

In their first action, at Belloy-en-Santerre, near Amiens, on 4 July 1916, as part of the Anglo-French Somme offensive, the RMLE lost 870 officers and men, including the young American poet, Alan Seeger. The fine weather had broken and heavy rain had turned the ground in front of the assaulting battalions into a quagmire. The RMLE attacked on a two-battalion front, the 2nd on the left, the 3rd on the right. At first the 2nd did well, overrunning the German defences and taking over 700 prisoners. Then the Germans counter-attacked, and before the day was over the two battalions were back on their start line.

After the war was over Alan Seeger's father came to France and gave a bell to the little church in Belloy-en-Santerre, in memory of his son. The bell is still there but Seeger is one of the missing of the Somme; his body has never been found and lies somewhere under the soil of Picardy.

Three days later the 1st Battalion of the RMLE was ordered to recapture a position called Chancellors

Trench, which had been lost to a German attack a few nights earlier. The first attack, at night, failed with some loss, including the battalion CO who died of wounds. Next day, supported by the 2nd Battalion, they tried again, but ran into massive machine gun fire which killed a further nine officers and 424 men before the attack was called off. The position was not taken for another three weeks. One of the men who distinguished themselves in the fight to take it was a German legionnaire, Adjutant (Sergeant-Major) Mader, of the 3rd Battalion.

The RMLE fought on in the Somme until winter arrived in early November and brought the offensive to a close. In the four months since the offensive began more than a million men had been killed or wounded for this piece of muddy ground. In return for their share in this catastrophe the British Fourth Army had advanced exactly ten kilometres. The RMLE was then transferred to Champagne where, in April 1917, it spearheaded General Maugin's spring offensive in the Chemin-des-Dames, and the death toll continued to rise.

The Legion is not composed of automatons, who accept death as inevitable. They may be soldiers and born to die in battle, but they like their death to have achieved some purpose. After these actions on the Somme and in Champagne, the Legion's officers – then, as now, the pick of St Cyr – sat down to consider if some better way could be found to counter the devastating effect of machine gun fire and artillery on troops advancing over open ground. Advancing in line was clearly stupid, for it exposed the troops to sweeping machine gun fire which rarely let enough of them reach the enemy trenches to do any good.

The solution they came up with was what is now called 'fire and movement' – squads of men working together, one squad firing at the enemy position, the other dashing forward, from one trench or shell-hole to the next, stopping to pour fire on the enemy while the first 'fire' squad comes up. The British, who had lost thousands of men while advancing in line on the 'First Day of the Somme', thought this form of tactics too complicated or difficult for the average soldier – a view in which they were almost certainly wrong – but then the legionnaires were not ordinary soldiers. They were told about the new tactic, they practised it carefully, and at their next battle they put it into effect.

The RMLE formed part of the Moroccan Division, a force of colonial troops, and their next assault on the German line went in on 17 April 1917. It was, perhaps predictably, a disaster. The German wire was uncut, their deep dugouts intact, and when the Legion advanced the Germans emerged from their underground shelters, coolly reoccupied their defences and opened fire with massed machine guns. Men went down in swathes before the scythe-like sweeps of the guns, with the officers suffering very heavily, but still the advance continued.

Pinned in the open between the trench lines, the legionnaires then formed small groups of survivors and began to 'pepper pot' forward, dashing from shell-hole to shell-hole, then into the German trench line, winkling out the machine-gunners with bayonet and grenades. They held what they had gained, beating off countless counter-attacks, and after four days of fighting held nearly five miles of the German trenches. Their losses were still terrible and included their commanding officer, Colonel Duriez. The new tactics clearly needed some honing but were worth trying again.

The hero of the hour was that German NCO of the 3rd Battalion, Adjutant Mader, who led an attack on a German pillbox, smashed his way in through the door and killed the defenders with bayonet and rifle fire. He then took a sack of hand grenades and began to tackle other pillboxes around the village of Vausdesincourt, driving the defenders into flight. As a final effort that day Mader and his squad of legionnaires overran a German artillery battery and captured six guns, an exploit for which he was awarded the Croix de Guerre.

After the battle, which went on in this fashion for five full days, the much-depleted RMLE regiment received a mention in despatches, a ribbon for their regimental colour, and a new commanding officer, Lieutenant-Colonel Rollet, a man who has remained one of the great heroes in the Legion story.

Lieutenant-Colonel Rollet was no stranger to the Legion. Before the war he had commanded a mounted company on the Morocco frontier, and he soon revealed himself as the ideal commanding officer for the Legion. Tough, relentlessly brave, astute, a born soldier and a fighting man, he was to lead the Legion to glory and became known in the process as 'The Father of the Legion'.

Rollet was the sort of man that soldiers follow and remember. He was a short, spare, wiry soldier, with a large and bushy beard and a good sense of humour. His time with the Legion in Morocco had clearly been the high point of his career to date, and when he joined the RMLE in France he continued to wear his old desert mounted company uniform, just a tunic with no shirt and boots without socks. This was hardly the warmest attire for a winter on the western front, but Rollet seemed not to notice the mud and the chill, the rats or the shellfire. He was back where he wanted to be, with his beloved Legion, and that was all that mattered.

Rollet first took his battered regiment back to Paris, where the President of the Republic personally pinned the ribbon of the Médaille Militaire to the regimental colours, and added the Croix de Guerre. Finally, as some public appreciation of their valour seemed called for, the RMLE was invited to take part in the 14 July parade down the Champs-Elysées. Then, having absorbed some fresh drafts, which increased the RMLE strength to some 2,500 officers and men, Rollet took the regiment to the Verdun sector, where they arrived in August 1917.

The Legion's task at Verdun was simple, but not easy. Their division of Moroccans had to recapture the ground lost by the French Army in the Verdun battles of 1916, especially the left bank of the Meuse, and the RMLE were to form the right wing of the assault, a task that was obviously formidable for one regiment, and one which even the senior commander felt could probably not be accomplished by a single brigade of infantry, however distinguished. In fact, the Legion stormed ahead before the initial barrage had lifted and had taken their first objective an hour before their assault was even supposed to begin.

Rollet and his men employed the same skirmishing tactics that had proved so successful on the Chemin des Dames. Having captured all their objectives and the village of Cumières, they then pushed on to take fresh ground and reached the banks of the Meuse, all for the loss of just 53 men killed and 270 wounded, very small losses indeed for a battle on the western front. Not only had the Legion done the impossible, they had demonstrated how the impossible could be done – and earned yet another Médaille Militaire for their regimental colour. This medal, and a great deal of well-deserved praise, was given to the RMLE by General Pétain, commander-in-chief of the French Army, at a special review of the Moroccan division after the battle ended in September . . . when the faded standard of the RMLE, now hung with ribbons and medals, received another one, the Légion d'Honneur.

Skirmishing tactics, fire and movement, were now seen to be the secret of successful, economical movement on the western front. Those commanders who threw their battalions in line against the defender's wire, machine guns and artillery saw their attacking battalions decimated for no appreciable gain, but the western front defences were vulnerable to infiltration. The Legion had absorbed this lesson well, and used similar tactics when they went back to the front line for their next engagement on the Mort Mare wood. This attack began with a seven-day bombardment, and on 8 January 1918 the RMLE went into the attack behind a 'creeping' artillery barrage, one that dropped shells on the enemy, just ahead of the advancing legionnaires.

Once again, these tactics paid off. The German front-line position was infiltrated and overrun, 1,500 Germans

A group of Free French Foreign Legionnaires at Bir Hakeim raise a cheer in the desert. Taken by Lt McLaren, 12 June 1942 *(IWM)*

The banner of the Foreign Legion flies at Bir Hakeim *(IWM)*

Fritz, a puppy captured at Narvik. He was said to be quite cosmopolitan and understood a number of languages *(IWM)*

Colonel Amilakvari, Commander of the 13th Regiment, with Battalion Commander Puchois and other officers of the Legion, studying a map at Bir Hakeim *(IWM)*

A more modern face to the Foreign Legion: a combat driver from 6ème REG Dinops in a covert offensive mission
(The Military Picture Library)

A signaller from 2ème REI stands guard in Chad *(The Military Picture Library)*

A pathfinder from 2ème REP at Calvi in Corsica, armed with a 9mm Heckler & Koch MP5SD silenced sub-machine gun *(The Military Picture Library)*

Foreign Legion paras from 2ème REP drop from C-160 Transals over Camp Raffali at Calvi during Ex Winged Crusader in conjunction with 5 AB BDE *(The Military Picture Library)*

Men from 2ème REI leap from their vehicle on a patrol, during the conflict in Chad *(The Military Picture Library)*

Sagaie armoured cars belonging to 1ère RHP deploying in Senegal
(The Military Picture Library)

Military policemen from the Foreign Legion on patrol in Djibouti
where they have a standing operational unit
(The Military Picture Library)

Sentries from 2ème REI, armed with Minimi machine gun and Eryx anti-tank, guard a pass near Mount Ingman in Bosnia-Herzegovenia *(The Military Picture Library)*

A Panhard ERC 90 F4 Sagaie armoured car of the 6ème Regiment, with the UN in Bosnia on a boulder-strewn mountain pass *(The Military Picture Library)*

were killed or wounded and the RMLE took 200 prisoners and a great quantity of enemy equipment – all for the loss of just 41 killed and 100 wounded. For some reason these effective Legion tactics, so sparing in manpower, were never introduced or shown to officers in the French or Allied armies, where every attack still produced an horrific casualty list.

The effective use of infiltration tactics was not lost on the Germans, and in March 1918, at the start of the 'Kaiser's Battle', 'Operation Michel', the last German offensive on the western front, they infiltrated their storm troops through the British lines around Arras, cloaked by a fortunate early morning fog, and after gallant resistance the British front collapsed. General Gough's Fifth Army, starved of reinforcements, was sent reeling back, but it did not break. In three weeks, though fighting desperately, the British armies were driven back towards the sea, being forced away from their French allies to the east. The RMLE was sent with the rest of the Moroccans to plug the gap, and on 25 April 1918 they attacked the advancing German battalions at the Bois Hangard.

The Germans were anticipating a counter-attack and had dug in to defend the wood, and this time there was no opportunity for 'fire and movement' or infiltration. This was one of those bloody, all-too-familiar Great War battles, and their head-on assault on the Bois Hangard cost the RMLE 850 officers and men, their highest loss in battle for almost a year. By the time the fighting ended the Legion had lost 1,250 men killed and wounded. These men could not be replaced, but on the other hand they were stemming the German advance. The war diary of the RMLE records one proud, grim fact: 'The question is answered – the Bosche, even when more numerous, will not pass through the front of the Legion.'

It is some indication of the fierceness of the fighting that the wood fell only after a battle in which the command of the 1st RMLE – the 1st Battalion of the regiment – fell on a legionnaire from Luxembourg, Legionnaire Kemmlet, after all the officers and NCOs had fallen. Legionnaire

Kemmlet mustered the men, rapped out fresh orders and led them forward with the bayonet. Much of the fighting in the Bois Hangard was hand to hand with grenades or bayonet, and the German position was overrun only after five days of terrible fighting. However, the gap between the British and French armies had been plugged and the two armies started to move forward again, an advance that did not stop until their triumphant forces stood on the banks of the Rhine.

The last six months of the Great War saw the RMLE continuously in action as the German Army, fighting stubbornly, slowly fell back towards the Rhine and the German frontier. At the end of May, the Germans counter-attacked at the Chemin des Dames and actually reached the Marne at Château Thierry before the RMLE were again sent in to stem their advance. In spite of everything the Germans could hurl at them, and with either flank giving way, the RMLE hung on until the arrival of American troops turned the tide of the battle.

At the end of June the much-depleted RMLE badly needed a rest and more men, but although the men arrived there was no time to rest before the regiment was ordered forward to take part in another offensive around Soissons. This attack, to clear the Soissons–Château Thierry road, began on 18 June and met with immediate artillery barrages from the Germans, followed by a strong infantry counter-attack. The battle around Aconin raged on for three days before the Germans withdrew, leaving a large amount of equipment and several hundred prisoners in Legion hands.

After Château Thierry, the time had come for a major advance, with all the Allied armies – British, French and the newly arrived Americans – advancing as one, moving like a great broom to sweep the Germans out of France and across the Rhine. This final offensive began on 18 July, with the RMLE always in the vanguard of the advancing French armies. The last great challenge for the Legion came in late August when they were ordered to break the 'Siegfried Stellung', better known as the Hindenburg Line, east of the Somme.

This was the main German defence line in France, a two-mile-wide system of trenches, dugouts and wired emplacements. The Legion bid to breach it began on 1 September and was immediately successful, though the fighting was heavy and against fierce German resistance, which employed poison gas, massed machine guns and incessant artillery. The entire breakthrough took twelve days, but on 2 September Terny Sorny was taken and three days later Sorny itself, to break through the last of the German defence line.

Once again skilful infiltration tactics were brought into play as the legionnaires advanced to Sorny. They broke up into small parties and attacked the machine gun nests surrounding the village with grenades and rifle fire, knocking out the German positions one after another without stopping their advance. Neuville, Vaxaille and Allemant also fell to the same tactics. More troops were pulled in and the advance continued for a full two weeks of continuous fighting until the Legion battered its way through to open country, enjoying for the first time the support of tanks. Then, as the men shouldered their packs and struck out for the east and the town of Metz, the news came that the Germans had asked for an armistice. At 1100 hours on 11 November 1918 – the eleventh hour of the eleventh day of the eleventh month – the Great War ended.

The cost had been high, and when the war ended the RMLE was disbanded, only to reform as the 3rd Régiment Etranger in 1919. In the three years from 1915 the RMLE earned the Médaille Militaire and the Légion d'Honneur and was mentioned nine times in despatches.

The RMLE saw a great deal of fighting and became the most famous unit in the French Army, but other Legion units were also in action, in other theatres of war, some of them as bloody as the western front. A new *battalion de marche*, the Régiment de Marche d'Afrique, composed of Zouaves and legionnaires, was raised in 1915 and sent to take part in the Anglo-French ANZAC landings at Gallipoli.

This three-battalion regiment suffered greatly in the

fighting against the Turks and was quickly reduced to just one battalion, mostly composed of legionnaires. After the evacuation the battalion received a draft of legionnaires from Indo-China and was despatched to take part in the Salonika campaign, where it spent the next two years fighting Bulgarians in the Balkans. Fewer than 200 legionnaires came back to Sidi Bel Abbès in 1919, where they were promptly and briefly enrolled in the ranks of the RMLE.

The RMLE took its heavily decorated standard back to Sidi Bel Abbès, where it eventually found a place with all the other Legion trophies. It was reformed as the 3rd Régiment Etranger, and Colonel Rollet was to command the regiment when he returned to Legion service in 1926. Rollet eventually became inspector general of the Legion, and when he died he was buried among the other Legion dead at Sidi Bel Abbès. There he lay until 1962, when his body was disinterred and taken by the Legion to its new home in Aubagne.

As for the Legion, the peace brought changes and new challenges. There was a proposal to form the Legion into what would now be called an 'Independent Brigade Group', with its own transport, artillery, engineers and cavalry, but after a year of discussion most of these plans were shelved and only the cavalry unit was formed. The Legion cavalry, which included a camel element, was formed in 1930, and it immediately attracted a large number of useful volunteers, many of them ex-cavalry officers from the Russian Army, driven from their homeland by the Russian revolution. These men were especially useful for the Legion was on the march again, and beginning a new campaign away to the west, in the Riff mountains of Morocco.

9

THE LEGION IN NORTH AFRICA: MOROCCO AND SYRIA, 1914–39

'During the War the Legion was my front line force, my last reserve'

General Lyautey, Resident General of Morocco, 1920.

The fighting in continental Europe during the Great War did not lead to any cessation in the fighting in Algeria or along the Moroccan frontier. Quite the contrary for, as in 1870–1, news of the war soon spread to the tribesmen of Algeria and Morocco and their efforts to expel the French from their tribal homelands duly intensified.

As related in a previous chapter, Morocco had become a French protectorate in 1912, but that not only failed to put a stop to the violence, it even increased it, with more trouble in cities like Fez and in the Riff mountains. The French decided to pacify Morocco as they had pacified Algeria, by seaming the country with roads on which their troops and artillery could reach any trouble spot with the minimum of delay, and as a step towards the colonisation of the country if they elected to go that far. This task was well under way, but by no means near completion, when war broke out in 1914, and General Lyautey, the governor-general of the protectorate, lost most of his best troops, including many of the Legion battalions, to the developing carnage in France.

The French soon realised that the war presented extreme manpower difficulties, and that just to hold on to the colonial territory they already possessed would be sufficient. They therefore asked Lyautey to hold on to Algeria and 'useful Morocco', that turbulent frontier strip already held by the relentless patrolling of the mounted companies, but to avoid any further entanglements until the war was over. Lyautey was even asked to prepare plans for the evacuation of the Moroccan protectorate, but this proposal was dropped when he pointed out that the first sign of weakness or withdrawal anywhere would lead to a general uprising by the Riff tribes and the spread of trouble throughout North Africa.

Trouble came anyway, a week after the outbreak of war, when a large Arab force attacked the frontier post of Taza and were only beaten off after a day-long battle culminating in a sweeping attack with the bayonet by a force of German legionnaires. Next day a party of 600 legionnaires was sent out to drive off the remainder of the Arab force, and this brought on yet another battle. Although the French finally drove the Arabs away, skirmishing, sniping and the ambushing of patrols continued on both sides of the border and, worryingly, in the Algerian Kabyle, where the tribesmen had found a new and charismatic leader in Abd-el-Malik, a grandson of the famous Abd-el-Kader. His forces had the French outposts under almost daily attack, the burden of defence and pursuit falling heavily on the *compagnies montées* of the Légion Etrangère.

On 24 March 1915, the *compagnie montée* of the 1st Legion Regiment was heavily engaged in a battle with a large Arab force at the jebel of Allava, a position the Arabs held and the legionnaires had to take. The *compagnie montée* left their mules at the foot of the jebel and stormed the position with the bayonet, meeting a fearful amount of rifle fire on the way up but overrunning the enemy position and driving the enemy away in disorder. This set the tone for much of the fighting in North Africa over the next four years, where aggression and fighting spirit were employed by the Legion to cover its deficit in numbers.

This mounted company was in action throughout the war, and in the spring of 1918 took part in one of the last operations, the storming of Abd-el-Malik's camp and the rescue of a Senegalese battalion that was surrounded by the Arabs and in danger of destruction. In all these battles the Legion relied heavily on the bayonet, and since their opponents were also willing to come to close quarters, many of these actions were hand-to-hand affairs, revolver and bayonet against sword and dagger.

Trouble was not restricted to Algeria. The tribes in Morocco had never accepted any rule, let alone that of the French intruder, and knowing that Lyautey had only twenty battalions to control both countries they were soon in the field, sending many *harkas* to attack camel trains, raid towns and ambush French columns.

The French replied with punitive raids against the tribal villages, but the Arabs were not easily cowed. In 1915 the commander of the garrison at Kenifra, Colonel Laverdure, attacked the camp of a local chief, Moha-el-Hamoud. The attack was successful, but on the way back to Kenifra the French column was attacked and halted by Moha's forces, and more Arabs arrived on the scene every hour, adding their rifle fire to that already flaying Colonel Laverdure's forces. The outlook for the survival of the French soldiers began to look bleak.

The Arab forces reached their peak at the moment when Laverdure's troops ran out of ammunition, and when the Arabs swarmed over them there was frightful slaughter, Colonel Laverdure and 613 officers and men being killed. What followed was even worse for the wounded, any prisoners being handed over to the women for prolonged torture. Only a few soldiers managed to reach the scant safety of Kenifra, where they managed to hang on, in a siege reminiscent of a scene from *Beau Geste*, until a relief column, including a battalion of the 2nd RE, managed to break through.

In 1918 Morocco was the scene of a great deal of bitter fighting between the Legion and the various tribes, culminating in a battle with a large *harka* near Sefalat in August 1918. A *compagnie montée*, and a force of French troops including two companies from a Battalion d'Afrique – a punishment battalion – were sent to intercept a Moroccan *harka* and brought it to battle among the palm trees of the oasis. Sefalat was a large oasis, sheltering some 150,000 people, and the battle raged among the palms and the mud houses, between French soldiers and the riflemen of the *harka*, a battle fought out among crowds of screaming fugitives, men, women and children, who wanted no part of the fighting but were shot down anyway, either directly or when running into crossfire.

As usual in a Legion engagement, the bayonet was eventually called into play and most of the final fighting was hand to hand. The commander of the Legion force was badly wounded, while his second-in-command, a Lieutenant Joel, was first wounded and then captured and stabbed to death. Another young officer, Second-Lieutenant Freycon, losing his own rifle, picked up a musket from a dead Arab and rushed about using it as a club, until a well-aimed shot brought him down. With every officer or NCO dead or wounded, the senior legionnaires took charge, organised their comrades into a firing line, leading the bayonet charges, and slowly, over an hour or so, they drove the Moroccans back.

This much was achieved only just in time, for the Moroccans had succeeded in breaking the ranks of the supporting French Senegalese and Tunisian troops, and the weight of the entire battle now fell on the legionnaires, who fought their way through the oasis and out to the open desert where the Moroccans did not care to follow. They had killed 50 legionnaires – including two officers and two NCOs who dropped dead of exhaustion – and wounded many more, but they had not routed the Legion and thereafter were reluctant to engage in all-out battle.

When the Great War ended Lyautey could report that he had not only held all the territory he had possessed in

1914, he had actually managed to increase it. Now that peace had come he requested strong drafts from France, in order to proceed with that part of the pacification programme delayed by the war – and these reinforcements were soon on the sea.

After the Great War, with the defeat of Germany and the collapse of both the Austro-Hungarian and Turkish Empires, the Legion expanded, receiving a great flood of recruits from these countries, many of them former soldiers of excellent quality and vast experience. The Legion was therefore reorganised into three new regiments, or small brigades: the 3rd Régiment Etranger d'Infanterie (REI) from the wartime RMLE, the 2nd REI from the old 2nd Régiment Etranger, which had been in Algeria but was now transferred to the Moroccan front, and the units previously in Morocco, which were reinforced and remustered into a new regiment, the 4th REI. The Legion also formed its first fully established cavalry regiment, the Régiment Etranger de Cavalrie, and all four units, plus horse artillery, were organised into a number of mobile columns for the Moroccan campaign which began in 1920.

The French and the Legion's chief allies in Morocco were the Berber people who live in the Atlas Mountains and are divided into three clans or tribes – the Glaoui, the Gundafi and the M'Tougi. The Berber chiefs, especially their leader, Hdj Thami, approved of the protectorate and supported French attempts to westernise the country. Not so the tribes of the Riff and the Sahara, and therein lay the problem, for these tribes were both well armed and warlike.

Morocco, then a network of tribal fiefs, now a kingdom and fully independent, is a varied land, with a rich coastal plain given over to agriculture, the mountainous Riff, which lies along the north coast, and the Atlas Mountains of the interior, which rise to over 3,000 metres and are only traversed by high passes, which are blocked by snow in winter. To the south lies the great Sahara, not all of which is a sea of sand dunes. Most of the Sahara is stony, arid and, like the Atlas, bitterly cold in the winter. As a campaigning ground Morocco is a place to test the fittest men with the stoutest hearts.

The first task of the French was to secure their protectorate by linking the great cities of Morocco, Fez, Casablanca, Meknes and Marrakesh with roads. While these were being built Lyautey hoped to proceed with the pacification of the Dissident Zones, and especially with the area around Taza, south of the Riff, and the Riff itself, and complete this task by 1923.

This campaign, which lasted five years, is the campaign that gave the Legion much of that legendary – even fictional – mystique which it retains to this day. This was the era of the early cinema, of *Beau Geste* and *The Desert Song* operetta, of long columns of blue-coated, white *képi*'d legionnaires trekking across the Sahara, bursting into song, harassed by brutal NCOs and the wily Tuareg, fighting and dying in desert forts. Films about the Legion poured out from the studios of Hollywood, some serious, if exaggerated, some frankly comical. *Beau Geste* was filmed several times, most memorably with Gary Cooper in the title role, while the comic version – *Beau Hunks* – in which the popular screen comedians Laurel and Hardy found themselves joining the Legion 'to forget the love of their life', contained the running gag that all the characters, including every other legionnaire and the Tuarag chief, all carried photos of the same girl.

Much of this was sheer fiction, but enough of it was based in reality to keep the legend of the Legion solidly based on genuine achievement. There *were* desperate sieges and dashing mobile columns and gallant patrol actions where small forces of the Legion stood and fought, and died and won, against overwhelming odds. In 1923, to give just one example, the 3rd/3rd, the 3rd Battalion of the 3rd REI, fought a twelve-hour battle against 2,000 warriors of La Ait Terschoren tribe, well-armed Arab horsemen who outnumbered this infantry battalion by two to one. The legionnaires took casualties, and saw their wounded cut to pieces before their eyes, but they carried on fighting and in the end the Arabs rode away.

The campaign in Morocco also escalated into a full-scale war, for in 1921 the Moroccan tribesmen found a leader, a doughty fighter who had already driven off the Spanish and was now equally determined to drive out the French. This was a warrior from the Riff Mountains, Abd-el-Krim, who first took the field against the French in 1921, after raising a well-equipped army of some four thousand men. El-Krim began his fight against Western incursions in the Spanish zone, defeating the Spanish Army with great slaughter at Anoual in July 1921. This success was the signal for a general rising in the Riff, and to counter it Lyautey moved two Legion regiments – the 2nd and the 3rd – up to Taza.

Abd-el-Krim was no uneducated savage. He knew exactly what he was up against, and he not only inspired the Riff tribesmen to join the resistance, he also equipped them with modern weapons, including bolt-action rifles, machine guns and field artillery, the latter manned by European and American mercenaries – and deserters from the Legion. He also engaged in a diplomatic offensive, sending well-educated Moroccans to plead the case for liberation abroad and in the European newspapers. Abd-el-Krim held the French off and even forced them back throughout 1923, 1924 and 1925, but the endemic disunity between the Moroccan tribes meant that success on the battlefield always led to the disintegration of the tribal alliances.

Fighting with the Riff tribes began in 1922 and went on for three full years, with 1922 providing the highest number of Legion losses in a year-long series of battles and skirmishes.

A legionnaire who served in the Riff, Jean Martin, recalls the Legion at this time: 'It is in these "*grandes affaires*" – "the big battles" – that you see the glory of the Legion – these formidable troops doing their work well, cool under fire, concerned only with not making mistakes as if the worst they had to fear was incurring the wrath of their sergeant . . . such an attitude makes cowardice impossible.'

In May two companies of the 2nd/2nd were building a road when they were attacked by a strong force of tribesmen, and while falling back to the post at Azinous their Senegalese comrades were overrun and fled. The two Legion companies, forming square and fighting back to back against a series of assaults, reached safety only after losing 25 men killed and six wounded. It is significant that even when fighting against a gallant and civilised leader like el-Krim, the Legion casualty lists in these North African battles always show more men killed than wounded, for a wounded man was immediately rushed by the tribesmen, and unless his comrades could get to his side quickly he would be knifed and killed, or dragged away for prolonged torment.

On that same day the 3rd/3rd were sent into battle near Skoura, at the northern end of the Middle Atlas, tasked to take and hold the strategically significant plateau of Tadout. The battalion had some artillery and some *goum* scouts, but were swiftly engaged by Moroccan tribesmen – known to the French as the *Shleuhs* – armed with magazine rifles and machine guns, as they approached the Tizi Adni position. The advance continued against stiff opposition but eventually the battalion had to fall back, with the *Shleuhs* advancing against them from every side.

Major Maire, a Legion officer, and one of the great Legion characters, recalls the retreat from the Tizi Adni position:

'The Shleuhs were everywhere and had pushed us back to the brink of a rockface, shouting and drunk with Victory as they saw it, indicating what they would do to us when we were prisoners, making the most bloodthirsty threats . . . then as we were thinking ourselves trapped, my orderly yelled out . . . "Captain . . . Behind you!"

'I span round and there was an Arab, pointing his rifle at my back, smiling at the thought of shooting me down. I could see his teeth below his moustache so I leapt at him and cut him across the face with my walking stick. I could do nothing else, my pistol was empty and there was no time to reload. Then I gave him a blow on the side of the head and he fell sideways but four more Arabs were rushing upon me – they did not shoot, they wanted to take me alive. I struck at the first two with my stick, then made for the rocks with the other two on my heels . . . and then one of my legionnaires saved me. He rose up from his position and struck one of them with his bayonet, skewering him . . . the blade went into the man's stomach and the point was out of his back . . . then the second Shleuh struck the legionnaire in the back with his dagger, and he fell dead . . . well, it was all like that, and I had to beat them off with my stick. We lost 118 men that day, with 64 wounded and the rest gone. As for my friend Captain Duchiez, the Shleuhs cut off his head, knocked the teeth out of his skull and dragged the headless body round their camps.'

Major Maire's account describes the nature of the Riff fighting most vividly, a battle with no quarter asked or given, and this was but one battle among many. At Bou Arfa in 1923, five Legion battalions got sucked into a terrible fight, which one experienced Legion officer, Prince Aage of Denmark, a descendant of the Legion's founder, Louis-Philippe, later described as the toughest fight in a lifetime of soldiering:

'The Shleuhs were not to be stopped – they had to be killed. If they ran out of ammunition they would attack with swords and knives and if these were broken they would attack with their bare hands and their teeth. The battle lasted all day, under a burning sun. I saw a legionnaire die, one of my men, with his throat torn out, another with his leg a bloody mess from an expanding bullet – over 100 of my men were killed that day . . . and the wounded . . . we only had wine to give them to dull the shock and pain but they took that and smiled and died.'

This fighting in the Riff eventually spread to the Berber tribes in the Atlas, for if the French were to be defeated by Abd-el-Krim, the Berbers wanted a share in the glory and the booty. There was fighting in the country around Taza close to the Algerian frontier, where 33 legionnaires were killed in a brief skirmish and a constant series of small battles around the *kasbahs* – mud-built Berber forts which proved surprisingly resistant to artillery fire. These actions were not large but attrition was at work and every battle took its toll of Legion strength. The men also had to cope with the cold and the snow, the autumn rains which went on for days at a time, and the constant ambushing and sniping which meant that there were few chances for rest and none at all for relaxation.

There was also the other side of pacification, the building of roads and public works. This included one of the Legion's most memorable feats, the boring of the Foum Zabel road tunnel, which ran for 65 metres though the heart of a mountain, the final tunnel being three metres high and eight metres wide. This work took months to complete in the summer of 1923, and when it was finished the men of the sapper platoon of the 3rd REI, who had hacked this tunnel through the rock with pickaxes and crowbars, put up a notice to remind the world what the Legion could do:

> This mountain barred our way.
> The order was given to make a pass through.
> The Legion carried out that order.

In 1950, after the French left Morocco, the local people marched to the tunnel and hacked the inscription to pieces.

On the face of it, this was a one-sided war, a group of tribesmen confronting a European nation – or nations, for the Spanish Army was also in the field, protecting Spanish enclaves in North Africa – which could and did deploy the full range of modern armaments – artillery, aircraft, machine guns and motor transport – against them . . . and still they would not be subdued. In practice, the 'Riffs', as the public came to call them, were superb guerrilla fighters, and in that rugged terrain they were more than able to hold their own.

In 1925 the French sent Marshal Pétain, the defender of Verdun and their senior soldier, to take command of the Moroccan campaign, and he soon had nearly 400,000 troops in the field, including 200,000 Spaniards, and against such a force – and the resolution to win which the commitment of such numbers revealed – Abd-el-Krim could do little.

In 1926, the French Army, spearheaded by the Legion, overran one Moroccan stronghold after another, and in May 1926, after two defeats at the hands of the 2nd REI, Abd-el-Krim surrendered. The campaign to pacify Morocco followed the same lines as that in Algeria – the 'war' was over, the 'struggle' continued – and the Moroccan tribes went on fighting until 1933, when the last Riff chief capitulated.

The Spaniards wanted el-Krim garotted, or imprisoned for life, but, as with Abd-el-Kader, the French opted for comfortable exile. El-Krim was sent to the Indian Ocean island of Reunion and granted living expenses of 100,000 francs per annum. He stayed on Reunion throughout the Second World War and in 1947 escaped from a ship taking him back to Morocco, during the traverse of the Suez Canal, and remained in Egypt until his death in 1962.

All that lay in the future, for by 1925 Abd-el-Krim could put some 25,000 well-armed and well-trained fighters in the field, many of them instructed by a former Legion NCO, a German, Joseph Klems, who had deserted in 1922 and lived for years among the Riff tribes.

Klems became a Muslim and took four wives, but one of them betrayed him to the Legion, who captured him in 1927. At his court martial he was sentenced to death but this was later commuted to life imprisonment in the 'Dry Guillotine', the prison on Devil's Island in French Guiana, where he served seven years before his release. He returned to Germany and took his own life during the Second World War.

This war was still going on in 1931 when the Legion celebrated its 100th birthday, with a big parade at Sidi Bel Abbès and the unveiling of the Monument to the Dead in the Quartier Vienot. The unveiling ceremony was performed by General Rollet, who had thought of commemorating the 100th anniversary with the erection of a memorial to the Legion dead. A legionnaire designed the memorial, the stone came from a mine the Legion reopened near Sidi Bel Abbès, and it was paid for by the donation of a day's pay from every Legion soldier, from general officer to legionnaire second class. The cost was 600,000 francs – about £8,000 in 1931 – and when the Legion left Algeria in 1962 the Monument aux Morts went with them and stands today at the new Quartier Vienot in Aubagne. The strength of the Legion stood at 30,000 in 1931 and their names, as contributors, are carved on the base of the memorial.

The fighting in and around the Riff went on for years, and while it might have seemed amusing in *The Desert Song*, that tuneful operetta, it was a hard war indeed in the rugged mountains. Finally, in 1932, the French decided to make a major effort and put an overwhelming number of troops into the field, to pursue the Riff tribes and go on pursuing them until they were brought to battle and defeated.

By 1933, the French has subdued many of the Berber and Riff tribes but the tribesmen of the Ait Atta, under their chief, Hasso Selan, were still in the field and were well equipped with modern weapons in their final stronghold, the Jebel Sagho. Two French columns of legionnaires and Zouaves marched out against the Jebel Sagho and their first assault went in on the morning of 13 February 1933.

This first attack on the Jebel, made by the Spahis and a force of *goums*, was a complete disaster, the troops driven back, their casualties considerable. The next attack, entrusted to troops of the Legion, was much more successful, but the advance was contested every step of the way by hidden marksmen, machine gun nests and small pockets of tribesmen who rushed out on the attackers with swords and knives. The Legion, Zouaves, *goums* and a handful of other fighting units attempted to break into the Moroccan positions time and time again but without success. Some positions really are impregnable, and the Jebel Sagho was one of them. Losses in some of the Legion companies attempting to take the position reached 50 per cent and after five days of fighting the attack was called off ... one of the few defeats in Legion history.

The Legion does not permit defeat. If direct assault should fail there are other methods, and these were now applied. The Legion and its comrades flung a belt of steel around the Jebel Sagho, and for six weeks nothing went in and nothing came out, not a mouthful of food, a wounded man or a drop of water. The suffering among the defenders was terrible and tragic, and in the end, bone thin, the gallant defenders surrendered, to be welcomed with warm food and doctors provided by their Legion opponents.

So, after twelve years of fighting in the current campaign alone, peace finally came to Morocco, but here, as in other parts of French North Africa, it was always fragile. The Legion built forts, and while the all-out wars ceased tribal outbreaks continued. Those Hollywood epics, filmed in the 1930s and 1940s which show legionnaires fighting off hordes of wild tribesmen circling their outposts on camels, are based on these periodic Moroccan and Saharan skirmishes.

The 1930s were not just the time of *Beau Geste*, though that novel brought many a romantically minded recruit to the Legion, where, one imagines, he was swiftly disillusioned. The thirties were also a time of massive unemployment in Europe and America, a time when many young men decided to leave home and prove their manhood, or simply find a source of food and shelter by serving a term in the Legion. Among them were some wealthy, even distinguished, people, like Prince Aage, a scion of the Danish royal family, who joined the Legion in 1922, served in the ranks, was commissioned, rose to the rank of colonel and died in 1940, while serving with the 13th Demi-Brigade in World War II.

While the Moroccan brawling continued, the Legion

had become involved in another colonial struggle, at the eastern end of the North African shore, in Syria, a territory that had formed part of the Turkish Empire but had been ceded to France in 1918 by the Anglo-French Sykes-Picot Treaty. Like the Palestinians, the Syrians had assumed that when the Turkish Empire collapsed they would get their freedom. Instead, they got another lot of new – European and Christian – masters, and the Syrians did not like it. The French did not care whether the Syrians liked it or not, and were quite ready to greet any opposition with armed troops. France had had interests in Syria since the time of the First Crusade, and saw the collapse of the Turkish Empire as a chance to win back territory that the Arabs had seized from them six centuries before.

The Arab group – or tribe – particularly opposed to French rule in Syria was the Druze, and when the pro-French Emir Selim of the Druze died in 1925, his followers threw off any French allegiance he had committed them to and took up arms, an uprising that soon developed into an all-out war. The Legion had only two battalions in Syria, the 4th and 5th of the 4th Regiment, plus a squadron or two of the newly formed Legion cavalry, a force that had seemed adequate for the sort of public order duties they had had to undertake between 1920 and 1925. This rebellion introduced fighting of a different order of magnitude.

Serious fighting began when a force of several thousand Druze laid siege to the French garrison in the fort of Souida. This fort was soon surrounded by thousands of Druze warriors who swiftly cut to pieces a relief column sent from Damascus. In such a serious situation there was only one thing to do, and General Serrail, the French commander in Syria, requested the help of the Legion, called them to Beirut, and sent them out to force a way to Souida and lift the siege.

The force had advanced as far as the little town of Messifre when their advance patrols were suddenly attacked by a battalion of Druze, around 1,000 strong, the vanguard of a much larger force. This second Druze force, estimated later to be 3,000 strong, and outnumbering the Legion infantry and cavalry two to one – fair odds for the Legion – crashed into Messifre just after midnight on 17 September 1925. The attack had been anticipated and the legionnaires had dug in, but Messifre was a small town, seamed with garden walls and alleyways, and the Druze were soon everywhere, their infantry creeping across the gardens, climbing onto roofs to snipe at the legionnaires, their horsemen charging up the main street or surging along the alleyways, firing pistols or swinging swords at the heads of the Legion infantry.

The Legion replied to this with fire from their 37 mm guns, but the fighting was soon too close to allow the guns to bear on the enemy, who were moving down the slopes of the nearby hills in large numbers, well deployed. Within a couple of hours the Druze had driven in the Legion picquets and the fighting moved down into the gardens and streets of the town. The Druze also put in mounted charges, one Druze warrior being shot from the saddle as his horse jumped the barbed-wire fence into a Legion position.

The Legion was heavily outnumbered and the situation was looking desperate when a flight of light bombers swept over the battlefield and attacked the Druze warriors with bombs and machine gun fire. About four in the afternoon, relief arrived in the shape of a battalion of light infantry and some armoured cars. There was more hand-to-hand fighting, of the sort at which the Legion excels, but the Druze were good soldiers and it was not until the following afternoon, after twelve hours of bitter fighting, that the Druze fell back and the road to Souida lay open.

The legionnaires in Souida presented arms to the 'Gamelin Column' as the relief marched in on 24 September. A sally by the Legion defenders then caught the Druze between the relief force and the garrison, but darkness fell before the battle could be concluded and many of these Druze fighters were in the front line when the battle began again at Rachaya.

The Legion cavalry regiment, which had lost all its horses at Messifre, soon received remounts and was in action again by the autumn as the French pushed into the Druze strongholds around Mount Hermon, and on 5 November a French column of the Legion cavalry and Spahis took up a defensive position in a ruined Crusader fort above the village of Rachaya, with orders that they were to hold the castle and the village at all costs – to the last man and the last round if need be. The commander of this small force, Captain Granger of the Legion, was the sort of man who carried out his orders to the letter. He occupied the village and the castle and put his men to work, turning the entire position into a well-entrenched fortress.

Here they were promptly besieged by over 3,000 Druze, who swiftly overran the outposts in the village below the castle, and brought the garrison under heavy fire at close range. The battle for Rachaya went on for five days, from 20 November to 24 November, with much of the fighting hand to hand, either during forays into the village or on the ramparts of the castle, as the Druze fighters attempted to overwhelm the garrison. One Legion position was overrun and all the defenders, including the wounded, had their throats cut, but the rest hung on and fought back, beating off a constant series of day and night attacks.

Captain Granger was killed by a sniper on 22 November when making an inspection of the ramparts, but repeated assaults on the position were driven off with machine gun fire and the bayonet, to which the Druze replied with accurate rifle fire and showers of grenades. Casualties mounted and the legionnaires were finally forced back into one portion of the castle tower. From there they prepared to *faire Camerone*, charging out to drive back the Druze, rising to meet the counter-charge, taking casualties, refusing to surrender.

At last, on the night of 23/24 November, rockets were seen lighting up the sky, a signal that help was at last on the way. There was another stiff attack at dawn and one last Legion counter-attack and then the Druze drew off. When the relief force drove up to the castle, the survivors of the garrison were outside the ramparts, fallen in at the 'present arms', in true Legion fashion. With that action the Druze rising slowly petered out, and Syria remained at peace until the Second World War put an end to the French occupation in 1941.

10

THE LEGION IN THE SECOND WORLD WAR, 1939–45

'Please inform Colonel-General Rommel that the Legion is not here to surrender'

General Pierre Koenig, commander of the
13th Demi-Brigade, Bir Hakeim, June 1942

The outbreak of the Second World War with Nazi Germany, in September 1939, presented the Legion with its now familiar problem, an influx of foreign volunteers and the need to separate the German legionnaires into battalions that could remain in Algeria while the rest went to France. This was an easy one to solve, given the experiences of 1914 and 1870, but the situation soon became more complicated.

Within a year of the outbreak of war, France had been defeated and occupied by the Germans, and the country was then split between two political factions, the 'Free French' of General de Gaulle, based in the United Kingdom, and 'Vichy' France, allied, often unwillingly as far as the ordinary French people were concerned, to Nazi Germany and headed by the 'Hero of Verdun', Marshal Pétain.

Algeria was part of France and under Vichy control, but a section of the Legion opted to join General de Gaulle's Free French. The rest elected to join the Vichy French forces which were, albeit reluctantly, allies of Nazi Germany. There were further problems, for the ranks of the Legion contained German Jews who had fled Germany in the 1930s to escape death in the concentration camps, and former soldiers of the Spanish Republic, who were fugitives from the firing squads in Franco's Spain. All these men were at risk when France allied itself with Nazi Germany. Among them was the writer Arthur Koestler, who, caught in France when the French Government surrendered in June 1940, thought it best to enlist in the Legion as Albert Dubert, a Swiss taxi driver. Koestler did not stay with the Legion long. He deserted in Marseilles and made his way to Oran, from where he eventually reached safety in Portugal.

With the Gestapo moving into France, to hunt down communists, Jews and anyone loosely defined as an 'Enemy of the Reich', the Vichy Legion units were no sanctuary and therefore became uneasy and unhappy battalions where desertion rates soared. It had not seemed that way when the war began and the Legion, as usual, expanded.

However, the Legion, even under Vichy, looks after its own, and these men were either protected by their officers or helped to escape. As for the Vichy Legion, it never fought alongside German units, though for a while between 1941 and 1943 it appeared that the two parts of the Legion might end up fighting each other in the Western Desert.

At the start of the war, with thousands of other recruits pouring in from countries annexed or overrun by the Germans, the Legion was able to form three additional Régiments de Marche Volontiers, the 21st, 22nd and 23rd RMEV. Two more infantry regiments, each of three battalions, were formed by recalling reservists, and a new force, a Legion reconnaissance regiment, equipped with armoured cars and light tanks, was formed as part of the Legion cavalry.

One of these new units, the 11th Régiment Etranger Infanterie, went into action on 11 June 1940 and was rapidly overrun and decimated by an onrushing German

145

Panzer division near Verdun. The battalion went into battle when a number of French Army battalions had already given up the fight and were in the process of disintegration. The 2nd Battalion of this regiment fought again at St Germain-sur-Meuse and burned its colours before digging in for a last stand against an oncoming German division.

This Regiment – or what was left of it – then fell back towards Paris and was still in action when France surrendered to the Germans on 22 June. Seven hundred legionnaires were taken prisoner, but the bulk of them promptly escaped and made their way by various means to North Africa, where they eventually joined General de Lattre de Tassigny's French Corps. Their sister regiment, the 12th REI, fought the German Panzers at Soissons, and then fell back, fighting a rearguard action until ordered to lay down their arms on 25 June.

There was then a certain amount of uncertainty. The Germans were torn between regarding German legionnaires as traitors and shooting them out of hand, or abiding by Legion rules and accepting that, for the term of their engagement, *Legio patria nostra* really meant what it said, even to a German legionnaire. Eventually a large number of German legionnaires – some accounts say up to 2,000 – were given the option of investigation by the Gestapo or enlistment in the 90th Light Division, one of the finest units in the about-to-be-formed Afrika Korps. Being sensible, most of them took up this offer, and the fine fighting reputation of the 90th Light may be due in large part to this influx of Legion soldiers.

At this time, in mid-1940, the Legion was well dispersed. Apart from the units fighting in France, there was the 6th REI currently serving in Syria, where it remained after the surrender of France as part of the Vichy forces. In Indo-China, the 5th REI was in garrison, and many of the Jewish legionnaires, or those Spanish legionnaires who had served the republic during the Civil War, were smuggled out of North Africa and France and sent to the 5th REI, beyond the reach of the Gestapo. They were not, alas, beyond the reach of misfortune and in 1945 the men of the 5th REI suffered grievously at the hands of the Japanese, who occupied Indo-China in 1941.

However, the great Legion unit of World War II, the one that established a reputation rivalling that of the Great War RMLE, was the 13th Demi-Brigade, a two-battalion force formed in February 1940 as a mountain brigade and one that still exists today as an integral part of the modern Foreign Legion. When this unit was mustered at Sidi Bel Abbès in February 1940 it included nearly 300 Spanish republican soldiers, recently released from internment camps on the north side of the Pyrenees on condition that they joined the Foreign Legion.

This 'mountain brigade' was originally destined to aid the Finns, who were fighting off an invasion from Soviet Russia in their 'Winter War' of 1939–40, but before this plan could be put into effect, Finland surrendered. The demi-brigade was sent to Norway in 1940 before the French surrender, as part of an Anglo-French expedition that aimed to evict the German Army which had just invaded that formerly neutral country. The demi-brigade left Brest on 20 April 1940 and went to Norway via Liverpool, disembarking near Narvik on 13 May 1940, just after the German Army thrust deeply into the heart of France and drove the British Army back to Dunkirk. This German thrust began on 10 May, and within five weeks had evicted the British and forced a French surrender.

The demi-brigade's first experience of Arctic warfare came on 14 May, when they were turfed out of their warm billets in Bajervik so that French soldiers could have shelter while the legionnaires slept in the snow. They then advanced to the German-held airfield on Lake Hartvigard, and pressing on in the face of air attacks from Stuka dive bombers and heavy artillery fire, they advanced towards the port of Narvik. On the way, the 2nd Battalion crossed the ice-covered Romlakfjord and fought their way along the railway line to Narvik, which fell to the 1st Battalion of the Legion on 6 June.

The capture of Narvik gave the Anglo-French expedition a naval base from which to develop operations in the mountains, but German air attacks took a heavy toll of British warships and the new German *blitzkrieg* in western Europe, which rapidly overran France, meant that the Norwegian operation had to be abandoned. The 13th Demi-Brigade returned with the rest of the expedition to Britain but then sailed on to Brest, landing the day after the Germans entered Paris. Not wishing to march straight into a prison camp the demi-brigade got back on to its transport ships and sailed back to Britain.

The demi-brigade, like a lot of other French soldiers who ended up in Britain after Dunkirk, now had some hard decisions to make. The Legion was a French force and France had surrendered. Moreover, the leader of France, Marshal Pétain, had allied his forces to those of Germany, so what was this Legion force to do? Should it stay in England and fight on – becoming traitors to the French Government – or accept the British offer of shipment back to Morocco where they could join the army of Vichy France? On the other hand, there was a French officer in Britain, a tall, spare tank commander called de Gaulle, who seemed to have other ideas and wanted to fight on beside the British.

'France', he said, 'has lost a battle, but it has not lost the war.' The war would go on, and he proposed to go on fighting it. He was going to raise a new force, the Fighting or 'Free French', here in Britain, and he called on all loyal Frenchmen to ignore the call for capitulation and the lure of Vichy and join him in London. This was fighting talk, the sort that many – but by no means all – French officers and soldiers wanted to hear.

The French officers of the Legion had little love for the British, and many of them believed that the Germans would soon invade and overrun Britain as quickly as they had France. They advised the legionnaires that, having sworn an oath of loyalty to the French Government, they would be regarded as traitors unless they took up the offer and returned to France. This advice was generally ignored.

Just why the British, in this desperate hour, even contemplated allowing any Legion soldier returning home to join the ranks of the enemy – and even provided the shipping for the journey – remains a mystery. In the end, the legionnaires agreed to differ. The 2nd Battalion of the demi-brigade elected to stay in Britain and join the Free French forces now mustering under General de Gaulle; the 1st Battalion chose to return to Morocco . . . and the Royal Navy escorted the ship that took them back to Africa to join the ranks of their enemies. The French have often said that the British are a curious people.

Among the officers who elected to remain in Britain and join the Free French were Major Pierre Koenig and Captain Amilakvari, a Russian from Georgia, both of whom were to render distinguished service to the Allied cause before the war was over. More French soldiers and a lot of other defiant Europeans were now arriving in Britain and the 2nd Battalion soon received enough recruits to reconstitute itself as the 13th Demi-Brigade.

The legionnaires that stayed in Britain included many French officers, but they had to be completely reclothed, and re-equipped with British weapons. Formed into a brigade, these legionnaires took part in operations against the Italians in Eritrea and were then sent to fight the Vichy French troops in Syria, then a French colony. Fortunately, the fighting in Syria was brief, though – as feared in 1940 – there came a day in July 1941 when legionnaires of the Free French 13th Demi-Brigade fought legionnaires of the 6th REI, the latter in the service of Vichy.

The 6th REI joined the Free French forces after the surrender in Syria and were with the brigade when it went to join the British Eighth Army in Egypt, where it arrived in time to make a significant contribution to the fighting around the Gazala Line. It was here on the Gazala Line, in May 1942, that the 13th Demi-Brigade made a splendid and memorable stand against Field Marshal Rommel's Afrika Korps, in the epic Legion battle at Bir Hakeim, a battle that ranks with Camerone and Dien Bien Phu in the glorious annals of the Legion.

The Arabic word 'bir' means a well, and the waterhole

at Bir Hakeim is all that distinguished this spot, at the south end of the Eighth Army's main defensive position, the Gazala Line, from anywhere else in the surrounding desert. The Gazala Line was not a continuous line of trenches and fortifications like the western front of 1914, but a series of defensive positions known as 'boxes'. These boxes were entrenched positions, hemmed in by barbed wire and minefields, which supported each other with artillery fire, while the open ground between the 'boxes' was patrolled by the armoured cars of the 7th Armoured Division – the famous 'Desert Rats'.

North of Bir Hakeim lay 'Knightsbridge', another 'box' held by a British Guards brigade, and another held by the 50th Northumberland Division, so the legionnaires were in good company when Field Marshal Erwin Rommel's Afrika Korps surged against the Gazala Line at dawn on 27 May 1942. Rommel's intention was to hook round the south end of the line, isolate the 'boxes' from support and supply and then roll them up from the flank, a process that would end when the Afrika Korps overwhelmed the South African garrison in the fortress port of Tobruk.

Much of the British line collapsed under the onslaught of the German Panzers but the Guards held 'Knightsbridge' with typical Guards stubbornness, refusing to budge from a position they had been ordered to defend, while away in the south, the 13th Demi-Brigade put up an equally memorable thirteen-day fight at Bir Hakeim.

The French commander at Bir Hakeim was Pierre Koenig, now a general, who had taken command in February 1942 and had kept the 3,500 men of his command fully occupied ever since, digging more and deeper defences, laying in supplies of ammunition, food and water, strewing mines before the wire. The defences were still not complete when Rommel attacked on the morning of 27 May, his onslaught spearheaded by the light tanks of the Italian Ariete Division.

Italian troops were not highly regarded in the Western Desert, but Rommel believed they could fight well if clearly directed, and they pushed home their attack at Bir

Hakeim with great tenacity, driving their tanks into the Legion positions, their infantry following close behind. In numbers they outmatched the Legion, but not in tenacity or fighting ability.

The legionnaires fought them off with two-pounder anti-tank guns and the famous French 75 mm field guns, and those Italian tanks that did break into the Bir Hakeim position were attacked with grenades, by legionnaires who leapt onto the tanks, prised open the lids on the turrets and flung in grenades, or sprayed the crew with tommy-gun fire. The Italian infantry were ravaged by 75 mm guns, flayed by machinegun fire and driven off by bayonet charges, and the day ended with the Ariete Division losing 35 tanks and a good number of infantry soldiers – and only one legionnaire was slightly wounded. General Rommel absorbed all this and sent in some of his crack troops.

German forces then probed the Legion lines that night, with fighting patrols, and tank and artillery fire from the notorious 88 mm gun. Having 'softened up' the Legion position, on the following day Rommel sent in a British prisoner under a white flag to demand the surrender of the Legion. Koenig tore up Rommel's note and ordered his artillery and infantry to open fire on any German they could see. As a reply this was better than words, but some memorable words came later.

The Afrika Korps now concentrated all their power on the 50th Division box which fell after three days of heavy fighting, on 1 June, and although the Guards were still holding on at Knightsbridge, Rommel felt able to turn his full might against the legionnaires at Bir Hakeim. On 2 June he sent in another message, requesting a surrender, since the Bir Hakeim position was now isolated and received a courteous reply: 'I am very sorry but please tell the Colonel-General that the Legion did not come here to surrender.'

Persuasion having failed yet again, Rommel hit the Bir Hakeim position with everything he had. Artillery, Stuka dive bombers, the elements of three divisions and 50 tanks – all this was hurled into battle, to take a position held by

3,000 men. The attack went on for a full 24 hours, and then General Rommel, who had great respect for good soldiers, again requested a surrender:

To the defenders of Bir Hakeim.

Further resistance will only lead to unnecessary bloodshed and you will suffer the fate of the British brigades wiped out yesterday. We will stop firing as soon as you hoist a white flag and come out to meet us. Those legionnaires who surrender will be sent to join their comrades in Morocco.

This appeal met with no response from the Legion trenches and General Koenig issued a general order, telling his men that having rejected three requests for surrender, they should expect the Afrika Korps to come on again with renewed vigour.

So it proved. Rommel was a great soldier but he did not take kindly to defiance and the rejection of his terms. He sent his crack divisions, including the 90th Light – a unit that contained more than a few ex-legionnaires – and each division came back from the attack having suffered losses and without having broken the stubborn Legion defence. In his war diary Rommel wrote: '. . . the French defenders were cut off from all aid yet their troops hung on grimly to their trenches and remained immovable.'

Shelled, bombed, strafed by fighters, short of food, ammunition and water – everything except courage – the brigade hung on, declining yet again Rommel's personal invitation to surrender, buying time for the British to re-form, beating off attack after attack, delaying Rommel's advance and causing heavy casualties among the German formations.

This was a real Legion battle, another opportunity to *faire Camerone*, for the Legion soldiers, Poles and Spanish, French – and German – had no interest in surrender. They fought because they were legionnaires, *c'est tout*.

After two weeks of fighting, much of it hand to hand in the usual Legion fashion, the Legion broke out of Bir

Hakeim on the night of 10/11 June and fought its way back to where the 7th Armoured Division was waiting. On the way out of the box, their rearguard, commanded by Colonel Amilakvari, was surrounded, and had almost been overwhelmed when the colonel rallied his men with the old cry of 'A moi, La Légion'. The war cry wrought its familiar magic, the legionnaries flung themselves at the enemy and the Germans were driven off. The Legion demi-brigade, much reduced but still full of fight, made its way back to the Eighth Army lines.

The Legion does not recruit women, but with them went an extraordinary young Englishwoman, Susan Travers, General Koenig's driver. Miss Travers had joined the Legion service in 1940 as an interpreter, and somehow managed to stay with them ever since – heaven alone knows how. She also managed to stay with the demi-brigade throughout the war, picking up a quantity of well-deserved decorations for her bravery in the field, and, having married a Legion NCO, left the Legion only in 1947. She drove Koenig's staff car on the break-out from Bir Hakeim, steering a path through the minefields under the general's direction.

The great fight at Bir Hakeim had cost the demi-brigade a third of their strength but earned them the admiration of soldiers everywhere, not least among the ranks of the Afrika Korps. The 13th Demi-Brigade pulled back to the Egyptian frontier and took up position close to the lines of the British 7th Armoured Division just south of a small railway station, at a place called El Alamein.

The Battle of El Alamein in October 1942 was the turning point of the Second World War. 'Before it,' said Winston Churchill, 'we never had a victory . . . after it we never had a defeat.' Not quite accurate, perhaps, but Alamein was indeed a famous victory for the Eighth Army, and one in which the Legion again played a significant part.

The battle began on the night of 23/24 October when the task of the 13th Demi-Brigade was to advance through the German wire and minefields just after dusk on the 23rd and take the hill of Heimeimat, which overlooked the Alamein line. From Heimeimat German guns could range at will over the surrounding minefields and enfilade the attacking tanks of the Eighth Army, and so Heimeimat had to be taken.

The task was given to the 13th Demi-Brigade, now commanded by Colonel Amilakvari. The legionnaires made their way through the minefields and were on the slopes of Heimeimat before the great Alamein barrage from over 1,200 British guns broke on the German lines. The brigade then stormed the German trenches, overran the Heimeimat position and by dawn were a mile behind the German lines. Colonel Amilakvari had been killed in the attack and the initial assault on the German lines was held up by some stubborn German resistance so the demi-brigade had to withdraw. The Alamein battle raged for ten days before the break-out, and then the Eighth Army began to pour west down the coast road, taking the demi-brigade and the 7th Armoured on a path that would lead them to the total defeat of Germany.

After Alamein, the 13th Demi-Brigade fought its way west with the Eighth Army, reaching Tunisia in early 1943, where it met up with many Legion comrades who had gone back to Morocco in 1940. These men had come over to the Allied side after the US forces landed around Casablanca in November 1942 and were now part of General Eisenhower's command. Their appearance was timely, for the Free French brigade was now down to about 1,000 men, but relations between the two Legion contingents were a little stiff for a while before the press of battle forced them back together.

This western, Moroccan, force – the 3rd Foreign Infantry Marching Regiment – had already seen some hard fighting under American command, including a heavy engagement with German tanks at the Jebel Mansour in January 1943. When the Germans in North Africa surrendered at Cape Bone in May 1943, the two halves of the Legion reunited and reformed and, as the 13th Demi-

Brigade, joined General Juin's French Army in Italy on 1 May 1944. This army, of five divisions, landed at Naples in April 1944 and was swiftly at the front.

Throughout the summer of 1944, the demi-brigade was involved in heavy fighting around Cassino in attempts to break the German defences of the Adolf Hitler Line – later renamed the Gustav Line – south of Rome. Rome fell on 5 June, the day before the D-Day landings in Normandy, and in August 1944 the demi-brigade formed part of the French contingent taking part in Operation Anvil, the landings in the South of France, when they landed at Cavalaire, near Hyères on the Côte d'Azur, on 16 August and began to push north up the Rhône Valley.

The legionnaires skirted Marseilles, a place all too familiar to most Legion recruits, and pushed north against stiff German opposition toward Lyons, which fell on 5 September. Then the 13th Demi-Brigade spearheaded the Allied advance into Alsace in early October, a thrust that might, had it been supported, have forced a rapid German withdrawal towards the Rhine. As it was, a shortage of fuel, and the sad fate of the British 1st Airborne Division at Arnhem, forced the Allies to halt their advance towards the Rhine and the German frontier, and before it could be resumed winter had come down and halted all advances until the start of the new year.

The Legion were next called into action to defend Strasbourg against a German thrust from what became known as the 'Colmar pocket', an event that almost provoked a breach between General de Gaulle, leader of the Free French, who, to put it mildly, was not the easiest man to get on with, and the long-suffering Allied commander, General Dwight Eisenhower. When the Germans struck west in the Battle of the Bulge in December 1944, they also made a supporting attack, Operation Nordwind, an operation launched from the Colmar pocket which, in spite of Eisenhower's orders, de Gaulle's forces had failed to eliminate.

Eisenhower ordered General Devers, the US commander on that front, to withdraw as far as necessary, giving up Strasbourg if need be, to absorb the first impact of the German assault. De Gaulle then announced that the French First Army – which included the 13th Demi-Brigade – would defend Strasbourg and he – de Gaulle – would not accept any orders to the contrary.

General de Gaulle had misjudged Eisenhower. De Gaulle was summoned to Eisenhower's HQ and in a frosty interview was told bluntly that if his troops were not prepared to obey the orders of the Allied Supreme Commander he – de Gaulle – should say so, but from that moment they would receive no further supplies of food, fuel or ammunition. He probably said a few other things, for his patience with de Gaulle had been sorely tried. General de Gaulle left Eisenhower's HQ in a slightly less arrogant mood, and in the end Strasbourg was held without further French tantrums.

The demi-brigade and other Legion units crossed into Germany in March 1945, and after a rapid advance in the last weeks of the war had reached the Alps when hostilities in Europe ended in May 1945. There was a small sequel to Bir Hakeim, when the Legion honoured General Koenig by making him both a corporal in the Legion and a *brigadier chef* (also a corporal) in the Legion cavalry.

The Second World War tested the Legion in many ways, not only on the battlefield. It had found itself a pawn between the warring nations, a football to be kicked about from country to country, and even *Legio patria nostra* was little comfort when parts of the Legion were serving in the opposing forces and even fighting in the line against other Legion units.

And yet, in spite of all the problems caused by divided loyalties, loyalty to the Legion as the Legion, not as part of any national force, finally triumphed. When the war ended it was widely dispersed, and much changed by five years of varied experience under British, Vichy and Free French control, but in the end the Legion remained the Legion. As soon as it could, it packed up its loot, discharged its time-served veterans, and set out on the march to Algeria and its old home in Sidi Bel Abbès.

There it regrouped and took up the old tasks of training recruits for Legion service, absorbing many of the refugees that would otherwise be starving on the roads of war-torn Europe, but that old familiar routine did not last long. The French were now attempting to reoccupy their empire and the task was not proving easy. In particular there was an increasing amount of trouble in the old colonies of Indo-China, where the communist forces of Ho Chi Minh were attempting to take control.

11

THE LEGION IN INDO-CHINA, 1945–54

'Chance plays a part in all warfare and guerrilla warfare is no exception'

Edgar O' Ballance, *The Indo-China War (1964)*

The end of the Second World War brought little peace to France and none at all to the Foreign Legion. France was in economic ruin and political turmoil and her empire, like those of the other colonial powers, Britain, Holland, Portugal and Belgium, was on the brink of disintegration. Within fifteen years the French Empire was to disappear, but the process began even before the Second World War ended, in the provinces of Indo-China, a territory that was to become better known as Vietnam in the 1960s and 1970s.

After the French Government surrendered to Germany in 1940, the Vichy Government of Marshal Pétain retained control of Indo-China but had to allow the Japanese Army to occupy the territory. The Japanese, who were nominal allies of Vichy France, allowed the French Army in Indo-China to retain its weapons but the men – mostly legionnaires – were forbidden to leave their garrison areas, or indulge in military training. Indo-China became, in effect, a Japanese territory, but the French settlers were left at liberty and spared the horrors visited on British and Dutch civilians caught in Malaya and Java, who were confined in labour camps.

As the years passed, many legionnaires deserted, either escaping to China to join the Allied forces fighting the Axis powers or returning to their homes in Europe, but there were still over 5,000 legionnaires in Indo-China when, on 9 March 1945, with the Allied victory in Europe, the collapse of the Vichy Government in France and the takeover by General de Gaulle's Free French forces, the Japanese struck at all the French and Legion garrisons in Tonkin and Cochin China.

Their first move was cunning, for the Japanese invited the Legion officers of the Lang Son garrison to a meal and their commander, General Lemonier, reluctantly gave them permission to attend. All went well until the end of the meal when, on a command from their host, the Legion officers were seized and bound. All who resisted were shot at once or bundled outside and beheaded. General Lemonier and the civil governor, Camille Auphille, were also arrested that night and presented with a surrender document. When they refused to sign it, they were first obliged to dig their own graves and then beheaded. These savage moves set the tone for what followed.

The Japanese used their customary brutality in their treatment of the legionnaires captured at Lang Son and Hanoi, where the legionnaires resisted Japanese attacks until their ammunition ran out. They then, as usual, elected to *faire Camerone* and went out against the Japanese with the bayonet. Most were killed in the fighting, but a number of wounded survived and were captured, lined up, shot in the feet or legs, and then finished off with swords or bayonets as they writhed on the ground. Other French soldiers suffered a similar fate. Those who refused to give up their weapons were shot down. Those who surrendered were shot, bayoneted or beheaded. The entire Legion garrison at one camp in Tonkin were beheaded by the Japanese after giving up their weapons. And so, in one way or another, the French garrisons in Indo-China were wiped out.

Fortunately, news of these initial massacres at Hanoi and Lang Son swiftly spread to the outlying Legion garrisons. The three battalions of the 5th Régiment Etranger Infantière – 5th REI – formed up for a fighting withdrawal of over 500 miles across North Vietnam and into China. This withdrawal was one of history's great fighting retreats as, harassed all the way by Japanese troops and aircraft, the Legion column fought their way over mountains and through jungle, to the uncertain security of the Chinese frontier. There was constant skirmishing with Japanese patrols, their food ran out and their boots rotted, and many of the legionnaires were barefoot and ill when the regiment finally reached safety in China. The survivors were hospitalised but eventually reformed as a *battalion de marche*, and these survivors of the 5th REI were still in the Far East when the war ended, returning to Saigon after the Japanese surrender.

The Second World War ended on 15 August 1945, after atomic bombs were dropped on the Japanese cities of Hiroshima and Nagasaki. Indo-China – or at least the part now better known as Vietnam – was then occupied by Chinese nationalist troops who moved to the North and by a British division which arrived in Saigon from the sea. The British had enough post war problems in their own empire and soon left, handing Indo-China back to the French who, in spite of pressure from the USA, announced their determination to stay.

The local people, and especially the political leader Ho Chi Minh and his military commander, a former schoolteacher turned guerrilla leader, Lo Nguyen Giap, had other ideas. They wanted an independent country, allied to the communist bloc, and when independence was refused by the French they took to the jungle and commenced a guerrilla war against the colonial power. Gradually, over the next few years, they took over the north of Vietnam, the region known as Tonkin, around Hanoi, and began to push steadily south. More Foreign Legion units arrived and began to push north, into the Central Highlands, while Giap and Ho Chi Minh crossed into China and began to seek arms and training facilities.

The French, like the British, were under pressure from

the USA to withdraw from their colonies. In 1944, even before the war ended President Roosevelt had said, 'The case on Indo-China is perfectly clear – the French have milked it for a hundred years and the people of Indo-China are now entitled to something better than that.' What the Vietnamese actually got was 28 years of continuous, terrible war until the US Army pulled out in 1973.

In 1945 the French response to US pressure to pull out was to set up a puppet government under the old Emperor of Annam, Bao Dai, and having persuaded him to ask for their assistance, they sent for more troops and began to raise an army to fight Ho's communist guerrillas. Ho Chi Minh's forces became known as the Vietminh, forerunners of the Vietcong, and, like the 'Cong', they were skilled in jungle warfare. Ho wanted general nationwide elections to settle the future of Vietnam and when this proposal was rejected by the French Ho set up a clandestine government in North Vietnam, based in the port of Haiphong.

Legion units poured into Indo-China from 1946, many, like the 13th Demi-Brigade, veterans of the fighting in the Western Desert and Europe, but none with any real grasp of how to fight a guerrilla war in the jungle. Among the fresh force were the 1st Legion Parachute Battalion (Battalion Etranger Parachutiste). Eventually there were two parachute battalions in Indo-China, commonly known as the 1st BEP and 2nd BEP, both formed in Algeria in 1948. The first man to join the 2nd BEP was Lieutenant Caillaud who was later to command the 2nd REP – the battalion later became a full regiment – at the end of the Algerian War and turn it into a para-commando regiment. The 1st BEP sailed for Indo-China at the end of 1948, arriving in Haiphong in November, while the 2nd BEP arrived at Saigon in February 1949; both units were soon involved in actions against the Vietminh.

However, the first operational Legion parachute unit was formed in Indo-China in April 1948 from volunteers of the 13th Demi-Brigade and the 2nd and 3rd REI. This first unit was of company strength and called the Compagnie Parachutiste du 3ème REI, and was commanded by Captain Morin. It was used for scouting purposes and became closely involved in the so-called 'battle for RC4', the French attempt to hold open the northern trunk road along the Chinese-Thai border.

The 2nd BEP, which disembarked at Saigon in February 1946, joined the old 5th REI, though this last unit was eventually returned to Algeria and for a while disbanded. Then came the 3rd Régiment Etranger Infanterie, or 3rd REI, the 13th Demi-Brigade and several more, including the first armoured unit, the 1st REC, which landed as an infantry force and fought in central Annam for a full year in an infantry role before being equipped with second-hand armoured cars and tanks from Britain and the USA. These were all large units, for following the end of the Second World War the Legion had plenty of men. Eventually it deployed 30,000 men in Indo-China ... and needed every one of them.

By 1946, the Legion was back in Algeria and flush with recruits from the shattered countries of western Europe. After the war ended, Europe was awash with refugees – homeless, often stateless, people usually known as DPs (Displaced Persons). Many DPs, having no other place to go to, found their way into the Foreign Legion. Among them were a considerable number of Germans, many of them refugees from the communist takeover of East Germany, but a lot of recruits came from the old divisions of the Waffen SS.

The Waffen – or 'Fighting' – SS were not the units that ran the concentration camps. They were hand-picked troops who served in conventional military units, usually SS Panzer – tank – divisions, but they were all committed Nazis, all members of the National Socialist Party, all tough fighters and, through their political connections, endowed with the pick of weapons and equipment. It is fair to add that many of them fought cleanly, but the Waffen SS were closely involved in too many massacres and acts of brutality – like the slaughter of the entire population of the French village of Ouradour in 1944 by the 2nd (Das Reich) SS Division, or the shooting of Canadian prisoners after D-Day by men of the 12th SS (Hitler Jugend) Division – to escape censure or enable the Legion to claim that these men were ordinary soldiers.

The acceptance of former Waffen SS men in the Legion caused an outcry, and the Legion was eventually forced to abandon its traditional secrecy over the identity of its men and circulate the names of the SS recruits throughout the newly liberated nations in case any man was wanted for a particular war crime, in which case he was arrested and handed over. One still wonders what the *bleus* from Hungary, Poland or one of the other countries ravaged by SS units felt when they found themselves serving alongside their former oppressors. It clearly caused some dissension, for in 1948 all the newly recruited Germans were taken from the usual mixed-nation battalions and formed into a new all-German battalion of 900 men, mustered in three strong companies.

Warfare was already sputtering into life in Indo-China as these units arrived, but the first major actions took place in November 1946 during operations to clear the Tonkin region of North Vietnam, a task allotted to a French corps which included the 3rd REI. In a few initial attacks against French outposts, the Vietminh killed 30 French soldiers, destroying the outposts and mutilating any captives or wounded, cutting off their heads and genitals.

In retaliation, the French Navy bombarded Haiphong, killing over 5,000 Vietnamese civilians and so – apart from committing an atrocity – started a series of tit-for-tat terrorist actions. General Giap sent his fighters to eliminate all the French positions he could find, and massacre the defenders to the last man. In return, the French Army and the Legion set out to comb the countryside for Vietminh and, failing to find any, took reprisals against the hapless peasant population. Within months of starting, the Indo-China conflict had become a very nasty war indeed.

One example of Vietminh savagery saw seventeen legionnaires, captured by the Vietminh in the Mekong Delta, crucified and nailed to trees. Some were still alive when a patrol found them days later. Henry Ainley, an Englishman serving in the Legion, recalls a friend who, when wounded and in danger of capture, blew his brains out with a .45 pistol, knowing that the Vietminh would cut his head off as soon as they reached him. Other French prisoners were stripped and staked over fast-growing bamboo spikes, which grew through their bodies. Still more, especially the wounded, were buried alive.

The Legion was not slow to take reprisals for these actions. Henry Ainley, who arrived in Indo-China in 1951, was shocked to discover that the company he joined routinely picked up, beat and tortured Vietnamese peasants, using rubber hoses, rattan canes or electric clips attached to a suspect's ears, lips and genitals. These interrogations frequently resulted in the death of the man being questioned, and those who confessed to involvement with the Vietminh were killed anyway.

On patrol the French soldiers and the legionnaires routinely raped, robbed, beat, tortured or killed anyone who crossed their path, losing men all the time to mines, ambush and the dreaded Vietminh 'elephant traps', concealed pits filled with sharpened bamboo stakes. It was not a glorious time, and the officers who should have stamped on such practices, like the formation of *Bande Noire* death squads which went out at night to raid villages or the poorer quarters of the cities, killing Vietminh fighters and bringing more prisoners back for brutal 'interrogations', were often deeply involved themselves.

The French Army in Indo-China used prisoners in order to function, and was not too particular where they came from or whether they were actually Vietminh. Prisoners were essential for cleaning duties, for gardening, for unloading stores, digging defences, cooking and hauling water. Every outpost therefore kept a supply of prisoners to do the hard work and the menial chores. After a while a commission was set up to visit the outposts, examine the prisoners and decide which were truly Viet-minh and which should be released, and this proved a more just and humane way of handling the prisoner problem.

These instances of terror and counter-terror are included as examples of what was going on in Indo-China in the early stages of the war. Such actions failed to do more than intensify the fighting and the bitterness that went with it, and represented, certainly for the French, a complete failure to implement any 'hearts and minds' policy that might have won the local people over to their side.

The Legion also had their women, their personal mistresses, or *congais*, young women who picked out a soldier, or were picked out by him, and lived with him during his service, the girl choosing another one when that soldier returned to Sidi Bel Abbès. There were also the girls – often rather old and raddled girls – of the BMC, the Legion military brothels. Some of these girls would be bought out of the brothel and live with a man as his *congai* for a while if a particular legionnaire formed an attachment to her – and it was not unknown for legionnaires to marry their *congais* or, indeed, to marry girls from the BMC. From time to time orders would come from on high, ordering the men to get rid of their *congais*, but this order, if obeyed at all, never had a great deal of effect. *Congais*, like beer and bullets, were part of life in Indo-China, and the French soldiers could hardly have functioned without them. Drugs were not yet part of the scene, but without women and alcohol, the fighting in Indo-China would have been unendurable.

The whores, says Henry Ainley, were a 'raddled over-painted lot, but cheerful and hard working'. They were also part of the battalion establishment and, like the men, developed a great *esprit de corps* for their particular regiment, and were, as a matter of course, invited to mess functions and even formal parades. As in Algeria, part of the money paid to these whores was used for mess and battalion funds, to buy presents for the children of the regiment or pay for battalion parties. Men were therefore encouraged to use the BMC rather than avail themselves of the freelance brothels and bar girls of Saigon, though a visit to the famous Buffalo Park near Saigon was considered part of the Indo-China experience for any soldier lucky enough to get leave. The Buffalo Park was *the* French Army brothel. It contained hundreds of whores, of every race, colour, size and shape, who plied their trade in a central courtyard of a country house and dragged their usually drunk clients off to a line of cabins, set up around the courtyard or in the surrounding park.

In early 1947, the all-out Indo-China guerrilla war had not yet begun and the war was fairly conventional, with some 20,000 legionnaires deployed in the country. By 1948, however, the Vietminh were attacking in strength, and in July of that year a strong force from the 316th Vietminh Division, estimated at 3,000 men, attacked the Legion post at Phu Tong Hoa, which was manned by 110 legionnaires of the 3rd REI. This attack came in as dusk was falling and began with an intensive artillery and mortar bombardment. Within an hour the post commander, Captain Cardinal, and his second-in-command, Lieutenant Charlotten, were both killed by mortar fire, and the command therefore descended on Second-Lieutenant Bevalot, who had been in Indo-China for less than a week, and knew hardly any of the men.

Just as he took over, the hail of shells and mortar bombs ceased and the sound of bugles announced an infantry attack against the shattered Legion position. These human-wave attacks after a heavy bombardment were to be the principal assault tactic of the Vietminh infantry, and a very effective one if they were prepared to take the losses. This attack came in from three sides of Phu Tong Hoa, and wave after wave of black-clad Vietminh were soon sweeping over the Legion positions, where they were met with grenades, rifle and machine gun fire and, of course, the bayonet. This was *faire Camerone* all over again, and the legionnaires did not falter. The struggle raged on in the darkness, and the legionnaires found one advantage in being outnumbered: anyone they shot or bayoneted was probably an enemy, while the Vietminh were coming in from all directions and frequently shooting each other. Then the moon came up and with it the sound of Vietminh bugles sounding the withdrawal. This again was a common Vietminh practice. They would bombard a French post and then send in their infantry, but their commitment was limited. If the position was not taken within a few hours they would withdraw and be well away in the jungle before any French relief force arrived.

The attack on Phu Tong Hoa was broken off at about 2200 hours, and by midnight the legionnaires were redigging their positions, having lost 23 men – which, coincidentally, was 23 per cent of their strength. A Legion relief force duly arrived two days later to find the post restored and Bevalot and his men drawn up outside in review to greet them, in the traditional Legion manner.

The French were startled by the size and violence of the attack on Phu Tong Hoa. The fact that Ho and Giap were now deploying 'divisions' and were prepared to commit thousands of troops in human-wave attacks to overcome one small outpost raised this guerrilla struggle to a new level of intensity. France could have withdrawn from Indo-China and might have done so but for the signal such a withdrawal might have sent to nationalist forces in her other colonial territories, especially Algeria.

Lest any sign of weakness in Indo-China should be taken as an indication that France's grip on her empire was slipping, they decided to stay on and fight the Vietminh to the finish, pouring in more troops to swamp the country with French forces. In they came by ship and plane, more than 100,000, of them, including another 10,000 foreign legionnaires, all set to pacify the country. For a time it worked, and as the guerrilla attacks declined, the French began to feel more confident that the Vietminh could be defeated and some political accommodation found with Ho Chi Minh.

Having driven the Vietminh away – or so it seemed – the Legion established fortified outposts at Bac Khan, around the city of Lang Son, and at many other places in Tonkin in the north of the country, each outpost occupied by a few wooden blockhouses, surrounded by trenches, foxholes and barbed wire with a mortar pit in the centre. In fact the Vietminh had only retreated to rethink their tactics and plan for what was clearly going to be a long war. In particular, they wanted to secure a viable supply line from China down a track inside Laos that came to be called the Ho Chi Minh Trail.

The French were – just – holding their own in Vietnam when in 1949 the communists took over in China and offered arms, money and a secure haven to Giap's guerrilla fighters. Within weeks the fighting in Indo-China flared up with growing intensity, concentrated around Route 4 (RC4), the main road from Hanoi towards Laos, which the French were anxious to keep open and the Vietminh were determined to close. Their first move was yet another attack on a Legion outpost at Dong Ke, which was overrun on the night of 17 September 1950, the few survivors escaping into the forest and taking shelter in the Legion fort at Cao Bang.

The key position on the RC4 was this Legion post at Cao Bang, strongly held by the 3rd Battalion of the 3rd Régiment Etranger and some Moroccan troops, about 1,500 in all, but the French decided that this outpost was untenable and decided to abandon it. The commander of this post, Colonel Charton, was ordered to evacuate the fort and march out towards Coc Xa and Lang Son. Charton's garrison was too small a force to march though Vietminh territory after Giap cut the road, so a large French force – 5,000 strong and codenamed Force Bayard, after the colonel who commanded it – was sent out from Lang Son to reopen the road and keep it open until Charton's force was safe. This force consisted of the 1st BEP and some Moroccan battalions who were to meet Charton's men at Dong Khe, another fort on the RC4.

This move was exactly what General Giap had hoped for. He wanted to score a major success, and if he could wipe out a large French force that aim would be achieved.

168

He therefore sent some 30,000 men – three full divisions – into the jungle to ambush the French and Foreign Legion forces as they advanced to Lang Son.

Charton and his men left Cao Bang as ordered, and shortly afterwards the Vietminh entered the fort and blew it up. Meanwhile, the Vietminh had already occupied Dong Khe, wiping out the two companies of the 3rd REI which held it. The 3rd REI were already in serious difficulties, for the Vietminh were in the jungle on either side of Route 4 and pouring fire on to the French column from both sides. Eventually the Vietminh succeeded in separating Bayard's force into various components which they then proceeded to eliminate one by one. Bayard elected to fall back towards Lang Son and posted the Legion paratroopers of the 1st BEP as a rearguard.

The paratroopers held off the onrushing guerrillas as long as they could, but were gradually forced back into the Coc Xa gorge where a massacre took place. When the legionnaires reached the edge of the gorge, a number of them were killed when Vietminh suicide fighters ran out of the jungle, flung themselves on the legionnaires and leapt off into space, dragging the legionnaires with them. Other guerrillas swept down on the French wounded, shooting and bayoneting the men as they lay on their stretchers. In this engagement alone over 100 legionnaires were killed. The fighting raged on.

The French of the Bayard force were now surrounded in the Coc Xa gorge where they were pounded by Vietminh mortars and raked by machine gun fire, unable either to advance or retire. The fighting went on all night, with no let-up in the attack, and at dawn the surviving soldiers of the Bayard group decided to break out and fight their way back towards Lang Son. Unfortunately, the officer now commanding the force, Colonel Lepage, decided to wait until dark for the break-out, not appreciating that darkness was the Vietminh's favourite time of day, and rejecting the advice of Major Segretain, commanding the Legion paratroopers, who urged him to make the attempt in daylight.

The result was another disaster. Many of the men were shot down as soon as they moved, the wounded were left behind, and those taken prisoner by the Vietminh were clubbed to death with rifle butts as the guerrillas did not wish to be burdened with captives. The only members of the entire Bayard force to get away were some of the Moroccan troops, who fled through the jungle towards Charton's little force of legionnaires from Cao Bang, which was still intact and coming on in an attempt to aid the troops surrounded in the Coc Xa gorge.

Colonel Charton had been left alone by the Vietminh while they annihilated the Bayard force, but now the full might of the enemy was turned upon them and the large crowd of civilians and peasants that had come with them from Cao Bang. Charton knew that without more men from the Bayard force his own party was doomed, but once again the tradition of Camerone told the legionnaires what to do.

They destroyed all the equipment they could not carry, sent the civilians into the jungle to find what shelter they could, and began to hack their way through the forest towards the sound of heavy firing and the place where the Bayard force was being wiped out. On the morning of 8 October, this small force reached a position on the edge of the Coc Xa gorge and linked up with some Moroccan troops fleeing from the débâcle below. Eventually, finding a distraught Colonel Lepage in tears and unable to command, Charton took his men into the fight, and the Vietminh swept in to make an end, wiping out the last resistance from Charton's force and the few survivors of the Bayard group – which effectively meant most of the 3rd REI.

Depending on what side you were on, the battle at the Coc Xa gorge was a great victory or a catastrophe. French losses totalled seven full battalions – about 7,000 men. Hundreds of legionnaires, French and Moroccan troops had been killed, very few of the wounded survived and only four legionnaires, including the gallant Colonel Charton, who had been wounded three times, were taken prisoner. The 1st BEP and the 3rd REI were wiped out almost to the last man, only three men surviving to reach the post at That Khe, which itself fell to the Vietminh a few days later. That apart, only a few dozen legionnaires led by a resourceful officer, Captain Pierre Jeanpierre, were able to break out through the surrounding Vietminh and return to safety.

The Cao Bang débâcle was a stunning tactical victory for General Giap and a shock to the French Republic. A large, well-equipped force had been cunningly ambushed and over 7,000 French troops were killed; this was not something that could easily be explained away as an incident in a guerrilla campaign. It was a major victory for Giap and the Vietminh, a foretaste of what would follow.

The disasters at Dong Khe, Cao Bang and in the Coc Xa gorge in September 1950 were the turning point in the Indo-China campaign, the first Vietnam War. The next place to fall was the city of Lang Son, which the French should have held at all costs, bringing up whatever forces were necessary to beat off the Vietminh. Instead, horrified by the slaughter at Coc Xa, the French ordered the garrison of Lang Son to withdraw before they too fell victims to Vietminh savagery. The French were evacuated by air, leaving behind a large quantity of armoured cars, artillery and machine guns which the Vietminh soon put to good use.

With the loss of Lang Son and these other posts along the northern frontier – and some 8,000 soldiers – the writing was on the wall for French rule in Indo-China. The northern half of the country and the vital R4 road were now under Vietminh control, which not only gave the Vietminh a secure base, but also enabled them to bring in vast quantities of weapons, ammunition and other supplies from China.

The French now turned to air power, hoping that their command of the air could be as decisive in this campaign as it had been during the recent war in Europe. The fact that the jungle gave the Vietminh perfect cover did not deter the French commanders from assuming that air power was the way to break the back of Vietminh resistance and their will to fight. They could not have been more wrong in the long run, but this policy did have some initial successes, which led the French into a fatal error at Dien Bien Phu some years later.

Meanwhile, the tactic was to bomb the Vietminh to the conference table while setting up a series of strong defensive posts which the Vietminh would be unable to storm. A number of such forts were linked together by mobile forces to form the De Lattre Line, which was established around the Red River delta in 1952 and manned by strong forces, largely legionnaires. These troops and forts did prove useful in stopping General Giap from deploying his forces in a conventional fashion and so escalating the war.

While the French held these strongpoints and command of the air, Giap was restricted to guerrilla warfare. However, after dark and in the jungle, the countryside belonged to the Vietminh, and slowly but surely they drove the French back and gained effective control over the northern half of the country. The man behind this defence line strategy was General Lattre de Tassigny, but he was ill with cancer and at the end of 1951 he was replaced by General Raoul Salan.

Flushed with success, Giap then made a mistake. He mustered all his forces and made a grab at Hanoi, daring the French to engage him in open battle. This was a grave error, for General Salan welcomed the challenge and thrashed Giap's forces three times in rapid succession, at Mao Khe, where the 5th REI distinguished itself, at Ngha Lo in October 1951, where the parachutists of the 2nd BEP avenged their comrades of the 1st BEP, at Hoa Binh, and finally at the Day River. In conventional warfare the Vietminh were no match for the Legion, and this was not a mistake Giap made again. He reverted to guerrilla warfare and began to mop up French outposts one by one, gradually taking over the rural areas.

During the latter months of 1951, and in the first half of 1952, Giap attempted to take over the central Amnam heights and sent his forces south through these mountains and towards Saigon and the Mekong Delta. Thanks to these infiltration tactics, fighting only when he chose and on ground that gave his men every advantage, his forces were soon firmly in control of the area between the Red and Black Rivers. From there he made a determined thrust at Na San, the main French supply centre and airbase, and it was only after three days of bitter fighting by the 5th REI that the Vietminh withdrew. The French managed to keep control of Na San, supplying it by air, when the surrounding jungle was swarming with Vietminh. This success sowed the seed for the tragedy at Dien Bien Phu two years later.

Throughout 1952 General Salan attempted to retrieve the deteriorating French position in Indo-China, by committing 30,000 troops to battle in the North. This expedition penetrated over 100 miles into Vietminh-held territory before it withdrew – at which point the Vietminh promptly emerged from the jungle and took over again. This withdrawal was yet another indication to the Vietminh that if they kept fighting, and just hung on, they would, eventually and by a process of attrition, wear down French resolve to stay in Indo-China at all. The French were still putting in more troops, among them the German battalion of the French Foreign Legion which was committed to the fighting along the border, where they were tasked to cross into Laos and interdict the Ho Chi Minh Trail, a route that was increasingly important to the Vietminh campaign in the South.

The Ho Chi Minh Trail was no muddy jungle track. It was a guerrilla motorway, many feet wide, well drained, equipped with rest houses and water points, concealed camps and hospitals. The Germans could not cut it completely so here, inside Laos, they became the guerrillas, ambushing Vietminh convoys, shooting up camps, raiding supply bases. They took no prisoners and treated harshly any Vietminh fighters who fell, however briefly, into their hands.

This brutality and the undoubted success of the German battalion along the Ho Chi Minh Trail brought the battalion to the attention of the media, and a storm of protest about their brutality – and the use of former SS troops by the French and the Foreign Legion – descended on the French Government in Paris. As a result the battalion was disbanded and legionnaires near the end of their enlistment discharged and forbidden to re-enlist (though many did, under yet another assumed name), the rest scattered among the other Legion units in Indo-China.

Matters were clearly coming to a head in Indo-China as the French and Vietminh mustered all their forces for one decisive engagement. During 1953 the new commander-in-chief in Indo-China, General Henri Navarre, elected to conserve his forces for an all-out thrust in 1954, when the newly trained National Vietnamese Army, the troops of Bao Dai, would finally take the field. The French Army therefore stuck to defensive operations and let the Vietnamese Army 'blood' its units in a number of small-scale operations against the Vietminh, but Navarre was well aware that a general like Giap would not stop his attacks simply because the French were holding back and that he needed to be kept in check.

In July 1953 Navarre employed three parachute battalions, including the 2nd BEP, in an attack on the Vietminh bases around that now well-worn battlefield, Lang Son. This attack was supported by an amphibious landing, and when the troops withdrew they brought with them, unharmed, the garrison of Na San, an outpost that had been standing off attacks from the Vietminh for over a year. The war was now at a turning point and great decisions had to be made. The French believed that the Vietminh could be defeated in pitched battles and could not drive French soldiers from well-constructed defensive positions. Therefore, if such a position could be created, which the French could supply and the Vietnamese would be obliged to attack, a great – even a decisive victory – was possible. This was an idea at least worth pursuing.

All this was a prelude to the great, final battle of the war, when in late 1953 the French decided to occupy the village and valley of Dien Bien Phu with parachute forces and the crack troops of the French Foreign Legion, and tempt the Vietminh to take it. The result, on a much larger scale, was a rerun of Camerone.

12

THE BATTLE OF DIEN BIEN PHU, MARCH–MAY 1954

'War is a contest of strength, for war settles everything'

Mao Tse Tung, 1938

The seven-week battle for Dien Bien Phu marked both the end of French dominion in Indo-China and a significant step towards France's overall decline as a colonial power. With the fall of Dien Bien Phu, the writing was on the wall for French colonial rule in Africa as well as in the Far East, and within six years of the Vietminh taking Dien Bien Phu the French Empire was effectively over.

For the Legion, Dien Bien Phu was another taste of the Camerone experience, a chance to show France, the world and a new generation of soldiers, that the spirit of the Legion was an enduring asset, that its worth as a fighting force was still considerable, and that they could and would fight to the death, whatever the odds, and go down fighting rather than surrender. This was a curious, even outdated, concept in the 1950s, but the stand of the Legion and the other French units – for the Legion was not alone in this trial at Dien Bien Phu – must rank as one of the great fights of military history, no less glorious for being a defeat.

As for the Vietminh, their victory at Dien Bien Phu marked a further stage in their long war against the imperial powers, a war that was to continue when, after the peace conference that divided Indo-China, the Americans, who were already paying the bulk of the cost of the French war, took their first faltering steps towards direct military involvement in what became the Vietnam War, which, in the eyes of Ho Chi Minh, General Giap and the bulk of the Vietnamese people, North and South, was simply a continuation of the same struggle. Fourteen years later military historians were to compare the stand of the Legion at Dien Bien Phu with the 77-day stand of the US Marines at Khe Sahn, though the outcome of those struggles could not have been more different.

From the military point of view, at Dien Bien Phu the nature of the war in Indo-China changed significantly, from a pure, if all-out, guerrilla conflict to a conventional war, involving the use of tanks and artillery by the Vietminh guerrilla forces. Wars are not won by guerrilla forces; they can keep the war going, and maintain the military and political pressure on the enemy, but to win a war an army has to come out into the open and fight in a conventional style, beating the enemy in the field. This Giap now felt able to do. By the time the French elected to fortify Dien Bien Phu, and invite General Giap to take it, the war in Indo-China had been going on for six years and the French were no nearer pacifying the country than they had been in 1945.

They had, however, learned a few lessons. One of them was that if and when the Vietminh could be brought to battle, the French Army could usually defeat them, especially with the use of air power, artillery and, increasingly, mobility. The trick therefore was to invite attack, and so bring on a major conventional battle where French firepower and aircraft could deliver a victory. The problem was that General Giap was also well aware of this fact, and had taken steps to neutralise French superiority in these weapons, and deploy similar weapons to his own advantage. General Giap was a great general, one of the 'Great Captains', a master of war, who ran rings around the French and, later, around the Americans. He did it, in both cases, by always being one step ahead.

In July 1953, General Navarre tested this theory of inviting the Vietminh into open warfare with Operation Hirondelle, when he dropped the 2nd BEP and two army parachute battalions close to the Chinese border around Lang Son. This parachute brigade raided Vietminh bases, killed a good many of the enemy and dispersed a lot of the remainder, before withdrawing to the Tonkin Gulf coast from where they were lifted out by landing craft, covered by a landing force of the 5th REI put ashore from the French fleet.

In August 1953, another combined operation evacuated the garrison from the French fort at Na San, without loss. These two successful operations convinced General Navarre that he had the measure of the Vietminh and could set a trap, which would bring on a general engagement and cause great loss to General Giap's forces.

The place chosen as bait for that trap was the valley of Dien Bien Phu, a long valley surrounded by jungle-clad mountains, which lies north-east of Hanoi, close to the frontier with Laos. The valley of Dien Bien Phu, if it could be held, could be developed as a patrol base that could inhibit or block traffic on the Ho Chi Minh Trail, still the main supply route for arms and supplies sent to the Vietminh forces in South Vietnam, vital to the continuance of the guerrilla struggle.

Dien Bien Phu was therefore a battle with clear objectives. The aim was to threaten the Ho Chi Minh Trail and so lure the Vietminh into a catastrophic battle, following which the Trail could be cut, the enemy brought to the conference table, *et voilà!* With all this to play for, in November 1953 the 1st Foreign Legion Parachute Battalion parachuted into Dien Bien Phu, to launch Operation Castor. The battalion landed without trouble and swept the valley clear of such Vietminh patrols as they could find.

It might have occurred to some of the French operational planners in Saigon to wonder why the arrival of this parachute force met with so little opposition from the swarming Vietminh battalions known to be in the area.

Perhaps someone did wonder, but no one on the French side seems to have thought that a trap can work both ways, that the Vietminh actually wanted the French to isolate a large force in this remote valley, where they could, in their own good time, surround it and wipe it out. As for the Legion paratroopers, they were happy to be where they liked to be, in the forefront of the battle. In the meantime they worked hard fortifying the valley against the troubles that were sure to come.

It has to be understood that the French predictions of victory at Dien Bien Phu depended entirely on air power. The valley was deep in Vietminh territory, close to the Chinese border, and it was reasonable to assume that the Vietminh could and would surround and isolate it. Indeed, if they failed to do so, the French master plan would have failed. On the other hand, what if the Vietminh appeared in overwhelming force from across the Chinese border? No matter, said the French planners; we will destroy the besieging forces with air power – and the more the better – and supply the garrison by air, and it will work because the Vietminh have no means of answering air power. They were, after all, a guerrilla army, without sophisticated weapons or anti-aircraft guns.

The existing small airstrip in Dien Bien Phu was swiftly extended, and a series of fortified defensive positions was dug on small hills on the valley floor to protect the airstrip. Reinforcements were then flown in to man them and by March 1954 the garrison of Dien Bien Phu stood at over 11,000 men, forming ten infantry battalions and their supplementary artillery and engineers. Five of these infantry battalions came from the Legion, two from the 13th Demi-Brigade, plus the 2nd and 3rd REI and the 1st BEP, commanded by Lieutenant-Colonel Jules Gaucher.

The rest came from four French Army parachute battalions, and troops from an Algerian, a Moroccan and two Thai battalions. These units were all deployed in that series of dugout fortresses on the valley floor, each one named – or so it is said – after one of the many mistresses of the local commander, Colonel de Castries, a cavalry officer: Isabelle, Beatrice, Elaine, Claudine, Gabrielle, Anne-Marie, Hugette.

These forts were arranged in a rough circle around the vital landing strip, with Isabelle some distance away to the south and defended by the 3rd/3rd Battalion of the Legion. So far there had been very little response from the Vietminh, which had led the local commander into his first cardinal error. The defences of the forts were neither naturally strong nor well prepared, the dugouts were not deep or well protected with head cover, and supplies of ammunition, especially mortar and artillery ammunition, were inadequate for a prolonged siege. All that apart, the defenders had not occupied the hills that surrounded the valley, which put them in a position described by a later American war correspondent as being like 'fish in a barrel' – waiting for the enemy to swoop down on them, which the enemy were now preparing to do.

General Giap, commanding the Vietminh forces preparing to invest the garrison, could hardly believe his luck when the French commenced their build-up in Dien Bien Phu. His scouts observed all the preparations in the valley and studied the ground carefully, while Giap moved his army forward and prepared to wipe Dien Bien Phu and its garrison from the face of the earth. To do this he was going to deploy a new army of some 50,000 men, equipped with heavy artillery – and anti-aircraft guns.

The story of how the Vietminh moved their men, supplies, ammunition and heavy weapons, including artillery pieces and anti-aircraft guns, up to the hills around Dien Bien Phu, without the French even suspecting what was going on, is one of the miracles of guerrilla warfare, but it came off because, even if the French had known that Giap had such weapons, they would never have thought it possible that he could get them over the mountains and through the jungle to the hills around Dien Bien Phu.

The task was completed, partly with the use of trucks supplied by the Chinese, but mostly with sheer guts and muscle power, as thousands of men and women, even children, pushed and hauled and sweated and bled, to manhandle the heavy guns and the ammunition through the mountains and jungle, on paths hacked out of the hillsides and into carefully concealed positions overlooking the unsuspecting French in Dien Bien Phu.

Even if the defenders had known what the Vietminh were doing they would not have cared too much. The French welcomed an attack on Dien Bien Phu. That is why they occupied the valley in the first place. They knew – or they thought they knew – what Giap would do and were convinced that their air power, with bombs, napalm and strafing from ground-attack aircraft, would cause heavy casualties to Giap's forces surrounding the forts.

Unfortunately for this ambition, General Giap was well aware of the French intention and had laid plans to counter it. The force now moving up to surround Dien Bien Phu was unlike any Vietminh force the French had fought before. To begin with it was very large and – as always – very well trained. The 16,000 defenders of the garrison were to be faced with some 50,000 Vietminh soldiers, drawn from four regular N divisions and a number of brigades, plus large amounts of heavy artillery. This force included a number of death squads, suicide troops who would carry haversacks of explosives right into the French bunkers and set them off, blowing themselves and the bunkers to pieces. Whatever it cost, the Vietminh were determined to take Dien Bien Phu and heavy casualties would not deter them.

The deciding factor, however, was control of the air over Dien Bien Phu, and for this Giap had a complete regiment of Chinese quick-firing anti-aircraft guns. He also had a quantity of 155 mm-calibre cannon – heavy guns with which to pound the French airstrip by day and night, besides shattering the defenders' ill-prepared trenches and dugouts before sending in human wave infantry assaults. The French knew the Chinese had these guns and could supply them to Giap, but surely he could not get them to Dien Bien Phu?

It sounded impossible, but Giap and his men did it, and

in complete secrecy, his trails over the mountains concealed under the jungle canopy, his troops heaving and dragging the guns, night after night across terrible terrain, to well-protected emplacements overlooking Dien Bien Phu – and until they opened fire on 13 March 1954, the French had no idea they were there. The shock was almost as terrible as the first shells.

The first position to be attacked, Beatrice, lay north-west of the airstrip, astride the road to Son La. Beatrice was held by the legionnaires of the 13th Demi-Brigade, and if any force could have held the position the 13th DBLE was the one to do it. The task was beyond even these fine soldiers, for a storm of heavy artillery fire fell on their trenches and dugouts and the pounding went on for several hours, shattering the defenders' positions and destroying most of their own artillery, which was unable to spot the Vietminh guns doing all the damage. Then, when the defences had been adequately reduced, the Vietminh infantry came in, flinging themselves on what was left of the wire, hurling grenades into the dugouts, swamping the defenders by sheer weight of numbers, though scores, hundreds, of Vietminh were shot down in the attack. The first attack was repulsed but after a further bombardment, mostly from mortars, the Vietminh attacked again.

A deluge of shells fell on the trenches and dugouts of the 3rd/13th DBLE and continued to fall for the next five hours, demolishing the poorly constructed defences. At 0100 hours on 14 March, the Vietminh swarmed in, in the first of several human wave attacks, swamping the defenders, with the death squads leaping into machine gun pits and command posts. Within minutes, other legionnaires listening to the battle at other positions along the valley heard Vietnamese voices on their comrades' radios, sounds of gunfire, shouts and screams ... and then the firing at Beatrice abruptly ceased.

Colonel Gaucher, commanding officer of the 13th DBLE, and commander of all the other Legion forces in Dien Bien Phu, was killed in one of the first attacks on Beatrice, and as the defences were gradually overrun the order was given to break out to the other strongpoints to the south around the vital airstrip. The resistance was swiftly overcome and Beatrice, which had been expected to hold out for weeks, fell to the Vietminh in less than eight hours.

Only 250 of the 1,100 legionnaires in this strongpoint escaped from Beatrice to reach other positions. Before long, these too came under attack, pounded by those terrible heavy guns.

As it began, so it continued. Colonel Gaucher's place was taken by Lieutenant-Colonel Lemeunier, who flew into Dien Bien Phu in a Red Cross helicopter. It had been hoped that the Red Cross would be respected by the Vietminh, but they fired on all the Red Cross aircraft approaching the landing strip and shot several down. Even night provided no respite, for the Vietminh gunners – who were mostly from the Chinese Red Army – swiftly ranged their guns on the airstrip and kept it under fire by day and night, gradually reducing the landing field to a pockmarked patch of mud. The fate of the wounded, with traumatic battlefield amputations, untreated wounds and the onset of gangrene, but denied evacuation by the enemy, is one of the more horrific aspects of the Dien Bien Phu story. More than that the steady reduction of the airfield, on which the entire defensive strategy depended, doomed the garrison to death or surrender.

On the next night, 14 March 1954, the Vietminh attacked Gabrielle, one of the smaller garrisons, isolated beside the road leading out towards Lai Chau. The entire 312th Vietminh Division attacked this position from three sides. The defenders had recovered somewhat from the shock of the initial bombardments and stood off the Vietminh attacks until dawn, though half the Doc Lap hill feature that contained the Gabrielle position fell into Vietminh hands. On the following morning, a counter-attack from Legion forces, supported by tanks, succeeded in retaking Gabrielle, but the defences had been so badly damaged that the position was untenable and the garrison withdrew to the main positions around the airstrip.

Reinforcements were clearly needed, and on the 15th a French Army parachute battalion was dropped into the valley, for aircraft landings in daylight were clearly impossible. It was already apparent that the French simply did not have enough bomber and fighter aircraft to subdue the attackers on the hills surrounding the valley, even if they could have located their positions, and the number of transport aircraft – there were just 75 transport aircraft in Indo-China – were not enough to sustain losses from anti-aircraft fire and still keep the garrison supplied. General Navarre had miscalculated and the troops now in Dien Bien Phu, French, Thai, North African and Foreign Legion, would have to fight it out as best they could.

Two nights after Gabrielle had been abandoned, another outlying position, Anne-Marie, was evacuated after three days of incessant bombardment, and the struggle began to concentrate around the central position, the strongpoints surrounding the airstrip.

In one respect, General Navarre's plan was working: the defenders of Dien Bien Phu were certainly killing a great many Vietminh. Over 3,000 Vietminh were killed in the first three days of the battle, but they were prepared for such casualties. Indeed, their tactics were based on accepting heavy losses in return for positive results, and these they were getting. By the 16th, the airstrip was out of use and all supplies for the garrison had to be dropped in by parachute.

This too caused problems. If the drop was from too high, a large proportion of the supplies drifted down to the enemy, but if the drop was made at low level the aircraft came under heavy and accurate fire from the Vietminh artillery; sixteen precious transport aircraft were lost in the first week, so the dropping of men and supplies had to be done at night, with obvious loss of control and accuracy.

Giap then proceeded with the central part of his plan. Having destroyed all the outlying positions except Isabelle, which was much further out, he started to enclose the central strongpoints in a circular trench system.

Every night, the Vietminh and their hordes of coolie workers would swarm to within half a mile of the main French positions and commence frantic digging. The French and the Legion sent out fighting patrols to fill in the trench and disrupt the work, and pounded the diggers with mortars, but the digging went on.

Eventually, within a few days, the garrison of Dien Bien Phu was enclosed within a system of deep, heavily manned Vietminh trenches. From this encircling position the Vietminh now proceeded to sap towards the French lines. The artillery continued to bombard the strongpoints but the big weapon now was the spade and, day by day and night by night, the unseen Vietminh crept closer.

The fight for Dien Bien Phu went on for another seven weeks, but after Beatrice fell the issue was never really in doubt. One after another the strongpoints fell and any hopes that the fortresses could be kept supplied, or the Vietminh deterred by air power, were soon proved to be false. Not even the wounded could be evacuated; Vietminh anti-aircraft guns shot down the transport aircraft and within days the only way supplies or reinforcements could reach the garrison was by parachute – and there was no way out at all.

The French fought hard against the tightening noose of the trench system, but by 20 March movement around the valley was becoming difficult, and on the 21st the daily fighting patrol that linked the main position with Isabelle was unable to get through. More reinforcements were needed, and on the 22nd another parachute battalion jumped into the battleground.

The French were still trying to make air power effective. That was still the main plank of Navarre's strategy and fighter aircraft, including naval fighters from the carrier *Arromanches*, cruising in the Gulf of Tonkin, were circling continuously over the valley, while bombers, dropping bombs and napalm, were ranging over the surrounding jungle, trying fruitlessly to detect the Vietminh batteries. Their effect on the ground fighting was negligible and the dying below went on.

Even so, by all accounts, morale in the garrison was high, especially among the Legion. Dien Bien Phu was by no means an exclusively Legion battle, but in many ways it was exactly the sort of battle on which the Legion thrived, a battle to the death, without hope of relief, and from all over Indo-China other Legion units volunteered to join their comrades in the fighting. They were not parachutists but they were legionnaires, and so they made their way to the battle.

Every night more legionnaires and volunteers from other French units were dropped into the valley. For many it was their first – and last – parachute jump, for they were not parachute-trained and they all knew that once in there was no way out. Once a man went into Dien Bien Phu he was there to fight and die, but that was the Legion way.

By 12 April, after a full month of fighting, the situation was getting desperate, and on the 12th two full parachute battalions, including the 2nd BEP, were parachuted in. Having joined the men of the 1st BEP, defending the central position, the two battalions were sent to counter-attack enemy forces occupying the valley between the central position and Isabelle. The fighting went on for a full day, and although the enemy were driven back, the 1st BEP was virtually wiped out.

On 22 April Dominique and then Elaine fell to the enemy, the survivors slaughtered as their positions were overrun. The Vietminh had now advanced, with the spade and artillery and a great sacrifice in lives, to within a few hundred metres of Colonel Castries' HQ by the airstrip, and for a week between 23 April and 1 May there was a pause in the infantry battle as Giap moved up fresh troops for the final push and let his artillery work to and fro over what remained of the French fortifications. Then, on 1 May 1954, he struck again.

The attack, on Isabelle and the central positions – Hugette and Claudine – went in after midnight, when waves of Vietminh infantry rose from their trenches and swept over the defenders' lines. They were met with machine gun fire, grenades, rifle fire, shells and the bayonet, but still they came on, shrieking and blowing bugles, unstoppable. The human wave broke only on reaching the strongpoints, and then only in order to find the entrances and fire into the weapon slits and trenches. The fighting was hand to hand, in driving rain and total darkness, lit by the light of flares and gunfire.

Six battalions of Vietminh, some 7,000 men, swept over Hugette and Claudine, overrunning the Algerian and Legion positions, and though they were driven out time and again by counter-attacks, they came sweeping back out of the night to try again . . . and again. Eventually, as dawn broke, the Vietminh drew off, leaving some 1,500 of their fighters dead or wounded in the French positions.

It was a small victory for the defenders but it brought them no respite. The artillery started to pound their positions, and two nights later the Vietminh tried again, eventually taking all the outposts surrounding the central position. A series of counter-attacks by the remaining legionnaires failed to dislodge them. The end was coming, for the defenders were exhausted and ammunition was running low. The trenches were collapsing, the dugouts full of wounded men, whose condition was pitiful, the ground around the outposts thick with decomposing corpses. Dien Bien Phu was a charnel house.

The Vietminh and the Legion – indeed all the defenders of Dien Bien Phu – had locked horns and sunk their teeth into each other, and this fight would go on, day and night, until the French and the Legion were overwhelmed or the Vietminh drew back. On 6 May the Vietminh attacked and again on the 7th. On the morning of the 7th Castries sent a message to Colonel Lalande of the 3rd REI at Isabelle, telling him to fire on Hugette and Claudine if he saw any Vietminh inside their defences, and by the afternoon of that day, with ammunition running low and his command post full of wounded men, Colonel de Castries prepared to surrender. When news of that intention reached his men, a groan of despair went up and a group of Legion paras, unable to accept the decision, fixed their bayonets and charged out against the enemy. A few minutes after they were shot down, de Castries surrendered and the Vietminh swarmed in.

That left Isabelle, the last stronghold of Dien Bien Phu, isolated from the rest, and defended for the last seven weeks by the 3rd Battalion of the 3rd Legion Regiment. While many of the Vietminh concentrated on the central positions, disarming and rounding up their prisoners, hunting through the trenches to wipe out the last signs of opposition, the legionnaires of Isabelle fought on.

They fought all that day, alone and surrounded, and all that night, until 0150 hours on 8 May. Then, with their ammunition gone, Colonel Lelande and his surviving men did what they had to do, being legionnaires. They fixed their bayonets and came out from their trenches and dugouts to *faire Camerone*, charging into the mass of the enemy until they were cut down. The battle of Dien Bien Phu, one of the epic struggles of history, was finally over, and it was time to count the cost.

The cost was appalling. General Giap had put 50,000 troops into the fight against 16,000 defenders and lost over 22,000 killed and wounded. The defenders of Dien Bien Phu lost over 9,000 men, and of the 7,000 who went into captivity only some 2,000 returned alive. The rest, especially the wounded, died of neglect, starvation or brutality in Vietminh camps, or during the 46-day, 600-kilometre march over the jungle-clad mountains from Dien Bien Phu to the prison camps in China.

Gradually, over the next few hours and days, the news of the fall of Dien Bien Phu filtered back to Sidi Bel Abbès, where the men were fallen in on the great parade ground to hear the fate of their comrades in Indo-China. The parade was taken by the commandant of the Caserne Vienot, and in a total silence the men heard him call the roll of the units that had fought to the end at Dien Bien Phu:

The 2ème and 3ème battalions of the 13ème demi-brigade?
The 2ème and 3ème battalions of the 3 REI?

The 1ère battalion of the 2ème REI?
The 1ère and 2ème parachute battalions?

There was no reply to this roll-call.

Nor was this dire toll the total of their casualties. The Legion's tradition of fighting to the last was reflected in the high proportion of Legion dead during the entire Indo-China conflict, where though the Legion supplied only some twenty per cent of the troops, it suffered 48 per cent of the total casualties.

These units had gone from the Legion muster rolls, at least for a time, and with them went the French position in Indo-China. The fighting continued for a while, but after such a catastrophic defeat the French position was no longer tenable, though General Navarre and his men were still willing to fight on, hoping to snatch a victory that would restore the position and bring the Vietminh to the conference table.

After all, the idea had been to bring on a big battle and kill a lot of Vietminh soldiers, and this had been done. Even so, Dien Bien Phu was a defeat – the Legion losses alone were 1,500 dead and 4,000 wounded – and the French Government had no stomach for more such defeats. General Navarre was relieved of his command, a conference was called at Geneva, and on 21 July 1954, eight weeks after the fall of Dien Bien Phu, an armistice was declared in Indo-China.

The final result of the peace negotiations was the de facto partition of the country into North and South Vietnam, the independence of the South being guaranteed by the United States, while Laos and Cambodia became separate states. The seeds of the next conflict were sown at this conference, but for the Legion at least the war in Indo-China was over. The fighting had cost the lives of 12,000 legionnaires – more, proportionately, than any other unit involved. Those who survived had another war to fight in North Africa, and in the country they left behind the Vietnam War of 1960–73 was about to begin.

13

THE LEGION IN THE
ALGERIAN WAR, 1954–60

*'This was a war of shadows, a game of hide-and-seek
with an enemy who refuses to fight but slips away to
return again and strike down more helpless victims'*

War Diary of the 1st Legion Parachute Regiment

While some 30,000 legionnaires had been fighting in
Indo-China and dying at Dien Bien Phu, another war,
much smaller but, for the Legion anyway, far more
destructive, had broken out in their homeland of Algeria.
This war of independence, which lasted for eight years
and ended in humiliation and withdrawal, brought the
Legion to its lowest point in all the 120 years of its
existence and culminated in the French leaving their
former colony and taking some two million French citizens with them – the biggest mass evacuation of civilians
since the Second World War.

The legionnaires who returned from Indo-China, and
especially those who came back from months of captivity
in Vietminh camps after capture at Dien Bien Phu, were
not in the best of condition, mentally or physically. Many
needed hospital treatment and all needed to rebuild a
confidence shattered by defeat at the hands of Giap's
Vietminh. In such circumstances a nice little war, fought
on ground they knew well, might have been a real tonic,
but there were deeper problems.

The Legion, which had always been regarded, and indeed regarded itself, as something apart from the mainstream of French life, had lost faith in the willingness or ability of France to maintain its imperial position and the empire that the Legion had done so much to create over the last century. If the French no longer had any interest in the French Empire, what would happen to the Foreign Legion?

The Algerian War of Independence was already going on when the legionnaires returned from Indo-China in 1955. Many Legion units, especially those based in Sidi Bel Abbès or Arzew, Mascara, had already been engaged with the forces of the FLN, the Algerian Front for National Liberation. The war was one of ambush, cordon and search and terrorism, and it was not going well. Rather more to the point, it was clearly very unpopular with the citizens of metropolitan France, who did not care for the *colons*, those French citizens who had settled in Algeria. The French of the 'metropolitain' referred to the French in Algeria as *pieds noirs* – 'black feet' – alleging that they were unsophisticated folk who wore sandals without socks and sat about in the sun watching the local Muslims do the work.

This snobbish attitude to their overseas fellow citizens was compounded by the fact that their sons, French national servicemen, called up at eighteen for two years' military service, were being employed against the *fellaga* or *fells* – the Algerian fighters of the ANL, the Army of National Liberation – and taking casualties.

The FLN, all descendants of men who had fought the French throughout the nineteenth century and had never really stopped fighting them since, had learned a few lessons from those long-ago campaigns. To begin with, they had learned that it was not advisable to engage the Legion – which, with the French paratroopers, *les paras*, constituted their main opposition – in open battle. Neither was it wise to make more than fleeting attacks on Legion outposts. They elected to fight a terrorist war, a war of hit-and-run, in the big cities like Algiers or Oran, backed by an all-out terrorist campaign in the countryside, attacking isolated French-owned farms, killing French men, women, and children, slaughtering any Algerian who failed to support the FLN, and torturing and killing any Algerian who openly supported the French position in Algeria.

The *fells* were wily fighters. The legionnaires learned to be constantly wary, to move slowly at night, holding a twig and letting it hang down lightly in front of them to detect any tripwires; blundering along in the dark was asking to walk into the blast from a tripwire-detonated grenade. Booby traps abounded. A French flag stuck in the ground by the road must be approached with care for the ground near it would be mined. A Coke can was the ideal container for a half a kilo of plastic explosive and a fuse. Entering an empty village house by the door – or carelessly through the window – sooner or later led the unwary into a blast of explosive and shrapnel, a compound of nails, scrap iron and glass. Caution was essential, and yet the provocation to impetuous action was constant.

The 1st REP war diary recalls a patrol coming on three Algerian farmworkers: 'one lay on the ground, his throat gaping open, from ear to ear. A few metres away lay another, disembowelled, his guts trailing in the dirt. Then there was the third, who had been drenched in tractor fuel and set alight.' Simon Murray, a British legionnaire who served in Algeria during the war, recalls his unit camping in the village of Sassel, a select village for the *colons* which had been attacked by the FLN *fells* in 1958 and in which 70-odd people had been killed. The Algerian War never attained the levels of activity and violence reached in Indo-China but it was a long war, and a dirty one.

The principal *fell* formation was the *katiba*, a company of 100–200 well-armed guerrillas, though these *katibas* would sometimes group together for a major attack, or to attempt a double ambush – first attacking a Legion patrol or convoy and then ambushing the unit that, summoned by radio, came to that patrol's assistance. As in all guerrilla wars, the advantage of surprise lay with the terrorists, who retained the initiative in making the attacks.

The Legion countered their activities by cordon-and-search operations in the *bled*, by roadblocks, constant patrolling, and the use of helicopters for rapid reaction following an attack or a contact with some roving *katiba*. This remained the backbone of French operations until the end while they lost men steadily to mines on the roads, sniping from the hillsides, and bombs and grenades thrown into bars and outpost stations.

During operations in Algeria, from 1955 to 1960, the Legion lost an average of 1,500 men killed or wounded every year from terrorist attacks, and experienced, as the war dragged on, an increasing amount of desertion, some deserters actually joining the *fells*, others drifting into the twilight world of the OAS, the French-Algerian terrorist group, where skilled gunmen like Legion deserters could always find shelter and employment.

The Legion probably misjudged the French will to hang on to Algeria, at least to begin with. The French did not want another humiliating defeat like Dien Bien Phu, and poured troops and equipment into the country, force levels reaching 400,000 men by the end of 1957. This was after the political débâcle of the November 1956 Anglo-French Suez operation, to which the French committed a number of crack units, including General Massu's 10th Parachute Division and a battalion of Legion paratroopers. The outcome of the Suez operation, the collapse of British resolve, the intervention of the United States and the United Nations, and the swift withdrawal of the invading forces, eroded Legion morale still further, and they returned to Algeria fully determined to stand no nonsense from the *fells*.

The conduct of the war in Algeria has to be seen against the backdrop of the political situation in France, where the public and eventually the government of General de Gaulle – who was summoned back to power to restructure the French state – were growing tired of these endless colonial brawls. Besides, the French had more than enough problems at home; French governments left office with startling rapidity in the fifteen years after the end of the Second World War and the entire nation was rent by internal dissension. The outcome of this situation, as it affected Algeria, will be explained in the next chapter, while this one concentrates on the Legion in Algeria between 1955 and 1960.

The *fells* began a campaign of murder and intimidation at the end of 1954 and were highly successful in driving the *pieds noirs* off their farms, partly by direct attacks on their property, mainly by murdering any Algerian Muslim unwise enough to stay in French employ. Many farm labourers were found with their throats cut, hanging upside down from carts and tractors. Livestock was slaughtered, crops burned, farms – and farm workers – set alight.

The very first attack of the campaign, on 1 November 1954, was made against a couple of young French schoolteachers, who had come to teach in a Muslim village school. They drove into an ambush, were dragged from their car and slaughtered. However, the main thrust of the FLN campaign was against their own, Muslim, people, especially those who committed the 'crime' of working for the French. In August 1955, a large number of Muslims were massacred at El Halia near Philippeville by a *katiba* of terrorists. Having shot or cut down scores of Muslims, men, women and children, the *fells* set fire to the village and threw explosives into the houses to flush out any survivors who might be sheltering inside. This group of *fells* was pursued and brought to battle by a fighting patrol of the 2nd REP, which killed several of the enemy and captured most of their supplies and equipment, before the band escaped over the frontier into Tunisia.

Such brutal intimidation was a useful, even essential, weapon for the FLN, for not all Algerians wished for independence; far from it. A large number, perhaps the 'silent majority', would have been happier with French *départemental* status, which would make Algeria an integral part of France, provided the benefits of that position

– full democratic rights, suffrage, positions of power and influence, access to education and the courts – were extended to the entire population and not reserved for the *colons* and the French expatriates.

A large number of Algerians served in the French Army or fought in irregular home-guard units – *harkas* – against the FLN. The men who served in these units, the *harkis*, took considerable risks. They and their families suffered from terrorist attacks throughout the war and were forced to flee to France when the war ended in victory – at the conference table if not on the battlefield – for the FLN.

The *fells* also had the advantage of safe havens in the neighbouring Arab states of Morocco and Tunisia, both of which had become independent after the Second World War, the first from French 'protection', the second from the Italians. The Arab governments of both countries were strong supporters of Algerian independence and here they were supplied with weapons, many coming from Egypt, and allowed to rest and train their recruits, before or between attacks, and plan further raids within Algeria.

In an attempt to stem the flow of terrorists into Algeria the French eventually constructed two barriers – *barrages* – covering both frontier zones. These consisted of an electrified fence – discharging 5,000 volts of electricity, enough to fry a man alive – and razor wire entanglement up to twenty metres thick, densely sewn with mines and fitted with arc lights and a warning system. At some distance behind these barriers, patrols of Legion or parachute troops, or motorised Legion cavalry, were on permanent stand-by, ready to go out and hunt down any group of *fells* that penetrated the barrier.

Constructing these *barrages* took time, for they ran for hundreds of miles, one along the Moroccan frontier from the Mediterranean to Colomb Bechar, the other along the Tunisian frontier from the sea to Negrine. Of the two, the Tunisian one, the Morice Line, was the more sophisticated, while the one along the Moroccan frontier was often no more than a minefield and a few coils of barbed wire. The real barrier was the men, usually from the

Legion or parachute units, who patrolled the country behind the *barrage* and brought the intruders to battle. The Moroccan *barrage* was covered by elements of the 5th REI, the 2nd Cavalry Regiment and the 2nd REP. This was one of the major snags of the entire *barrage* concept. Unless they were covered by troops they were virtually useless, and by 1958 no less than 80,000 front-line troops were tied down on the Morice Line alone.

That these *barrages* were effective in discouraging *fell* attacks and infiltration was hardly surprising, for they were both covered by machine guns and field artillery batteries, as an account from the 4th REI diary reveals: 'At 1800 hours, harassing fire along the barrage was commenced, using heavy machine guns and 75 mm cannon. This fire straddled the barrage and included fire beyond the Tunisian border. Six motorised patrols then went out, and patrolled the tracks and roads behind the barrage until daylight when they withdrew to guard post positions and continued to watch the countryside until dusk when the process of harassing fire and night patrols began again.'

The war diaries of the Legion regiments are full of accounts of fighting along the *barrage* line, on both frontiers. On Camerone Day, 30 April 1958, two large FLN groups, each several hundred strong, succeeded in crossing the *barrage* from Tunisia just after midnight. Abandoning preparations for their annual festival, Legion paratroopers flung themselves into trucks and helicopters and rushed to the area of the breakthrough, flinging a cordon around the area where the terrorists might be found. In fact, unable to penetrate the guard posts, artillery concentrations and patrols that lay behind the *barrage*, these two *katibas* abandoned their attempt at a breakthrough and tried to return to Tunisia.

However, the action was not over. At dawn the legionnaires found the Muslims trapped on the Algerian side of the *barrage*, unable to find their way through. Spotting the Legion patrols debussing before their position, the *fells* scraped trenches and prepared to hold off an attack. They did not stand a chance. The legionnaires swept through their position, firing submachine-guns and automatic weapons from the hip as they came, tossing grenades into the hastily dug trenches, overwhelming the position with shouts of '*Camerone*'.

Once again the *fells* discovered how unwise it was to meet the Legion in pitched battle. The Legionnaires worked in pairs, one firing while the other moved, taking it in turns to work their way forward and outflank the *fell* positions. The action took about five hours and resulted in the death of some 200 *fells* . . . only eight prisoners, all wounded, were taken. The Legion also made a good haul of weapons, mostly Russian models, familiar to those legionnaires who had fought in Indo-China, and with this booty and their prisoners crammed into their trucks, the legionnaires returned to their Camerone festivities.

The officer in charge of this operation, Colonel Pierre Jeanpierre, was typical of the kind of men then commanding Legion units. An outstanding St Cyr cadet, Jeanpierre had been posted to the Legion on receiving his commission in 1936. In 1941 he was wounded fighting against the British in Syria and repatriated to France where, on recovering from his injuries, he left hospital and joined the French Resistance – the Maquis.

In 1943 he was wounded again while attacking a German convoy, captured, tortured by the Gestapo and sent to the concentration camp at Mauthausen, near Vienna in Austria, where it was expected that he would either be executed or worked to death in the infamous Mauthausen quarry, where starving men were routinely beaten to death. Somehow, Jeanpierre survived. After the war he returned to the Legion and volunteered for service in the newly formed parachute battalions, joining the 1st BEP in 1948.

Posted to Indo-China as a company commander, he was one of only three Legion officers from the 1st BEP to survive the battle on the Coa Bang ridge. He then returned to Algeria to command a training battalion, going back to command the re-formed 1st BEP in time to be dropped into Dien Bien Phu. He was in command when the 1st BEP was again cut to pieces in that battle. Surviving Vietminh captivity, he returned to Algeria in 1955, re-formed the 1st BEP – for the third time in eight years, now as a regiment, the 1st REP – and dropped with the battalion at Port Fuad, during the Suez operation of November 1956.

Now he was leading his regiment on these sweeps against the *fells* from the front, and taking as many risks as any other legionnaire. The outcome was perhaps inevitable. A few weeks after this Camerone Day action, Colonel Jeanpierre was killed when the helicopter in which he was flying was hit by ground fire and crashed. It is hard to say that he would have wished to die like this, but such an end was the one he expected, after a life spent where he wished to spend it, at the cutting edge of battle.

Algeria certainly gave the Legion plenty of experience in small-unit actions. This was a 'corporal's war', which usually means a junior officer or senior NCO's war, where the bulk of the fighting, and nearly all the hard work that produces a 'contact' with a terrorist group, is done by small bodies of men, at squad or platoon strength. The actions are usually short, often unexpected and always violent: a sudden burst of fire, a charge by a line of men, the exchange of grenades or bursts of automatic fire, the screams of a wounded man, shocked at the blood pouring from his body, and then, suddenly, it is all over, and there is nothing to do but fire some rounds at the fleeing enemy, gather up the dead, help the wounded – and get on with the war.

By such painful methods, in 1959 the 3rd REI killed or wounded over 1,000 *fells* and captured a vast quantity of arms and explosives. The 1st REP, rightly regarded as a 'crack' unit, killed 972 *fells*, for the loss of 140 paras, killed or wounded. Many of these actions took place along the border, in the country behind the *barrages*.

But not all the action took place in the *bled*. As the years passed the mountains and the borders became the operational areas of the Legion and the French Army parachute units, while the French infantry units, which largely contained conscripts, concentrated on containing FLN activity in the farmlands and in the cities. The cities, especially the large ones like Oran and Algiers, soon became hotbeds of terrorist activity, centres for the distribution of propaganda, the collection of funds and the purchase of arms, as well as contributing a growing number of terrorist attacks, usually with grenades, on French troops and civilians walking the streets or sitting in bars and cafés. Eventually, when the army and the police seemed unable to contain this situation, the Legion and the French paras were summoned to the capital, to take part in a counter-terrorist operation that has entered history as the 'Battle of Algiers.'

There is no doubt that the French and the Legion acted brutally towards FLN suspects during the Battle of Algiers. Had they not done so, they might not, in winning the battle, have lost the war, for the brutality and torture rebounded on them – and any popular support for the continuation of French rule in Algeria – when news of what happened reached the outside world. There is no need to present another side to the argument, for the French officers who took part have never denied the accusations of brutality, including the use of electrical and water torture on the men and women suspected of involvement with the FLN. General Massu, who commanded the operation, has admitted that he tried out the electric torture devices on himself, to see what happened. Thus equipped, the Legion and the French paras descended on Algiers in January 1957, and tore it to pieces.

It has to be added that the situation in Algiers at that time called for strong measures. The FLN were living openly in the *Kasbah*, emerging by night and increasingly by day to bomb any French property, civilian or military, that looked vulnerable, and shoot any French citizen or Algerian sympathiser who attracted their attention. The bombs, made of plastic explosive, were the great weapon of the FLN in the cities and the *plastiquers*, the bombers, used them freely, regardless of who was killed or maimed in their attacks.

The *pieds noirs*, the usual victims, retaliated with bombs of their own, killing 70 Muslims in the Algiers *Kasbah* in one attack alone. Most of these Muslim people were completely innocent, and such senseless brutality provoked reprisals and counter-reprisals in a steady escalation of violence. In September 1957, the FLN planted bombs in a city centre milk bar, a place popular with the children of the *pieds noirs*, and at the Air France terminal. Scores of young people were killed or injured by the milk bar bomb, and although the Air France bomb failed to go off, the governor-general of Algeria, the Indo-China veteran General Raoul Salan, had had enough. If the conscripts and the police could not stamp out the *plastiquers*, he would see what the Legion could do.

The sweep against the *plastiquers* was no secret operation. Massu's men marched into the city of Algiers in full battle order, parading through streets lined with cheering *pieds noirs*, to take up positions around the souks and bazaars and occupy the police stations. Massu then divided the city into map squares and sent in his men to round up everyone within each square, get their details on file, and then bring in any suspects for interrogation. Each street had to find a street leader, each block of flats had to appoint someone who could vouch for, or report on, the rest of the inhabitants. The Legion clampdown was rough and total and it produced a reaction, a general strike called by the FLN on 28 January 1957.

The legionnaires and the paras broke the strike. They brought armoured cars into the city, backed them up to the shops and tore the metal shutters off or dragged the shopkeepers from their homes and forced them to open up. Their ploy having failed, the FLN ordered their activists to step up the bomb attacks, but one or two *plastiquers* were captured and under torture revealed the names of their colleagues and the location of the main bomb factory. So, slowly, under the pressure exerted on individuals by the Legion and the paras, the FLN organisation in Algiers began to crumble.

This did not happen overnight. The Battle of Algiers went on for eight months, until September 1957, when a prisoner broke silence under torture and revealed the hideout of the FLN commander in Algiers, a twenty-year-old student called Said Yacef. The task of capturing Yacef was given to a company of Colonel Pierre Jeanpierre's 1st REP, which surrounded Yacef's hideout on the morning of 23 September. The legionnaires were spotted as they raced down the street, and Yacef had time to slip into a secret cubbyhole under the bathroom. This did not help him for long, for the legionnaires knew of the cubbyhole's existence and smashed their way into it with pickaxes. Yacef then opened fire with a pistol, and threw a grenade which slightly wounded Colonel Jeanpierre and three of his men. The Legion then attached an explosive charge to the outer wall of the hideout and gave Yacef five minutes to come out before they blew the charge. Faced with death, Yacef surrendered.

Capturing Yacef was a considerable coup, but then came tragedy. Another Legion patrol had been sent to round up a thirteen-year-old FLN message-runner, Ali le Point, who had also taken refuge in a hidden cavity. When he refused to come out, an explosive charge was triggered and ignited the bomb cache young le Point was guarding. The resulting explosion killed le Point and a score of innocent Muslims in the adjoining houses – as well as injuring three legionnaires. So ended the Battle of Algiers, with the crushing of the FLN within the city, but the erosion of France's claim to rule in the country in a democratic, liberal fashion, as a bastion against terror, was almost total. Besides, French rule, so harshly enforced in Algiers, was still being disputed by the FLN in the countryside.

Algeria had never been an entirely peaceful country. In the entire 130 years of French rule, few had passed without some sign of resistance. Many of the centres of fiercest resistance during that period proved equally hard to crack during the Algerian War, after the local tribesmen acquired modern weapons and took up the fight against the French. The Aures Mountains, home of the Chaouia tribe, were one such place, where harsh terrain gave the terrorists an additional advantage. The Aures had few roads or negotiable tracks, and the mountain weather was frequently vile, with heavy rain and snow driven by freezing winds making them a hard place to soldier in. Legion patrols, dropped in by helicopter, attempted to keep the Aures neutralised, but the FLN declared them a no-go zone for French troops and attempted to turn them into a Military District – a *Willaya* – the base for up to thirty well-armed and fully manned *katibas*.

The Legion was not going to tolerate even the idea of a no-go zone in their operational area. The Aures were in the region patrolled by the 3rd REI, which had the 1st REP as its back-up force, and in October 1960 these and other Legion units took part in a major operation against the Aures *katibas*.

For this cordon-and-search operation, five Legion regiments, including both parachute units, were deployed around the mountain range, while strike forces, backed by aircraft and artillery concentrations, moved in to flush out the *fells*. One *katiba*, pinned down by a company of the 3rd REI, lost 120 killed, and 26 surrendered before the few survivors broke free. In the course of this operation, which lasted five weeks, the Legion killed, wounded or captured 575 *fells* . . . after which there was no more talk of no-go areas in Legion territory.

These successes in the field could not stave off the relentless decline in the French commitment to a continuing presence in Algeria. The Battle of Algiers had left a bad taste in French mouths, the Third World and the UN were furious, and the continuing round of tit-for-tat atrocities was wearing down French resolve to stay in the country – as indeed it was designed to do. In April 1958 the FLN executed three captured French conscripts, an event that triggered massive riots in Algiers by the *pieds noirs*, in support of a demand that the war against the FLN should be prosecuted with increased vigour and all talk of a compromise solution ended.

General de Gaulle did not succumb to this demand but he agreed to one more military effort, replacing General Salan, the governor-general, with an air force general, Maurice Challe, charging him with the task of inflicting such casualties on the FLN that they would forgo the battlefield and come to the conference table.

Challe was a good officer and a sound strategist, and having taken a look at the security situation he decided on some radical changes. Guerrilla wars consume a lot of men uselessly, employing them to guard places that might be attacked rather than sending them out into the country to hunt down the enemy. France had nearly 400,000 troops in Algeria, but Challe estimated that no more than 20,000 were actually employed against the FLN in the field; the rest were guarding bridges or public buildings, or simply hanging about, waiting for something to happen. He decided to change all that.

His first move was to form a large number of surveillance forces called *commandos de chasse*, paras or legionnaires with Muslim *harkis* attached, small groups who would live in the *bled*, tracking and observing FLN *katibas* and calling in helicopter-borne troops to surround and eliminate them. These follow-up forces would come from a central reserve of paras and legionnaires who would have no other task but to hunt down and kill FLN fighters, and once the FLN had been detected and engaged there was to be no let-up in the pursuit until they had all been destroyed.

Challe's strategy and these close-pursuit tactics were highly effective, especially in terms of the use of helicopters which were quickly seen as war-winning aircraft. His *commando de chasse* teams soon located the *katibas* and the follow-up forces from the 10th Parachute Division and the Legion ran them down and brought them to battle. In three weeks they killed over 1,600 FLN and captured another 400, twice the number in one month than the best regiment in Algeria, the crack 1st REP, had previously managed in a year.

So it went on, with Challe making ever more use of the

Muslim *harkis*, the locally raised scouts, whose numbers expanded from a few hundred to over 60,000. In April 1959 Challe launched a major operation in the countryside around Algiers, using helicopters in large numbers to move his troops about and block the retreat of FLN *katibas*. As in other guerrilla wars of the period, in Malaya, Aden and Borneo, the helicopter was a battalion-enhancing weapon, but most of the aircraft had previously been used to taxi senior officers around or carry stores. Challe told the senior officers to walk and turned every helicopter he could find over to the front-line units.

In July 1959, Challe launched the Legion paratroop regiments on Operation Jumelles in the Kabyle mountains. This operation was carried out above the 2,000-metre mark, in freezing conditions, but it succeeded in breaking up the *katibas* in the hills. It was not carried out without loss. One Legion company stumbled into an FLN ambush and lost twenty men in the first burst of fire, and several helicopters were shot down by ground fire. The enemy's main force was finally located dug in along a ridge, and after their position had been raked by machine gun fire from helicopters, the legionnaires put in a frontal assault, moving up the slope in an assault line, breaking into pairs as usual, to grenade the enemy trenches, shooting down any *fell* attempting to flee. The final battle took less than ten minutes, 53 *fells* were killed – and no prisoners were taken.

In previous engagements that might have been enough, but Challe's rules required immediate pursuit or a continuation of the search. This produced another action in which more *fells* were killed, the pursuit continuing all day until the legionnaires reached the 'stop line' provided by the men of the 13th Demi-Brigade ... at which point some legionnaires were detailed off to go back to the battleground and hack of the heads of the dead FLN fighters in order that those killed could be identified and removed from the 'wanted' lists, a gruesome task for any soldier.

Thanks to these successful operations, the French soon

had the FLN on the run. The kill ratio was now ten FLN fighters for every French soldier, and as a result of that grim statistic the FLN were now surrendering rather than fighting to the death. This in turn led to more contact information, supplied by the prisoners, and hence to more contacts and still more kills. Challe forbade the use of torture and took a hard line with any man breaking this order, reducing NCOs to the ranks and dismissing officers. 'Hearts and mind' operations began again, schools were repaired or rebuilt, roads and bridges brought back into use. The Algerian people, the chief sufferers in this interminable war, began to breathe again, while for the French the scent of victory was in the air.

Challe's tactics had paid off in the field and filled the French and Legion soldiers with confidence. They were winning this war and they knew it, but they did not know, at least in 1960, that victories on the battlefield were not enough. The FLN refused to discuss anything but terms for independence, and the war, so unpopular in France, therefore looked likely to continue, further disrupting the even tenor of French life. France had other political ambitions, in the Common Market, and these could not be pursued until this war was ended, no matter how.

In 1960, General Challe was recalled to France and General de Gaulle sat down for peace talks with the FLN. When that happened, with the prospect of a surrender to the FLN a serious possibility, a new revolt broke out in Algeria among the European *pieds noirs*, the French paras – and the French Foreign Legion. For the first time in their history, the Legion took part in a mutiny.

14

MUTINY: THE LEGION LEAVES ALGERIA, 1960–62

'The OAS is filled with thugs, deserters and fanatics, who were the scum of the Army . . . particularly from the units of the Foreign Legion'

General Charles de Gaulle, President of France, 1961

Algeria was not only home to more than a million French settlers, the *colons* or *pieds noirs*, many of whom came from families that had been in Algeria for generations, it was also home to the Foreign Legion, and the idea that it could be given up and handed over to the rebel *fells* was anathema to the bulk of the legionnaires. The Legion had virtually created Algeria, building the roads and the ports, defending the frontiers, suppressing rebellion, pacifying the interior, shedding Legion blood in a thousand engagements, almost since the time of their creation.

Now they were fighting again, with hardly a pause for breath after the débâcle of Indo-China, they had the *fells* on the run and, with all that achieved, the politician in Paris – *le grand Charles* – was proposing to give it all away. This was not justice, and the Legion took it personally. They were fighting for their home, for Sidi Bel Abbès, the Legion base for more than 100 years, for their tradition, their Monument to the Dead, for the barracks and facilities that their predecessors had built with their hands and defended with their blood. Besides, the Legion had no home in France and there were well-founded fears that if the Legion went back to France it would soon be disbanded.

This being so, when the *colons* decided to fight the French Government's decision to leave Algeria, and discovered that some senior French generals were willing to conspire against the government, and overthrow it if need be, the conspirators found a ready ally among many of the French and Legion rank and file, including most of the French Army parachute regiments, and especially among the 1st REP of the French Foreign Legion, the crack unit among the French forces in Algeria.

By the end of the 1950s, the Legion was in any case becoming disenchanted with its role in Algeria. To begin with, until General Challe took charge, the war was not being won or fought in a way that would lead to victory. There was no foreseeable political settlement available, and by 1960 the war had been going on for six years, with great loss of life and increasing brutality, without an end in sight, though, as has been shown, General Challe's new tactics were proving highly effective.

This success had come a little late, for the Legion suspected – rightly – that the anti-colonial mood of the times, a mood intensifying in France as the casualties mounted, would eventually lead to the French Government seeking some form of compromise with the FLN. Within Algeria, the Europeans and the Legion and the thousands of *harkis* were rock solid in their determination to see this trouble through and remain in charge of the country, and though they conceded that greater attempts must be made to integrate the native Algerians into the running of the country, the idea of *Algérie française* would not be abandoned lightly.

However, the *colons* and the Legion were well aware that the French public in metropolitan France had quite different views. The French in general were sick of these endless colonial wars. Unlike in Indo-China, French conscript soldiers were fighting and dying in Algeria, survivors taking terrible tales back home. Here lay the big division, between the *colons* and the citizens of the Métropolitain, and between the regular army and the conscripts . . . and the conscripts had more votes and, like their parents, supported the move towards a compromise.

The Legion was well aware that the only 'compromise' the FLN would accept was a French evacuation of Algeria and total independence. If that happened they feared that their home in Algeria – and perhaps their very future – would be lost. There was also a considerable amount of well-justified fury about the fact that while they had been fighting this war for the last six years, and seeing at first hand what the FLN could do, their elected leaders, the politicians, were prepared not only to talk to the FLN, but give them whatever they wanted in return for peace.

That was the nub of the Legion dissatisfaction, the background to the mutiny of April 1961. The Legion had then been in Algeria for 130 years. It had built its own town – Sidi Bel Abbès – and had large land holdings in the surrounding countryside, including plantations purchased with Legion funds and run by Legion staff. It even had its own fishing boat, a trawler called the *Anne-Marie*. It had schools, hospitals, a large number of pensioners, wives and children in Algeria. Algeria was 'home' in every sense of the word, not least the emotional one, for the Legion had bought a stake in the country with generations of Legion blood. Now the French Government of General de Gaulle was proposing to give it away.

The Legion saw no need to pull out of Algeria. There were plenty of Algerians anxious to retain French rule, and many of these, the *harkis*, served with Legion units. Were the Legion to leave, the fate of the *harkis* and their families at the hands of the FLN *fells* was sure to be terrible. To the Legion, fighting the enemy in the field was more than a war, it was a moral crusade.

Challe's tactics were paying off and there was no short-age of good troops. The rates of Legion enlistment and re-enlistment were high in 1960, as recruits poured in, attracted by the prospects of war, which always stimulated Legion recruitment, and also by large bonus payments,

50,000 francs for the first five years and 12,000 francs – i.e. about £1,000 – for every year after that. These were large sums in the early 1960s and the legionnaires flourished. They had war, and money . . . and doubts.

Scratch a legionnaire in the early 1960s and you might well find a man who had a considerable degree of sympathy with the Muslim Algerians' position, though not with the terrorist *fells* who tortured and murdered anyone who disagreed with their 'liberation' programme, as well as any French soldier who fell into their hands.

Matters began to come to a head in 1958 with the election of General de Gaulle, wartime leader of the Free French, to the presidency of France. De Gaulle was not a sympathetic character. He had a deep belief in *gloire* – the glory of France – but this was matched by an equally strong belief that he – and he alone – knew how that *gloire* could be achieved in these difficult times. He was also overweeningly arrogant. At an international conference one delegate summed him up by nodding at the General and remarking quietly to a colleague, 'There, but for the grace of God, goes God.'

De Gaulle was a patriot and a soldier, but he was also a pragmatic realist. Before he took charge in France in 1958, post-World War II French governments had sometimes lasted a matter of days only before collapsing, and the country had had more than 30 governments in the last ten years. De Gaulle was a man with a clear grasp of priorities, and he saw that the first priority for France was to end the Algerian War. He saw that the 'Imperial Dream' of Louis-Philippe and Napoleon III was long since over, and that the divisions in French society caused by the Algerian War had to be healed, for the sake of France itself. He therefore decided on a pull-out, though to begin with he kept that decision to himself.

In May 1958 there was a major *pied noir* demonstration in Algiers after the FLN had executed – or murdered – three French prisoners in reprisal for the execution of three Algerian terrorists. The *pieds noirs* kept the city in uproar for two full days, occupying many government buildings, and the local police and army units expressed their solidarity by declining to intervene. This demonstration was widely reported in France and was soon followed by a counter-demonstration in Paris – *against the army in Algeria*. The country was falling apart and the French people finally called on de Gaulle to take the presidency and restore order.

Immediately after taking office, de Gaulle visited Algeria, and after touring Oran and Algiers he called on the Legion depot at Sidi Bel Abbès where he was taken on a tour of the Legion museum and shown the battle flags, the Monument to the Dead and relics of the fallen, after which the curator asked him: '*Mon President*, have all these men died for nothing?'

De Gaulle made no reply and went back to Paris to brood over his plans. Over the next year, as described in the previous chapter, the French Army in Algeria, under Challe, made considerable headway against the *fells*, and felt that they were on the brink of winning the war. It was therefore with shock and dismay that they heard de Gaulle's next major speech on Algeria, when, in a broadcast from Paris on 16 September 1959, he offered the Algerians – the Muslim Algerians, the FLN, the *fells* – a stark choice: complete independence, union with France, or self-government under French rule. Whatever they decided they could have, for France had no intention of continuing with the war. De Gaulle may have regarded this as a shrewd move. The *pieds noirs* and the Legion regarded it as a sell-out. After all, what had the *fells* been fighting for but an independent Algeria – so could there be any serious doubt as to which of the three options they would choose?

This speech caused particular dismay among the ranks of the Legion and the French paras, but de Gaulle made it very clear that, while he understood their concerns, professional soldiers – legionnaires or French – were to have no say in the matter. They were men under orders and their job was to obey those orders, however unpalatable. This point was soon driven home when General

Massu, commanding the 10th Parachute Division, the one that had parachuted into Port Fuad during the Suez operation of 1956 and conducted the notorious Battle of Algiers, was unwise enough to criticise the de Gaulle broadcast in the press. Massu was promptly summoned to Paris, relieved of his divisional command on 18 January 1960 and sent off to command the garrison of Metz, one of the most dreary postings in all France. This warning shot across the bows of the French military, a hint that dissension would not be tolerated, was not enough to stop the simmering discontent coming to the boil . . . and not only among the military.

When the news of Massu's sacking reached the public, the National Front, a right-wing party, called for a general strike over the Algerian issue to commence on 24 January. On the 23rd, the 10th Parachute Division was called back from operations in the Kabyle and used to break the strike, but it was soon reported that the Legion, and the paras, were fraternising with the protesting *pieds noirs*, who had gathered at the city university, and sympathetic to their views. Murmurs of mutiny began to spread among the battalions, which included those of the crack 1st Parachute Regiment of the Foreign Legion, the 1st REP, commanded by Lieutenant-Colonel Henri Dufour. As a result the 10th Parachute Division battalions were sent back to their barracks and replaced in the field with the 25th Parachute Division, flown in from France.

The *pieds noirs* were allowed to leave the university with their arms and were escorted to the 1st REP barracks, where some of them were recruited into a uniformed force called the Akazar Commando. Clearly, the Legion paratroopers, if not the entire 10th Parachute Division, were hand in glove with the *pieds noirs*, and in an attempt to break up this alliance the division was sent back on operations in the *bled*. Had the men been allowed to get on with the war, the discontent might have died out, but when a large FLN force was detected near the Tunisian frontier, the 1st REP was ordered to leave it alone.

Dufour sent a strong protest to Paris, asking why they

were not to be allowed to engage the enemy, and was promptly relieved of his command. This action escalated the discontent and gave the mutineers another chance to express their disapproval of French policy. When a French commanding officer leaves his unit, he personally hands over the regimental colours to his successor as a sign of transfer, but Dufour went on unofficial leave, taking the colours of the 1st REP with him, so the transfer of command could not take place. He was supported in this move by Lieutenant Roger Degueldre, one of his company officers, and a leading figure in the mutiny. Dufour also made contact with two French generals in Paris, where a plot was being hatched to keep Algeria French.

By the early summer of 1960, General Challe, the air force officer who had done so much towards winning the Algerian War, had been posted back to France, and the French Government was in open talks with the FLN over the future of Algeria. At the end of the year de Gaulle made another broadcast to the French people, declaring that he had set in motion a process by which the government of Algeria would pass from French to Algerian hands. Clearly, whatever the wishes of the *pieds noirs*, de Gaulle was determined to be shot of the Algerian problem. One result of this announcement was that the 1st REP refused duty, declaring that they saw no point in hunting and killing the men who would soon be ruling Algeria.

De Gaulle – who never lacked courage – decided to visit Algeria, arriving in Algiers on 9 December, where his visit was greeted with violent demonstrations by the newly formed FAF – the Front d'Algérie Française, a *pied noir* organisation which had plans to assassinate or kidnap the president. The riots in Algiers and Oran brought the Muslims on to the streets, and there was a great deal of intercommunal violence before French paras were deployed in Algiers and stopped the fighting with tear gas and rifle fire.

De Gaulle's staff suspected – with good reason – that the 1st REP were closely involved in these riots, if not in the proposed assassination of the president, and all officers were relieved of their commands and sent back to France, as was General Jouhard, the garrison commander in Algiers. This action, intended to nip another protest in the bud, simply spread the infection, and the 1st REP moved a stage closer to open mutiny. Meanwhile, public order in Algeria began to crumble.

Violence now became endemic in Algiers and the other towns, with Arabs killing *colons, colons* shooting Arabs and French troops from the Métropolitain caught in the middle, trying to contain the trouble and keep the peace. The plot against de Gaulle and his supporters continued to develop, the generals behind it – Challe, Salan, Jouhard and Zeller – forming a new terrorist organisation, the OAS, or Secret Army Organisation, which in its methods was no different from the FLN. The OAS was ruthless in killing anyone believed to support the idea of Algerian independence, and determined to stop the transfer to Algerian rule.

It is not hard to have some sympathy with these generals. Soldiers are not mindless automata, and there were serious doubts, in France as well as in Algeria, about the legality of de Gaulle's actions. He may have had a mandate from the French people, but were his actions constitutional? Algeria had been part of France for 130 years and tens of thousands of people had been killed to keep it that way. Did one man, even the president of the republic, really have the right to give it away?

In early January 1961, de Gaulle grasped this nettle and announced that he would hold a national referendum to determine if he indeed had a mandate to negotiate with the FLN over the granting of Algerian independence. The referendum was held two weeks later and the French people gave de Gaulle an overwhelming mandate to proceed with talks. Meanwhile military operations against the FLN went on, though on a much reduced scale, while terrorism in Algiers by the OAS continued to escalate and the plotters went ahead with plans for their coup.

The final blow came in April 1961 when de Gaulle announced that the French would withdraw from Algeria and hand over to a government comprised of FLN leaders and their political supporters. The sense of shock and betrayal that swept through Algeria, the French Army, the Legion and, to a lesser degree, all France is hard to underestimate. There were riots and the tricolour was burned in the streets of Algiers and Oran, but the order to withdraw was gradually accepted, except by certain French generals, who at once began to muster support among the *colons* and plot a mutiny.

Matters came to a head yet again on 20 April when Generals Challe and Zeller left their posts in Paris and were secretly flown into Algiers in an air force plane. Once in Algeria, Challe set up his HQ and announced that he and a group of generals proposed to seize power in Algeria, destroy the FLN and set up a Franco-Algerian state. As Challe was making his broadcast the 1st REP was boarding its trucks and setting out for Algiers to join his forces.

With the 1st REP on the move, Algeria exploded. Word of a mutiny reached the rest of the Legion, including the 2nd REP, on 22 April. This unit was about to go out on yet another 'search and destroy' sweep against the FLN when they were ordered to stay in their barracks. Orders changed regularly throughout the day, and it soon became obvious that something was afoot, with rumours that de Gaulle had been assassinated. Then word came that the 1st REP had taken over Algiers, occupied all the government offices and captured the radio station; this was mutiny on a grand scale, an anti-government putsch.

Algiers radio was soon broadcasting *Algérie française* messages to the delighted *pieds noirs*, and it appeared that the 1st REP, commanded by Major Saint Marc, in the absence of its new commanding officer, Colonel Maurice Guiraud, was at the centre of the rebellion, supported by the 1st and 2nd Legion Cavalry but not, as yet, by the 2nd REP. That evening de Gaulle made a passionate speech to the French nation and the French Army, ordering the troops back to their duties, threatening harsh punishments for those who were leading this uprising. This may have done something to stem the rush of other units to the rebel side. Nonetheless the 2nd REP left its barracks in Philippeville and drove the 500 kilometres to Algiers, meeting crowds of cheering *pieds noirs* along the way.

The French commander in Algeria, General Gambiez, saw the Legion paratroopers leave their barracks and set off to halt them, but was unable to do so. He therefore followed the paratroopers into Algiers and saw them occupy public buildings and the radio station; clearly this was a well-planned coup and the 1st REP were in it up to their necks. A broadcast from the radio station then told the citizens of France and Algeria that the army in Algeria was determined to resist de Gaulle's plan for the country, and would fight to do so if need be.

This broadcast contained some considerable exaggerations. The bulk of the French Army in Algeria did not support Challe, the OAS or the coup. The support came from the 1st REP, certain parachute units of the 10th Division, various other Legion units, mostly from the Legion Cavalry, and some members of the 2nd REP who drove in from their camp near Philippeville to occupy the airport. However, the bulk of the Legion, though supporting the motives of the *pieds noirs* and the generals, stayed true to their salt and remained in their barracks. Challe and Salan had bargained on their support spreading if their initial coup was successful but this failed to happen, and wild talk of sending the 10th Parachute Division to drop on Paris and arrest de Gaulle only alarmed the more moderate elements in the army, and the general population in Algeria.

By that evening, wiser counsels had prevailed and de Gaulle's words were having an effect. The Legion mutineers and the paras who were supporting Salan and Challe were very much in the minority. The bulk of the French Army stayed loyal to their government, and since there were some 200,000 French troops in Algeria, and less than 20,000 legionnaires, if it came to a fight the odds were against them. The cause was anyway dubious. Loyal French troops were now hurling words like 'traitor' at every para and legionnaire they met, and there were a growing number of clashes between loyal and rebel units. By 25 April, four days after first word of the coup, the rising was seen to be a failure. Challe and Salan fled, loyal officers arrived to disarm and arrest the mutineers, and the mutiny, so short-lived in time, so devastating in effect, was over. Now it was time to punish the guilty.

The 1st REP gave up their positions in Algiers and returned reluctantly to their barracks at Zeralda, where they were soon hemmed in – but left strictly alone – by hundreds of police and soldiers. Salan and Challe fled to Spain and went into hiding, and a large number of Legion and para deserters took off their uniforms and disappeared into the clandestine world of the OAS, which carried on its terrorist campaign in Algeria and France.

The mutiny, the coup, the revolt – these events had a number of names – had collapsed, and now de Gaulle prepared to exact retribution, beginning with the men of the Foreign Legion. The officers of the 1st REP were arrested and court-martialled. On 30 April the 1st REP, that crack unit of Dien Bien Phu and Indo-China fame, was disbanded, some men imprisoned or sent to serve in punishment units, some discharged with dishonour, the majority dispersed to other, 'loyal' units. As they were driven away from Sidi Bel Abbès the men of the 1st REP littered the road with medal ribbons torn from their tunics and according to most accounts, sang – instead of 'Le Boudin' – a song by Edith Piaf, 'Non, je ne regrette rien'. The 1st REP has never been re-formed.

The 2nd REP was not allowed to return to its barracks but it stayed in being while its fate – and that of the other Legion units – was being decided. As for the generals, they were all sentenced to death *in absentia*, though their sentences were eventually commuted to terms of imprisonment and remitted entirely in de Gaulle's amnesty of 1968. With his enemies at home dispersed or dismayed, de Gaulle sat down with the FLN leaders at Evian and began to hammer out the details of a peace and the final handover.

Meanwhile, back in Algeria, the war against the FLN went on in the *bled*. The FLN had no intention of giving up the 'armed struggle' just because their leaders were also talking peace. They had scores to settle and enemies to kill, and besides, there was the OAS, which was turning into a serious menace.

The OAS was determined that whatever was decided at Evian they could keep *Algérie française* by making the country untenable unless their demands were met. The leader of the OAS in Algiers was a former Legion officer, Captain Roger Degueldre, and under his direction the OAS proceeded to make Algiers and Oran cities of terror and death. Plastic explosive was a new weapon then, ideal for making powerful bombs which were detonated by the OAS in buses, mosques, hotels, bars and restaurants.

In the first few weeks of spring 1961, over 1,500 plastic bombs went off in Algeria, killing and maiming hundreds of people. Muslims were kidnapped in the streets and found with their throats cut, women and children were shot down. Commissionaire Roger Gavoury, the Algiers police chief, a man seen as sympathetic to the FLN, was shot dead by an ex-legionnaire gunman. Atrocity begat atrocity, and the Muslim and Christian communities, which had lived peacefully side by side for over 100 years, were soon at each other's throats, their animosity reaching a crescendo on 1 November when more than 60 Arabs were killed in street rioting in Algiers. The *colons* also burned down the library and the laboratories of Oran University, to keep the Algerians from having them.

On 7 April 1962, Roger Degueldre and some of his closest allies – mostly Legion deserters – were caught in Algiers, shipped back to France, swifty tried and sentenced to death. General Salan, who had returned secretly to Algeria, was arrested at the end of the month and was lucky to escape a similar fate, especially when the OAS responded with a spate of attacks and bombings, destroying every European building they could reach – factories, power stations, commercial property – determined to leave nothing to the new rulers of Algeria.

On 27 April a referendum in France voted overwhelmingly to grant independence to the Algerians, and after that it was only a matter of time until the FLN were in charge. Under the terms of the temporary ceasefire the *fellagha* were already moving into urban areas, and acts of terrorism between them and the *pied noirs*-backed OAS increased daily. Even those *colons* leaving Algeria were not safe; on 5 July 1962, over 2,000 unarmed *colons,* waiting in Oran for shipment to France, were massacred by the FLN – and Paris ordered that the French Army and the local police should not intervene. On the following day, Roger Degueldre was shot by firing squad at Fort d'Ivry, near Paris. Degueldre went to his death wearing his Legion uniform and all his decorations, and his instruction to the firing squad, telling them to get on with it, and his singing of the 'Marseillaise', so unnerved the soldiers that it took five volleys, and several bullets from the NCO in charge, to finish the job.

Morale in the Legion and among the regular soldiers in the French Army slumped. Even the crack 2nd REP lost men, over 130 in three months, a number joining the ranks of the OAS. The men had no soldiering to do now, and were either confined to their barracks or deployed on labouring tasks, digging roads that led nowhere, laying lorry parks that Legion transport would never use. Only a visit by General Lefort, the inspector general of the Legion, in December 1962, when he assembled the men and assured them that they did have a role in the French Army and that the Legion would not be disbanded or further disgraced, saved morale from plummeting deeper still.

Meanwhile the French Army began to withdraw and with it the *colons*, the *pieds noirs*. Not since the Israelites left Pharaoh's Egypt has North Africa seen such an exodus. More than a million French citizens gave up their homes and businesses in Algeria – which in most cases meant everything they had – and left for France. Men, women, children, babies in arms – they left by air, on transport aircraft or crammed on to ferries or troop-ships, carrying whatever clothes and valuables they could.

Behind them their homes and farms were taken over by the FLN, without payment or compensation of any kind. They had their lives and that was all. These people did not want to leave; they hated France for forcing this fate upon them and they had no idea what they would do in the future. Many settled in the Languedoc and began again as *vignerons* and farmers, but all knew that life would never be the same again.

The independence of Algeria was declared on 3 July 1962, but the Legion stayed on for a while, packing up its treasures and wondering about its future. The 2nd REP had been forgiven for its part in the mutiny and restored to duty in May, many members taking part in the last parade at Sidi Bel Abbès on 24 October, when the Legion formally gave up its home and left for France.

With them went all the treasures of the museum, their colours, Captain Danjou's hand and the Monument to the Dead, the stones carefully dismantled and packed away for re-erection in their new home, wherever that might be. Most of the Legion dead remained in Algeria, but three bodies were disinterred and taken away, those of General Rollet, of Prince Aage of Denmark and, to represent the 35,000 legionnaires who had died for France since 1831, the body of Legionnaire Zimmerman.

The Legion found a new home at Camp de la Demande, a set of World War II barracks near Aubagne, a small town a few miles from Marseilles, in Provence. When the first elements of the Legion arrived they found Camp de la Demande distinctly depressing, and the locals far from friendly.

Work began at once to turn the camp into a barracks fit for legionnaires. Eventually Camp de la Demande became the Quartier Vienot as the caserne in Sidi Bel Abbès had been, and the Legion re-erected the Monument des Morts and re-established the Voie Sacrée, as well as building a first-class museum to house Captain Danjou's hand and the other Legion relics.

As more legionnaires arrived, so more buildings were erected, but it was eventually decided that, while Aubagne should be the Legion depot and headquarters, the training function and the various units needed to be dispersed. The old recruit assembly point in the grim Bas-Fort St Nicolas in Marseilles was no longer needed, so that was closed down, as were a number of the recruiting offices in the provinces.

The 2nd REP, which had now taken on a role not unlike that of the British SAS, as an intervention and counter-guerrilla force, went to Calvi in Corsica, where their very presence was a strong hint to Corsican nationalists that trouble would not be tolerated. The training battalion went to Castelnaudrey, near Carcassone in Languedoc-Roussillon, and since then thousands of volunteers – now known officially as the *engagés volontaires* but still referred to as *les bleus* by the trained legionnaires – have got their first taste of Legion life in a town hitherto famous only for the taste of *cassoulet*. The commando and mountain warfare cadres were established with other commando units of the French Army at Mont Louis on the Cerdagne plateau above Perpignan, and the Legion Cavalry, equipped with armoured cars and light tanks, is now based at Orange, the old Roman town in the Rhône valley.

The home for disabled or elderly former legionnaires, the Domain Capitaine Danjou, is at Puyloubier near St Maximin, at no great distance from Aubagne, so that veterans can still attend Legion festivals and pop in now and again to see that standards are not slipping. Every legionnaire, of every rank, still contributes a day's pay a year to maintain these old soldiers in suitable comfort.

To an outsider these places are superior in every way to the locations the Legion used to inhabit in Algeria, but even the casual visitor can detect a longing for the old days, for the time when the Legion lived a life apart, sticking together in the *caserne*, knowing they had few friends outside the walls. Modern legionnaires are just as physically tough as, and better equipped and probably better trained, they have ever been, but the mental toughness that came from serving in a Legion of self-inflicted outcasts seems to have declined somewhat.

The Legion is part of the French scene now, and that is not really where the legionnaire belongs, even after 160 years. Action defines the legionnaire, and to find action is why many legionnaires join. Therefore, as soon as their training is completed, the legionnaires prefer to be sent to one of the Legion outposts, far from the comforts of the Métropolitain.

So, with their new bases established, in 1963 the Legion settled down to finding a new role, much of it in the former colonies of the old French Empire.

15

POST-COLONIAL CONFLICTS: CHAD, DJIBOUTI AND KOLWEZI, 1963–95

'An elite unit only becomes such when those in it consider themselves already dead. Dying is what the Legion is all about.'

Douglas Porch, *The French Foreign Legion*

The Evian peace talks on Algerian independence ended with the handover of Algeria to the FLN; the final agreement was concluded on 19 May 1962. Troop withdrawals and a mass exodus of *pieds noirs* and those *harkis* wise enough to flee began almost at once, but under the transitional arrangements some units, including the Legion, were permitted to stay in the country for another year, though the Legion units were given exactly four months to get out of a country that had been their home for 130 years. In fact some Legion units stayed on until 1964, packing up their treasures. What they could take with them they were allowed to take; what they had to leave behind the FLN happily destroyed.

At the end of March 1962, as the FLN provisional government prepared to move in from Tunisia and take control of the country, the 2nd REP moved to Telergma and six months later to Mers-el-Kebir on the coast, where they were kept busy for a while building a new camp.

222

Since Mers-el-Kebir was a French naval base and, under the terms of the independence agreement, would be retained by France for a further five years, many Legion units gathered there. New buildings were hardly necessary, for with the withdrawal of many French Army and naval units the Mers-el-Kebir base was full of empty barracks. It was clearly a pointless task, something to keep the legionnaires busy while the powers that be in France considered their future.

Throughout 1962 their future did not look too promising. General de Gaulle had not forgiven the Legion's 'treachery' and took no interest in their fate, and the Legion had to look on in Algeria while the FLN took over the country, drove out the *colons* and exacted a vicious revenge on the *harkis*. Only 15,000 *harkis*, and a few of the many thousands of Muslims who had supported the French, were permitted to enter France, and it is estimated that up to 100,000 *harkis* were killed, many after torture, at the hands of the FLN. After the FLN Government took over their *katibas* came swarming down from the hills and, while warily skirting any Legion patrols, proceeded to indulge in mass acts of revenge against the *harkis*. Meanwhile there was internal fighting among the rival groups within the FLN as they fought it out for positions of power within the new government.

In July 1962 the 2nd Legion Cavalry were disbanded and those legionnaires with sufficient time left to serve were transferred to the 1st REC, which actually remained in Algeria, in the French enclave at Mers-el-Kebir, until repatriated to France five years later. The 2nd REI had been fully occupied guarding French nuclear installations and test sites in the Sahara until it too returned to Mers-el-Kebir and thence to Aubagne in 1969, after which this unit too was disbanded.

The Legion was shrinking as more men, recruited for the Indo-China or Algerian wars, earned their pensions and retired or finished their terms of enlistment and declined to sign on for a further tour. By the mid-1960s the Legion strength had dropped to 10,000 men and it has remained at around that level ever since. The 4th REI was disbanded in 1964, and some of the units that were retained, like the 13th Demi-Brigade and the 5th REI, were sent to occupy isolated garrisons in some far-flung corner of the shrinking French Empire; no one fully trusted the Legion and the French felt safer if its units were widely dispersed.

The final wrench was giving up Sidi Bel Abbès. Legionnaires had built this town with their own hands; Legion architects had laid out the streets and designed the facilities. Once it had been a *bidonville*, a ramshackle hamlet on the edge of nowhere, selected as the Legion home because no one else wanted it. Now that it was a prosperous thriving town, they had to leave and hand it over to the FLN, who would soon eliminate any sign that the Legion had ever been there. The last parade at Sidi Bel Abbès took place on 24 October 1962, when the remaining 700 legionnaires paraded for the last time. The Black Flag banners captured at Tuyen Quang were burnt, and in the glare of those flames the legionnaires sang 'Le Boudin' for the last time in Algeria.

All their treasures and trophies (which mean nothing at all in themselves but meant everything to the Legion) were packed up and sent to France, to await whatever fate the future held in store. Over the next weeks and months the more permanent memorials were dismantled and shipped out, but eventually there was nothing more to move and the last *képi blanc* mounted the last lorry and drove away through silent crowds to Oran and the boat for France.

Very few people visit Sidi Bel Abbès today – Europeans are not welcome or safe in present-day Algeria – and in the last 30 years the local authorities have worked hard to expunge all memory of the Legion. The caserne has been bulldozed flat, the facilities turned over to the public, though most of them – like the great swimming pool and the cinema – have crumbled into ruin or been allowed to rot. The Legion church has been desecrated and Legion memorials and tombstones overturned or dug up. Sidi Bel

Abbès is a shadow of its former self; less than 30,000 people now live in the town created and maintained by the Legion, for now that the Legion has gone Sidi Bel Abbès has no reason to exist.

Matters began to look up in January 1963 when the 2nd REP received a new commanding officer, Lieutenant-Colonel Caillaud. Colonel Caillaud has some claim to be the first Legion 'para', starting his parachute training in Indo-China in 1945 but – owing to various distractions, like the Indo-China War – getting his jump wings only in 1961. He was a dedicated Legion officer, full of enthusiasm for parachute soldiers, and he had plenty of ideas concerning the future of the 2nd REP.

Caillaud proposed turning the 2nd REP into the Legion equivalent of the British SAS, in the form of a para-commando regiment. The Belgians already had such a force, raised from former members of the World War II No. 10 (Inter-Allied) Commando, and the Belgian Troop of the SAS. If Caillaud had his way, the 2nd REP would become as good as any para-commando unit in the world, the men fit and well trained in the full range of special force skills – sabotage, sniping, amphibious techniques, mountaineering and skiing, parachuting (both static-line and free-fall), canoeing, unarmed combat, and long-range reconnaissance. The 2nd REP would become a rapid-reaction force, the élite of the élite. The only way into the unit was via the Legion; first a man must qualify as a good legionnaire, and then the best of them would be permitted to volunteer for the 2nd REP and undergo a further gruelling series of selection tests.

Simon Murray, a British legionnaire, and one of the first members of the new-style 2nd REP, recalls that one of the tests was to jump into the sea from the 100-metre-high roof of a warehouse. Water gets remarkably hard when hit from higher than about 30 metres, and having managed the first terrifying jump Murray elected to do it again. This time he was not so lucky; one arm drifted away from his side as he fell, and the impact with the water dislocated his shoulder. Such tests – and some enthusiasts actually *dived* 100 metres off the roof – soon weeded out the unfit or the unsuitable.

Caillaud's plan met with the approval of the French Government and aroused considerable enthusiasm in the Legion. 'Morale has been given a gigantic shot in the arm,' Simon Murray recorded in his diary. 'We're back in business and someone thinks we can do something except build bloody roads all day and there is a feeling of moving forward again.' The Legion is full of good soldiers and the best of them wanted to be in the 2nd REP. It offered them an élite status and the possibility of action, which has always been the big attraction of enlisting in the Legion for adventurously minded fighting men.

Caillaud had the new REP formed and functioning inside two years, and the unit was installed in its new base at Camp Raffali, Calvi, Corsica by the middle of 1967, where the training intensified. As a sign that the Legion had been forgiven for the Algiers mutiny the 2nd REP became part of the 11th Parachute Division, itself part of France's rapid-reaction force. The first call to action came in April 1969, when two companies of the 2nd REP were sent to join other Legion units assisting the president of Chad, a former French colony in central Africa, against two rebel groups attempting to overthrow his government.

The French Empire might have gone, but French influence has been maintained in the francophone states of Africa. None of these could reasonably be described as democracies, but the French find it useful to support the current tyrant, and do not hesitate to deploy French troops, usually from the Legion, if one of their clients is in danger.

One of these rebel groups was raiding into Chad from across the Somali border and the other was causing trouble in the north of the country, along the barren fringes of the Sahara, where the dissidents were being armed and trained by the Libyans. The Somali problem was quickly resolved by the deployment of Legion patrols along the border. These patrols swiftly hunted down and killed any intruders and, after a few brisk actions, put an end to that problem.

The trouble along the fringes of the Sahara took longer to solve and looked at one time as if it might involve Chad – and France – in war with Libya. These Saharan patrols were a return to Legion life as it had been in the nineteenth century – patrols on foot or by camel, as well as by tracked vehicle and helicopter. The dissidents knew the country well, and there were a number of brief but bitter actions in which seven legionnaires were killed and over twenty wounded.

The problems in Chad have simmered on for years, and Legion companies have been flown out on a number of occasions to signal French support for the current government or to discourage Colonel Gaddafi, the Libyan leader, from developing his harassment into full-scale war. In 1984, Gaddafi announced the annexation of Chad's valuable uranium deposits in the northern frontier region, probably hoping that this uranium could provide the raw material for his nuclear weapons programme, but once again the deployment of Legion units proved sufficient threat to prevent a takeover.

In February 1976, trouble arose in the former colony of Djibouti in the Horn of Africa, at the foot of the Persian Gulf, and the Legion forces based in that country rushed to intervene. Djibouti is actually the name of the principal port and town. The French Somali-Djibouti territory is bordered by Ethiopia and the Republic of Somalia, which became independent in 1960, and is made up of the former Italian Somalia and British Somaliland. The Republic of Somalia at once declared its intention of incorporating French Somalia (which elected in 1958 to become a French overseas *département*) into its territory, and, but for the presence of French troops, it would probably have done so.

Attempts to destabilise the territory of Djibouti began at once and have continued ever since, partly through crude attempts at subversion, sometimes through even cruder cross-border raids. France maintains a strong garrison in Djibouti, a garrison that always contains at least one Legion contingent, usually the 13th Demi-Brigade, though the 2nd REP often visit the country for desert training. On 3 February 1976 a group of well-armed Somalis were retreating to the border after a raid when they came on a bus full of French and Somali schoolchildren which they hijacked and drove to the border. There the bus was stopped by French border guards, but the raiders threatened to kill the children unless they were permitted to pass.

French troops then surrounded the bus at a discreet distance, but while this stand-off was going on the confidence of the raiders grew. Within an hour, the leader of the Somali force was demanding not only free passage across the border for his men and their hostages, but the release of all terrorists held in Djibouti, immediate independence for the territory and the immediate departure of all French troops . . . or else the children would be shot, one by one.

The French had no intention of granting any of these demands but their first priority was the lives of the children. A local woman, Madame Jeanne Bru, offered to board the coach and comfort the children and the terrorists allowed her on board, carrying soft drinks and sandwiches for the children, whom she found very excited by all the fuss but not at all worried. Meanwhile, a company of the 2nd REP had taken up position near the border and had the bus and its passengers under surveillance.

The stand-off continued for some hours, without resolution, and then the legionnaires began to move in, their actions greeted with fire from Somali Army positions across the frontier. The legionnaires returned fire, and the shooting alerted the terrorists on the bus. The terrorists then drove the bus to a position close to the frontier and the legionnaires had reason to believe that they were being reinforced by Somalis from over the border.

The situation was clearly deteriorating, and at 1630 hours the legionnaires stormed the bus. Three squads rushed the position, shooting down two of the terrorists in the first burst of fire. The other terrorists then counter-attacked, wounding a Legion officer, but one of the sergeants shot them down and Legion snipers covered the bus while an assault group, led by Corporal Larking, swarmed on board. Two more terrorists were killed on board but, sadly, two children were caught in the cross-fire, one being killed outright and the other dying later. The Somali Army positions were hosed with cannon and machine gun fire from armoured cars of the 13th DBLE and the Somali soldiers fled.

In the following year French Somalia gained its independence as the Republic of Djibouti, but French troops have remained in the territory ever since, to guarantee that independence – and to prevent Djibouti sliding into the state of anarchy and chaos that has engulfed Somalia in recent years.

These incidents helped to keep the legionnaires on their toes and Legion exploits in the newspapers, but in May 1978 something much bigger arose in western Zaire, the former Belgian Congo, when a strong party of rebels from the FLNC, the Congolese National Liberation Front, crossed over from Angola into the Zaire province of Shaba. Shaba was formerly known as Katanga, a part of the old Belgian Congo that was anxious for complete independence from the shambles that has engulfed Zaire. This well-armed group, some 2,000 strong, captured the town of Kolwezi.

Kolwezi is a copper-mining town. Apart from a good deal of industry and a local population of over 10,000, in 1978 it contained about 2,300 Belgian and French mine managers and technicians, together with their families. The FLNC rebels, backed by Cuba and with armoured cars in support, were after money and arms, but they were not averse to looting, which led within hours to rape and murder.

At first, they concentrated their violence on the Zairean population, but when they discovered that the whites had more to offer they started rounding up the white expatriates and gave themselves over to a positive orgy of savagery and violence. Women were raped, children terrified, men who worked in the state-owned mines beaten up, hauled before people's courts, accused of working for the 'Traitor Mobutu', the president of Zaire, and then shot. Over the first two days the level of violence increased until the entire population of Kolwezi were in fear of their lives. There was, and is, very little law in Zaire, and no assistance was available from local forces.

Fortunately, before all communications had been cut, a radio operator at one of the mines had managed to get a message out, telling the world what had happened and calling for urgent assistance. Zaire had been independent for eighteen years but the Zairean Army was quite incapable of dealing with the threat – and quite capable of carrying out similar atrocities itself, given the chance. In any event, the Zaire Government and army were not over-concerned about the fate of a few hundred Belgian expatriates and, after a few days of hesitation, the Belgian Government, as the former colonial power, determined to intervene while there were still lives left to save. Belgium then decided *not* to intervene but to restrict its efforts to offering 'humanitarian aid' and issuing pleas for the lives of the prisoners. This was no great help to the people in Kolwezi, but the Belgians had been through all this before. If people were foolish enough to work in countries with unstable regimes, they must take the consequences if something went wrong.

Belgium had already intervened twice in the former Congo, once immediately after independence in 1960, when the local Congolese defence force, the Force Publique, mutinied and went on the rampage, raping and killing any white they could find, and again in 1964 when the 'Simbas', another terrorist movement, held a few hundred white hostages in Kinshasa and chopped a few Belgians to pieces each day in the town centre.

On that occasion Belgian para-commandos parachuted directly into the town and rescued the survivors, but after that affair Belgium let it be known that it was not prepared to go on intervening in its former colonies, and anyone unwise enough to take employment in one of these countries was on their own if things went awry. That threw the

Kolwezi problem back into the lap of the leader of Zaire, President Mobutu, and he asked the President of France, Giscard d' Estaing, for military assistance. This was a job for the Legion, and the 2nd REP were ordered to intervene.

The order to commence Operation Leopard, the hostage rescue at Kolwezi, reached Colonel Eurlin, the commander of the 2nd REP, at Calvi on the morning of 17 May. Colonel Eurlin put the regiment on six hours' notice to move, and sent out radio messages and parties of NCOs to round up all the legionnaires out on training exercises and get them back to barracks. By 2000 hours that evening the REP was fully kitted up with arms and ammunition and ready to move.

At 0800 hours on 18 May the first detachment flew out of Corsica, *en route* for Kinshasa in Zaire, 6,400 kilometres to the south. By the end of the day the rest of the regiment had followed, landing either in Kinshasa or at Lubumbashi, capital of Shaba province, and the closest airfield to Kolwezi. By that evening Colonel Eurlin and his staff were at Kinshasa, arguing with the Zairean military and working out plans for a combat drop on the town. There were no maps, very little information on what was happening, and a shortage of parachutes and parachute aircraft.

Sufficient parachutes were obtained from US sources and there were four C-130 and a C-160 aircraft available, rigged for dropping parachute troops. Five aircraft were not enough to carry more than half the battalion, but there was no time to be lost. The men had not had much sleep for two days, but at mid-morning on 19 May the five aircraft, carrying 400 Legion paras, took off for Kolwezi. The flight took four hours, and just after 1500 hours the paratroopers jumped over Kolwezi, with no clear idea of what would greet them on the ground, but knowing they faced odds of five to one – and could expect no help until the following day.

The important thing, having jumped and revealed that rescue was coming, was to get into the town and free the hostages without delay; as the Belgians had found in the past, the first action of Congolese rebels faced with a rescue force was to turn on their prisoners and hack them to pieces. With this thought in mind, the legionnaires rolled out of their falls, shucked off their parachute harnesses and set out for the town centre.

This first drop, on DZ Alpha, north-east of the town, was greeted with a certain amount of ground fire, but the big canopies of the US chutes softened the drop and all the men, from HQ and the 1st, 2nd and 3rd Companies, landed safely. On reaching the outskirts of the town, they ran into confused opposition from FLNC fighters deployed in shacks and alleyways. As they beat these off, and pushed on into the town, they found ample evidence that for some of the population their arrival was already too late.

Swollen, decomposing corpses, black and white, men and women, littered the side streets or lay sprawled in the gardens, or along the verandas of the houses. The stench of rotting corpses hung heavily in the air as the legionnaires pressed on towards the town centre, where they met even stiffer opposition but also found scores of civilians, ragged, dirty, and terrified, coming out of hiding and running down the streets to meet them. These people were now in danger from crossfire and were hustled away to a temporary aid station which the REP medical staff had set up in a school. The chief centre of FLNC resistance was around the main hotel and the police station, both of which were eventually taken by frontal assault.

The fighting in Kolwezi went on all afternoon. By the time dusk fell, the Legion felt they had the situation under control, but the rebels were still probing their positions and showed no signs of retreating. As dusk fell the rebels even put in a strong attack, backed with fire from their three armoured cars, against the Legion positions in the Old Town, but this attack was not pressed home in the face of showers of grenades and accurate rifle fire from the legionnaires. During the night, Legion patrols clashed repeatedly with wandering bands of FLNC, but dawn brought the roar of aircraft engines and the second drop, another rifle company plus the mortar platoon and the recce platoon, the men in it anxious to get a share of the action. These men had managed to get some sleep and came surging into the town and began to winkle out FLNC snipers in the New Town area, finding still more hostages in the process.

Some 80 FLNC were killed at this stage in the action, and during the day the Old and New Towns were gradually cleared; the Legion were taking few prisoners, for the sights they were uncovering were not those that inclined men to mercy. In one house they found the chopped-up bodies of at least 38 men, women and children, lying in a thick, fly-swarming pool of blood. The ground floor of the Impala Hotel, where the FLNC had held their 'trials', was awash with blood and littered with the hacked-off flesh of dead victims.

Many of the surviving hostages were badly wounded or deeply shocked, and once the nearby airstrip had been cleared Colonel Eurlin was able to call aircraft in, aircraft that brought in Belgian soldiers for the necessary humanitarian tasks, doctors to treat the injured and distressed, most of whom were then flown out to Kinshasa and back to Europe.

On the following day, the Legion transport, jeeps and trucks, arrived from Lubumbashi and the 2nd REP began to move out, pushing the rebels back towards the Angolan border, hunting down the remainder of the FLNC fighters and either forcing them to flee or shooting them down. During this pursuit the legionnaires found the bodies of a further 40 white hostages, men and women who had been taken away by the rebels in their flight and murdered later in the bush.

The legionnaires also collected a large quantity of arms, which they destroyed before they were flown back to Kinshasa and, on 4 June, back to Corsica. Operation Leopard had cost the Legion five dead and 25 wounded, but although 240 whites and at least as many black civilians were killed by the FLNC in Kolwezi, the Legion paras had saved the lives of at least 2,000 whites, and their arrival spared the entire population from further assault and bloodshed.

For the Legion it was a most satisfactory operation, a sign that their glory days were not yet over and that such dangerous tasks were well within their operational capacity.

Their next operation, though less dramatic, was certainly just as tricky. In the summer of 1982 the 2nd REP formed part of a multinational force charged by the UN with escorting Yasser Arafat's PLO from their camps around Beirut in Lebanon to the port of Tripoli, from where they would be shipped to safety in Morocco. The REP formed part of the French contingent and were sent to take and hold the dock area which they did successfully, seeing off any truculent militiamen looking for trouble until the evacuation had been successfully completed.

Since that time the Legion has remained at the cutting edge of France's military operations. During Operation Desert Storm, the Gulf War of 1991–2, the Legion deployed troops in the desert, patrolling out towards the Iraqi lines, masking the deployment of the armoured forces that crushed Saddam Hussein's much-vaunted Republican Guards in just a few hours of heavy fighting. Legion units have been deployed in a number of trouble spots, in Bosnia and Croatia, as part of the UN peacekeeping efforts, and are on permanent stand-by to go into action if any French interest is threatened or any French ally requires assistance. One hundred and sixty-five years after its foundation, the Légion Etrangère still has a front-line role.

16

THE LEGION TODAY, 1997

'The Legion offers an active outdoor life, sometimes somewhat rough'

Foreign Legion recruiting brochure, 1996

There is still a career to be had in the Foreign Legion for a good fighting man. Over thirty years ago, after the Legion finally left Algeria in 1964, there was a widespread belief that it would be disbanded. The actions of the 1st REP had shocked many people in the army and in French political circles and damaged the Legion's reputation as a loyal fighting force. On the other hand, the circumstances surrounding the mutiny were so unusual that many people were secretly sympathetic, and felt that one brief lapse of judgement could not obscure the Legion's reputation as a superb fighting force. The real question was what sort of fighting force did France need, now that her colonial empire had vanished?

The legionnaires needed to know, for with withdrawal from the one country – Algeria – that had been regarded as their home to one – France – where they could not legally serve and were anyway unwelcome, their very future seemed uncertain. All that was to change, as we shall see, and the Legion today is still a hard-hitting, well-equipped force, at the forefront of France's military establishment, widely deployed about the world and, as part of France's Rapid Reaction Force (FAR), ready for action at the sharp end, wherever it might occur. This RRF contains an Alpine and a parachute division, with a full range of support including artillery and engineers, but the 2nd REP is the hard edge of this 20,000-strong force, the one on the front line available for instant deployment.

The Legion today is smaller than it has ever been, with an establishment of around 8,500 men. It still contains a wide mix of nationalities, with a number of recruits arriving from Bosnia, Croatia and the other states of the former Yugoslavia, as well as a number of East Germans. There are also a considerable number of British legionnaires, many of them ex-soldiers, and usually about twenty Americans. The core of the modern Legion is the 2nd Régiment Parachutiste Etranger, normally based at Calvi in Corsica. This is virtually a Legion demi-brigade, mustering some 1,500 men, all trained parachutists, all well equipped with a full range of special force skills.

As already described, the 2nd REP is part of FAR – France's Rapid Reaction Force – which includes all the other Legion units now dotted about South France: the 1st Foreign Cavalry Regiment is based at Orange in the Rhône delta; the 2nd Foreign Infantry Regiment is at Nîmes, just across the Rhône, and the 6th Foreign Combat Engineer Regiment is at Avignon, a pleasant city on the banks of the Rhône, so all the Legion units, with the exception of the 2nd REP, are within easy reach of one another. The policy of dispersing Legion units was abandoned years ago.

Apart from the Legion units based in metropolitan France, there is the 3rd Foreign Infantry Regiment, which guards France's space research station in French Guinea and patrols the jungle border with Brazil and Surinam, mostly on the lookout for drug traffickers. This regiment also runs the French Jungle Warfare School in French Guinea. The 5th Combat Engineer Regiment is based in the South Pacific, on the island of Tahiti, and helps guard and maintain the French nuclear test ground in the Moraroa atoll. The famous 13th Demi-Brigade of North Africa fame is based in Djibouti in the Horn of Africa.

The 13th Demi-Brigade usually has a company deployed to the Comores, a group of islands off Madagascar where, in 1994, they suppressed a mutiny against the Comores Government. The final, sometimes active, unit deployed is in the central African republic of Chad, which is under periodic threat from Colonel Gaddafi's Libya.

Those who join the Legion today can therefore expect to see something of the world, and if France engages in any military adventure, either on its own or as part of a UN Force, the Legion will certainly be represented. This being so, the Legion does not lack for recruits, but joining is not easy, and the Legion today is small enough to be highly selective. About 6,000 men apply to join the Legion every year and only about 1,000 are accepted.

The would-be recruit must first become very fit and then make his way to France. Information about the Legion, the period of engagement, the pay and the prospects for promotion can be obtained from any French embassy or consulate, though the French do not actively recruit in other countries. The usual response to any telephone or written enquiry is a glossy brochure in various languages – Italian, English, German, and Spanish – which informs the would-be recruit that in the Foreign Legion 'you will lead an active, outdoor life, sometimes somewhat rough, devoted to honour and work. You will participate both by weapons and by tools to the maintenance of a prosperous peace and to the equipment of underdeveloped countries.' This faintly pious statement sounds better in French.

It goes on to add: 'The Foreign Legion will be a large family for you where you will find friends and help. When you are discharged this family will look after you. Available to you will be welfare services, convalescent homes, rest centres, retirement houses, veteran clubs. After fifteen years service you get a retirement pay and it you wish the Legion will facilitate your establishment in France and your naturalization.'

The Legion looks after its own and anyone who serves in the Legion, and abides by the Legion code, will not lack for help in hard times.

The Legion maintains recruiting offices, manned 24 hours a day, around the country in place like Dieppe, Paris, Metz and Nice. Volunteers can also enlist at any French Army recruiting office, of which there is one in every large provincial town, or even at police stations, from where the recruit will be speedily sent on to the nearest Legion recruiting office. From these sixteen offices a steady stream of applicants is sent every month to the HQ of the Legion, and the depot of the 1st Foreign Regiment, the Quartier Vienot at Aubagne, near Marseilles. Quite a number of recruits also turn up at the Legion gates, asking to join. After an interview, if they seem sober and sensible, they will be shown around, invited to talk freely to serving legionnaires from their own country and, again if both parties are happy, invited to stay on and join the next intake of trainees.

It is no use going that far if you are not aged between seventeen and 40, extremely fit and active, carry some form of personal identity, are very sure about what you are doing, and willing to sign on for five years' service. In 1831 the minimum term of enlistment was two years but for the last century five years has been and remains the minimum term. That can seem an eternity for a young man, and the thought of a five-year stint makes quite a few have second thoughts.

Those who have not already changed their minds or been turned away now face a three-week selection process. This allows time for the Legion reception centre to carry out a full range of physical, psychological and intelligence tests, while the Deuxième Bureau, the French intelligence service, carries out an investigation via Interpol and the recruit's national police force, to ensure that the would-be legionnaire is not a psychopath, on the run for some major crime, or a political agitator. It will also ensure that he is not a hired killer or political assassin – Carlos, 'The Jackal', would never have survived a Legion investigation. The recruit's behaviour is also studied for signs of chronic alcoholism or – a more likely failing these days – drug abuse, either of which would get the volunteer

238

an immediate discharge. If all goes well the recruit is accepted for Legion training, signs on and is given his *paquetage*, his kit and clothing, tunic, boots, green tie and beret, even his *képi blanc*, though he is not allowed to wear it yet. The Legion supplies everything he needs, for his own clothes are taken away and sold. He will not be allowed to wear them again and the training he is about to undergo means that in a few weeks they would not fit him anyway.

The recruit is then sent to the training depot at Castelnaudary, to the Quartier Danjou, for sixteen weeks' basic training, and at that point his official legionnaire record begins. More recruits drop out week by week as the training progresses, the drop-outs usually deserting across the nearby Spanish frontiers. The Legion makes no great effort to recapture such men, but their names and descriptions remain on the Legion and Deuxième Bureau files. A surprising number of Legion deserters returning to France after an absence of years, perhaps on holiday, have been identified, arrested and returned to Legion service.

After a few weeks' training, the recruit will receive his *képi blanc* during an evening ceremony at which the recruits swear to serve France – or to be more precise the Legion – with *honneur et fidélité*, in accordance with the Legion motto. It has already been made clear to the *bleu* that the *real* object of this training, apart from producing a battle-ready legionnaire, is to inculcate a sense of comradeship and loyalty *to the Legion*. Anyone who fails to feel this growing commitment and *esprit de corps* will not go far in his new career, or be happy in the Legion's ranks.

Legion training, once legendary for a harshness strongly tinged with brutality, is still hard, but far more sensible. Modern soldiering requires an intelligent soldier, not a brutalised automaton, and the Legion will not tolerate men who are little more than brutes. The recruits come from a wide range of social classes and a large number of nations, and there are sometimes problems as they shake down and become legionnaires; fist fights are not uncommon and a Legion recruit has to know how to take care of himself, and defend himself, if need be, against aggressive comrades. Internal aggression tends to disappear as the new legionnaires get to know each other and discover a common tongue – French.

The standards required are high, but a willing recruit can reach them and will receive every assistance in achieving top results, though unlike in many other armies there are no rewards or extra pay for any qualification other than parachuting. Expert marksmen are expected to devote their time to helping less gifted legionnaires reach their level of proficiency, and since the Legion range course, covering an entire range of weapons from the MAS assault rifle down to pistols, sub-machine guns and anti-tank projectiles, lasts a full nine weeks, the standard eventually achieved is extremely high. This same rule – that the strong and experienced help the weak and the beginner – exists throughout the Legion, so that the whole force is united in reaching the highest possible standards.

The legionnaire is never idle; indeed one of the common complaints is that more time still seems to be spent on *corvée* – fatigue duties, cleaning up around the camp – than on actual military training. Finally, before 'passing out' and transfer to one of the Legion regiments, the legionnaire goes on a five-day final exercise – or *raid* – in which all his skills, fitness and tenacity are put to the test, in whatever weather, always without much sleep. This will include a 100 kilometre march in full kit, which must not take more than two days. The Legion has always been a marching regiment, and it remains one to this day.

Then comes the application of other skills, in the use of helicopters, in navigating across country by day and night, in rappelling, demolition, patrolling and living in the field in all kinds of weather and terrain. The country around Castelnaudary is ideal for such training, with the Pyrenees a few miles away offering scope for mountain and winter warfare training, plenty of high summer temperatures to make any route march gruelling, and the sea close by for amphibious exercises. Commando training is now imposed on every recruit and takes place around the little fortress town of Mont Louis on the edge of the Cerdagne plateau in the Pyrenees, a chilly place in which to train in the winter months.

During all this time the recruit will be rapidly acquiring proficiency in French, partly through daily lessons, mainly because French is the language of the Legion and no other tongue is tolerated during working hours. Even an English legionnaire will soon be heard chatting in French to another English legionnaire – it is simply easier that way. To help the process along, each non-French-speaking recruit is now paired off with a French-speaking buddy, who helps him get a grip on the language. Within a few weeks, most recruits are managing to speak French adequately, and within a few months most are quite fluent.

Throughout the months of training the legionnaire also learns about the all-embracing life the Legion offers, the one described in the recruiting brochure. Not many recruits care much about pensions or retirement – that sort of thing lies well in the future and most new legionnaires expect to be dead or discharged before they need such help – but they soon learn that the Legion looks after its own and that in this respect they have a part to play, not least by contributing funds and carrying out maintenance and social work with former legionnaires. One of the most striking features of the Legion is its ability to find men within its ranks who can handle any task. Men trained in almost every profession can be found, and these non-military skills – those of architects, doctors, lawyers or plumbers – are always welcome and freely used should the need arise.

The Legion maintains its own hospital and convalescent home. It has a retirement home for old or crippled legionnaires to which all serving members contribute money. It runs farms from which fresh produce arrives in Legion kitchens – these farms are also used for survival exercises. It even runs its own hotel in Marseilles where legionnaires can go on leave; modern legionnaires get a month's leave a year, with discounted travel on the French railways. Legionnaires always wear uniform, in

241

and out of barracks, though after three years a man in good standing, who has reverted to using his own name, may be permitted to wear civilian clothes off duty.

All that lies well in the future when the recruit tramps back into the Quartier Danjou at the end of the final exercise. Now he has to join his regiment and the first dispersal begins. The goal of many recruits is the famous 2nd Régiment Etranger Parachutiste – the 2nd REP, currently based at Calvi in Corsica.

The 2nd REP is a parachute formation but is best imagined as the Legion equivalent of the SAS. It is organised in 'troops' on SAS lines, and the men wear the green beret with a mailed fist and dagger badge. 2nd REP recruits take the standard French Army parachute course of six jumps, one of them at night, before obtaining their silver wings, but their training is not over then. Elements of the 2nd REP are deployed to sensitive areas and likely trouble spots, and those at Calvi are on permanent stand-by, able to move in at least company strength to anywhere in the world within 24 hours. Each company in the 2nd REP has a special function as well as forming part of the whole.

One company concentrates on mountain and arctic warfare and is trained in climbing, skiing and winter survival. Another is the Night Company, trained to operate at night and equipped with night vision equipment such as image intensifiers. A third is the amphibious troop, containing scuba divers, small-boat handlers and reconnaissance teams. Another contains sabotage and demolition experts, and the last company specialises in the use of HALO (High Altitude, Low Opening) parachutes. The 2nd REP can produce teams of highly trained experts for every conceivable situation, and competition to enter its ranks is considerable.

During training the Legion assesses the *bleus* to see which are ready for promotion. Promotion is worth having as it means extra pay and fewer turns at *corvée*, but the rules governing suitability for promotion seem to vary. This has always been the case and it can be confusing.

When Englishman Simon Murray served in the 2nd REP in the 1960s, during the Algerian War, his chances of promotion were frequently stalled for no good reason, though he was an outstanding soldier and a good legionnaire. He joined the Legion in February 1960 and it was not until the end of 1963 that he was sent on a corporal's course . . . and passed out first of his class.

On the other hand, Henry Ainley, who joined the Legion at Sidi Bel Abbès in 1950, was sent on a corporal's course immediately after training and had to fight off attempts to send him on a sergeant's course after that. Ainley joined the Legion in order to fight communism and wanted to be sent to Indo-China, where the war against the Vietminh was at its height. Both men agree that their time on the Legion corporal's course was one of the hardest parts of their service.

Ainley's course lasted four months and the legionnaires on it were told on arrival at the Mascara NCOs' school that at the end of that time they would be 'either corporals or corpses'. All movement, everywhere, was to be at the double. The first week was a retake of their recruit training, with yet more pressure on them to reach ever-higher standards of drill and turnout. The slightest mistake meant hours of doubling around the parade ground with a full pack, and the entire intake was punished for the failings of any one man.

Ainley had a break in the middle of his course when the Legion celebrated Camerone Day, but on that day he and another man had a fist fight with two of their instructors. There was no official reaction, but from then on the two instructors made Ainley's life hell. By the time the course ended he had lost 4.5 kilograms in weight – on top of the 7 kilograms he had already lost during his recruit training – and was ready to give up from sheer exhaustion. He still managed to pass out eighth out of fifty. He was then made a corporal-instructor, but a month later was detailed for the four-month-long sergeant's course. This might have seemed complimentary, but as Ainley said, 'after nine months of pounding round barrack squares and North

African goat tracks, my feet and morale could not stand any more training'.

Simon Murray attended a corporal's course run especially for men of the 2nd REP, 'an in-house effort for the regiment required 20 corporals'. This course was another four-month-long trial, from the end of May until mid-October 1963. The Legion had clearly not softened in the intervening thirteen years for the account of Murray's course reads like a nightmare. Every day began at 0500 hours with an eight-kilometre cross-country run. Barrack rooms were inspected three times a day and if any fault was found – and fault was always found – the barracks were inspected again at midnight and at four in the morning. Sleep became rare and precious. Afternoons were spent in the hills on field training or map-reading exercises, all exercises ending in a forced march.

Within a week attendees were on speed marches, often returning to find the barrack room wrecked, their kit and clothing sprayed with a fire hose, with orders that they must restore it to pristine glory within two hours, or else . . . somehow, they did it. When a mosquito was found in the barracks, Murray had to dig a trench 1.5 metres deep and bury it.

It was harsh, but it worked. Within two weeks these men, already seasoned Legionnaires, were fitter, tougher, better trained and more efficient than they had ever been, and they were the cream of the regiment to get on the course in the first place. Moreover, the actual instruction was of a very high standard, and it produced NCOs who were not only extremely fit and mentally tough but who knew their jobs.

The Legion has a dread of boredom. The men have to be kept active, and traditionally if there were no wars to fight then they were employed in public works. A large number of roads in Algeria and Morocco were built with Legion labour, and those men who grumbled that they had joined to fight, not swing a shovel, soon found themselves in the guardroom. This part of Legion life has faded away, partly because modern armies need to train constantly, partly because the trade unions do not like the use of unregistered labour, but the Legion is still insistent that the men must be kept busy. Otherwise they may suffer *le cafard*.

To those outside the Legion *le cafard* might seem like a joke, another of those tall Legion tales from the desert wars of the last century, but men living a life of great hardship on some lonely outpost, without mail from home or any entertainment other than that arranged by themselves, are prone to let their thoughts prey on their misfortunes, let petty squabbles become a source of irritation, and eventually these pent-up emotions can lead to suicide or violence. The answer, in lieu of any other relief, like drink, leave or women, was – and is – to keep the men busy on any task, however pointless, so that when the working day was over they had no energy for quarrelling or mutiny, but would fall into a dreamless sleep before the routine started again on the morrow. Even today, Legion service is not well provided with leisure or luxury.

Some things, of course, are different. The Legion barracks have every facility and if the home comforts are lacking the Legion ranks still contain plenty of men who are more than capable of building a cinema, directing a play or organising a concert. It also helps that the Legion is stationed in populated places in agreeable parts of France, although the overseas postings, in places like Chad, Guiana and Djibouti, are still fairly bleak ... *le cafard* is still a possibility so the men, as always, are kept busy.

All that said, in the Légion Etrangère some things never change. 'Le Boudin' is still sung at Legion ceremonials and in the officers' mess before lunch, the ceremonies of Camerone Day are still held, like semi-religious rites. The training is still hard, the *corvée* relentless, and the men who join are still looking for something, though most of them would be hard pressed to say what.

A man joining the Legion today will find himself a member of an élite unit with an outstanding battlefield record and a curious history. The stories in this book are all true, but all form part of the Legion legend, and have a place in the Legion tradition, that collection of rules which says that the Legion does not surrender, does not abandon its dead, and when all hope has gone and the ammunition is expended charges out against the enemy with the bayonet. These stories, this legend, that tradition, all go to make the Legion a formidable fighting force, but they also create, for those who join its ranks, a unique way of life, one that marks a man for the rest of his days, and continues to exercise an influence on him long after he has obtained his *libération*, his certificate of discharge, and gone on his way.

In some ways a Légionnaire never really leaves the Legion. It has Old Comrades associations in many countries, including the UK, and these men get together on Camerone Day, or on Remembrance Sunday, to recall their service and the traditions of their famous corps. The Legion *is* another country, and those who have lived there never really escape its pull.

Legio patria nostra, once, now and always.

SELECT BIBLIOGRAPHY

The Algerian Problem, Eddie Behr, Hodder, 1961

The Battle of Dien Bien Phu, Jules Roy, Carroll and Graf, New York, 1984

Bir Hakeim, Jacques Mordal, Presse de la Cité, Paris, 1970

Devil's Guard, George Elford, New English Library, 1978

Devils, Not Men, Roy C. Anderson, Hale, 1987

Doctor at Dien Bien Phu, Paul Grauwin, Hutchinson, 1955

Elite Forces, Walter Lang, Guild Publishing, 1987

The Foreign Legion, Patrick Turnbull, Heinemann, 1964

The Foreign Legion, Charles Mercer, Arthur Barker, 1964

The French Foreign Legion, John Robert Young, Thames and Hudson, 1984

The French Foreign Legion, Nigel Thomas, Wayland Publishing, 1973

The French Foreign Legion, Douglas Porch, Macmillan, 1991

French Foreign Legion Paratroops, Martin Windrow and Wayne Braby, Osprey, 1985

Hell in a Very Small Place, Bernard Fall, Lippincott, New York, 1967

The Indo-China War, Edgar O'Ballance, Faber and Faber, 1964

In Order to Die, Henry Ainley, Burke, 1955

Képi Blanc; A History of the Foreign Legion, Regnary, Chicago, 1956

La Légion, Pierre Sargent, Presse de la Cité, Paris, 1985

Legionnaire, Simon Murray, Sidgwick and Jackson, 1978

March or Die, Tony Geraghty, Guild Publishing, 1986
Mourir pour Cao Bang, Marc Dem, Albin, Paris, 1978
The Reluctant Legionnaire, Michael Alexander, Hart Davis, 1956
A Savage War of Peace, Alistair Horne, Penguin, 1977
Strange Company, Adrian Liddell Hart, Weidenfeld and Nicolson, 1953